DISPELLER OF OBSTACLES

The Heart Practice of Padmasambhava

RANGJUNG YESHE BOOKS ♦ WWW.RANGJUNG.COM

PADMASAMBHAVA ♦ *Treasures from Juniper Ridge* ♦ *Advice from the Lotus-Born* ♦ *Dakini Teachings*

PADMASAMBHAVA AND JAMGÖN KONGTRÜL ♦ *The Light of Wisdom, Vol. 1, Vol. 2, Vol. 3, Vol. 4, & Vol. 5*

PADMASAMBHAVA, CHOKGYUR LINGPA, TULKU URGYEN RINPOCHE, ORGYEN TOPGYAL RINPOCHE, AND LAMA PUTSI PEMA TASHI ♦ *Dispeller of Obstacles*

YESHE TSOGYAL ♦ *The Lotus-Born*

DAKPO TASHI NAMGYAL ♦ *Clarifying the Natural State*

TSELE NATSOK RANGDRÖL ♦ *Mirror of Mindfulness* ♦ *Empowerment* ♦ *Heart Lamp*

CHOKGYUR LINGPA ♦ *Ocean of Amrita* ♦ *The Great Gate* ♦ *Skillful Grace* ♦ *Great Accomplishment*

TRAKTUNG DUDJOM LINGPA ♦ *A Clear Mirror*

JAMGÖN MIPHAM RINPOCHE ♦ *Gateway to Knowledge, Vol. 1, Vol. 2, Vol. 3, & Vol. 4*

TULKU URGYEN RINPOCHE ♦ *Blazing Splendor* ♦ *Rainbow Painting* ♦ *As It Is, Vol. 1 & Vol. 2* ♦ *Vajra Speech* ♦ *Repeating the Words of the Buddha*

ADEU RINPOCHE ♦ *Freedom in Bondage*

KHENCHEN THRANGU RINPOCHE ♦ *King of Samadhi*

CHÖKYI NYIMA RINPOCHE ♦ *Present Fresh Wakefulness*

TULKU THONDUP ♦ *Enlightened Living*

ORGYEN TOBGYAL RINPOCHE ♦ *Life & Teachings of Chokgyur Lingpa*

DZIGAR KONGTRÜL RINPOCHE ♦ *Uncommon Happiness*

TSOKNYI RINPOCHE ♦ *Fearless Simplicity* ♦ *Carefree Dignity*

DZOGCHEN TRILOGY COMPILED BY MARCIA BINDER SCHMIDT ♦ *Dzogchen Primer* ♦ *Dzogchen Essentials* ♦ *Quintessential Dzogchen*

ERIK PEMA KUNSANG ♦ *Wellsprings of the Great Perfection* ♦ *A Tibetan Buddhist Companion* ♦ *The Rangjung Yeshe Tibetan-English Dictionary of Buddhist Culture & Perfect Clarity*

MARCIA DECHEN WANGMO ♦ *Confessions of a Gypsy Yogini*

COMPILATION ♦ *Precious Songs of Enlightenment*

DISPELLER OF OBSTACLES

The Heart Practice of Padmasambhava

Padmasambhava
Chogyur Lingpa
Jamyang Khyentse Wangpo
Jamgön Kongtrül Rinpoche
Tersey Tulku
Karmey Khenpo Rinchen Dargye
Dilgo Khyentse Rinpoche
Tulku Urgyen Rinpoche
Orgyen Topgyal Rinpoche
Lama Putsi Pema Tashi

Translated by Erik Pema Kunsang
Compiled and edited by Marcia Schmidt

Rangjung Yeshe
PUBLICATIONS
Boudhanath, Hong Kong & Esby
2006

Rangjung Yeshe Publications
Flat 5a, Greenview Garden,
125 Robinson Road, Hong Kong

Address letters to:
Rangjung Yeshe Publications
Ka-Nying Shedrub Ling Monastery
P.O. Box 1200, Kathmandu, Nepal

www.rangjung.com

1 3 5 7 9 8 6 4 2

First paperback edition published in 2014

Printed in the United States of America

Distributed to the book trade by:
Publishers Group West

Publication data: ISBN 978-962-7341-96-6 (pbk)

Dispeller of Obstacles, The Heart Practice of Padmasambhava
Padmasambhava, Chokgyur Lingpa, Jamyang Khyentse Wangpo,
Jamgön Kongtrül Rinpoche,
Tulku Urgyen Rinpoche, Orgyen Topgyal Rinpoche,
Karmey Khenpo Rinchen Dargye,
Tersey Tulku & Lama Putsi Pema Tashi

Translated from the Tibetan, based on the teachings of
Kyabje Tulku Urgyen Rinpoche by
Erik Pema Kunsang (Erik Hein Schmidt)
Edited and compiled by Marcia Dechen Wangmo [Marcia Binder Schmidt]

Photos courtesy of Graham Sunstein
Cover photo courtesy of Chris Zvitkovits

FIRST EDITION

CONTENTS

PREFACE

Marcia Dechen Wangmo

This book, *Dispeller of Obstacles, The Heart Practice of Padmasambhava,* is the first in a new series presented by Rangjung Yeshe Publications. This series will offer videos, audios, photos, and commentaries as supports for the practices of the Three Roots. The Three Roots are the inner practices of tantra connected with sadhanas for the lama, yidam, and dakini. As is often said, "The lama is the source of blessings, the yidam the source of accomplishment, and the dakinis and protectors are the source of activity."

Apparent differences, such as gender or peaceful versus wrathful modes, do not ultimately define these three, because in essence they are identical—the display of the empty, cognizant, awake nature, rigpa. However, due to our varying dispositions as sentient beings needing to be tamed, they manifest in myriad ways to accomplish the utmost benefit. The qualities of each deity are the fully perfected qualities of our buddha nature; we undertake this deity training in order to connect with and accomplish that nature. Thus, we should practice whichever deity moves us most profoundly.

As Tulku Urgyen Rinpoche said, "True blessings are the oral instructions on how to become enlightened in a single lifetime, which you can receive from a qualified master." In a practical way, we can experience this ourselves, since our guru is the source of guidance, inspiration, and strength for the Vajrayana path. He or she is the most vital, meaningful person in our lives, dispelling hindrances so we may progress in this tradition. Living in this degenerate age, we must seriously study whatever we intend to practice. These sacred texts, our teachers' words, and our own intellect and experience need to harmonize, in order to clear away any misconceptions and doubts. The gift of teachings that we receive and apply expands our ordinary way of seeing reality and breaks down our normal, conditioned concepts.

Having a direct bond with a qualified, living teacher is our sole means of being introduced to the nature of our minds and being able to recognize and train in it. In the moment of love for our guru, we experience a gap, an opening free of mental constructs and internal gossip. This space offers the possibility to come into direct contact with the nature of our mind, true awareness. The Nyingma and Kagyü traditions especially emphasize devotion and consider it indispensable. This is another reason why guru practice is so exalted, because we reach enlightenment by stabilizing the momentary recognition of our mind's nature and by continually maintaining that recognition. Without this, although the path may be a very enjoyable one, it will definitely be quite long.

Guru practice offers an infusion of direct insight, whereby each step brings us closer to accomplishing our teacher's mind, as our teacher is no different from the primary figure in any Three Roots practice. The *Tukdrub Barchey Künsel* cycle of teachings presented here serves as an example and framework, although any other guru practice will suffice. While the specifics relate to this cycle of teachings, which I have chosen because I have the most familiarity and precious material for it, the principles outlined are universal and applicable to all guru practices. Such topics include development and completion stages, with guidance on the three samadhis; the fourfold stakes of recitation; the four recitation intents; and feasts, as well as advice for structuring a retreat. As with guru practices, all sadhanas follow the same basic format; only the liturgies differ. Thus, I have tried to offer teachings and advice that are general to all sadhana practices.

This cycle of *Tukdrub Barchey Künsel* is a vast and profound *terma,* "hidden treasure," a revelation with a rich history that unfolds throughout the book. This presentation is special, because it contains not only the root text and classical commentaries by the *tertöns,* "hidden treasure revealers," Chokgyur Lingpa and Jamyang Khyentse Wangpo, but also explanations by modern-day masters, such as Tulku Urgyen and Orgyen Topgyal Rinpoches.

This extensive cycle contains teachings and practices that encompass the preliminaries up to and including the Great Perfection. Moreover, the main sadhanas come in varying lengths, ranging from a few pages up to a few hundred pages, and the subsidiary sadhanas consist of separate practices for each of the main deities. Linking to a fresh terma has the power to imbue us with hot, juicy blessings that invigorate our being and generate profound devotion and joy.

Gratitude goes to all the people who have helped to make this book a reality. It has been a journey involving a living, breathing mandala of Dharma friends and teachers, magnetized by the inexhaustible, inconceivable love for Padmasambhava. With joy, it is offered to all receptive and fortunate beings, so we may all become inseparable from the Lotus Master and reunite in the sublime mandala of *Sangdok Palri*. In particular, thanks go to Erik Pema Kunsang for the primary translation, Zack Beer for the secondary translation, Graham Sunstein for photos and research, Anne Paniagua for editing and copyediting, Maryann Lipaj for the cover design, Joan Olson for the book design, and Lynn Schroeder and Michael Yockey for proofreading.

Once again, we are greatly indebted to Richard Gere and the Gere Foundation and to its undaunted director, Mollie Rodriguez, who continue to believe in our work and support it with graciousness.

This book was joyfully completed at the sacred place of Padmasambhava, the Asura Cave in Pharping, Nepal, on the tenth day of the twelfth lunar month in the year of the Water Snake (2.9.2014) by Marcia Dechen Wangmo. May it be auspicious and may all countless beings benefit.

Tukdrub Barchey Künsel Guru

THE HEART OF PADMASAMBHAVA

Jamgön Kongtrül Rinpoche

All the secret paths whereby a person of sharp faculties can attain the great state of unity within a single lifetime are included within two types: the means for dispelling the obstacles and the means for attaining the siddhis. By the power of the former, the latter is easily accomplished. To practice both of them based on the blessed path of guru sadhana is the profound meaning of all secrets. The cycle of *Lamey Tukdrub Barchey Künsel* is the intent of the root tantra, *Magical Net of the Vidyadhara Gurus.*

This terma cycle is an extract of the heart of Padmakara, the knower of the three times, and it is the single unique treasure concealed under the earth in Tibet. It is like the great treasury of the universal monarch, filled completely and unmistakenly with all the means for accomplishing the supreme and common siddhis.

In terms of the sections of tantra, this profound path is based on the Great King of Tantras, the *Peaceful and Wrathful Manifestations of the Magical Net of the Vidyadhara Gurus,* which is the root of blessings belonging to the category of the *Eight Sections of the Magical Net.* Due to the certainty of oral instructions, there is no conflict in that it also belongs to the category of *Lotus Speech*, among the *Eight Teachings of Sadhana Sections.*

In short, it is like the extracted essence of the meaning of all stages of development and completion as well as the activity applications of the tantra and sadhana sections.

(top) Chokgyur Lingpa, (above left) Jamyang Khyentse Wangpo,
(above right) Jamgön Kongtrül, the first

A SHORT INTRODUCTION TO THE *BARCHEY KÜNSEL* CYCLE

Kyabje Dilgo Khyentse Rinpoche

The *Barchey Künsel* is the heart essence of the accomplished master Padmasambhava, who perceives the three times in their entirety. It is the quintessence of one billion heart sadhanas of the guru, the most unique terma, buried in the land of Tibet. It is also the first of the *Four Cycles of Guru Sadhana*. This *Guru's Heart Practice That Dispels All Obstacles* contains in completeness all the profound key points of the view, meditation, and conduct of the three inner yoga tantras. It manifested from the secret treasury of the great wisdom, the vast realization of the Second Buddha of Uddiyana, as the self-existing, natural vajra sounds in perfect, melodious tones.

Its expressions, which are unmodified by the intellect of ordinary people; its words, which are without delusion; and its meaning, which is unmistaken, are exclusively due to the kindness of the three powerful knowledge holders, Khyentse, Kongtrül, and Chokling, the great beings of the three families, who incarnated as masters to compile and propagate an ocean of secret teachings. It is exclusively through their kindness that this teaching was established in writing, as the splendor of unending welfare and happiness for the disciples in the Land of Snow, and propagated to flourish everywhere.

This pure and perfect teaching, which effortlessly bestows, in accordance with one's wishes, the all-encompassing supreme and common siddhis, temporarily and ultimately, was an unprecedented diffusion of the gemstones of the profound meaning, opening up the treasury of the universal monarch.

Padmasambhava

PADMASAMBHAVA

Tulku Urgyen Rinpoche

In our own present world age, one thousand Buddhas will appear. Each one will be accompanied by an emanation of Guru Rinpoche to carry out the Buddha's activities. In the present age of Buddha Shakyamuni, all the Buddha's activity appeared in one emanation in the form of Padmasambhava, the Lotus-Born One. He was born from a lotus flower in the middle of a lake. In his life story, he recounts, "I appeared from a lotus flower, without a father, without a mother." In this way, he was spontaneously born, but there was another reason for this as well. As a miraculously born human being, he was endowed with great miraculous powers to subdue not only human beings but also spirits and other classes of non-humans.

Padmasambhava lived for a very long time. After his birth, he continued living in India for about one thousand years. Afterward, he arrived in Tibet and remained there for fifty-five years. At the end of his stay in Tibet, he departed for a place called Gungtang on the border of Nepal, accompanied by his twenty-five chief disciples as well as the king of Tibet. At that site, mounted upon a fabulous horse called Mahabhala, he flew off into the sky escorted by dakinis of the four classes. His companions, who were left behind, watched his image grow smaller and smaller as he slowly disappeared.

According to the story, he made his first descent in Bodhgaya, where he remained for some time. Later, he went on to his own pure land called *Sangdok Palri*, the Glorious Copper-Colored Mountain. Geographically, this place is situated somewhere out in the ocean, southwest of Bodhgaya. It is a type of subcontinent, which is inhabited by *rakshasas*, "cannibal spirits," on the lower levels. According to a prediction given by Buddha Shakyamuni, at a certain period in history, when the average life span of human beings will be twenty years, these cannibal spirits will invade the known world, subjugating and destroying all human beings. In this way, mankind would be in great danger. However, the Buddha also predicted that Guru Rinpoche would go to this land and conquer all these raksha-sas. He did just this to fulfill the prediction.

The main mountain in the center of the island is copper colored and descends deep below the ocean into the realm of the *nagas*. Its summit pierces the skies, even to the heights of the *brahma-loka* in the realm of form. On the very peak of this mountain, a miraculously manifested bud-dhafield exists, created by Guru Rinpoche. There are three levels: Above is the *dharmakaya* level, where the main aspect of Guru Rinpoche appears as Amitayus; on the middle level dwells Avalokiteshvara; and at the ground level dwells Guru Rinpoche himself in the familiar form. He is surrounded by the eight manifestations.

Appearing in this world, Guru Rinpoche is the body emanation of Buddha Amitabha, the speech emanation of Avalokiteshvara, and the mind emanation of Buddha Shakyamuni. Before manifesting in our world, he first appeared in the *sambhogakaya* realm as the five families of Tötreng Tsal, then as the eight and twelve emanations, and so forth, until fifty manifestations had appeared. Finally, countless different mani-festations of Guru Rinpoche appeared.

Before Padmasambhava left Tibet, he made many predictions, hid many teachings to be revealed in the future, and blessed his close disciples to be inseparable from him. In this way, they would reincarnate in the future, reveal the hidden teachings, and be as powerful as Guru Rinpoche himself, endowed with great miraculous powers, such as flying through the sky, freely traversing solid matter, and unimpededly expounding all the sutras and treatises as well as the meaning of the tantras.

In particular, he prophesied the coming of 108 great tertöns, "hidden treasure revealers." World history fluctuates, causing particular difficul-ties to arise at different times. Having foreknowledge of these historic intervals, Guru Rinpoche designed special practices that specific tertöns would reveal at the appropriate times, in order to aid human beings. The tertöns discovering these termas, "hidden treasures," would then give a totally fresh, up-to-date teaching meant for that specific time and situa-tion.

Just as we prefer to have fresh food prepared in a way that will not make us sick because it's rotten, in the same way, the terma teachings revealed with the "short lineage" are endowed with a very special quality. By virtue of having a short lineage, the teachings have not been inter-rupted by any damage or samaya breakage. They have not been interpolated by anyone else, but have come directly from Guru Rinpoche by means of the revelation of one of his disciples appearing as a present-day incarnation, who then spreads the teachings to people for their immediate practice.

The *Lamey Tukdrub Barchey Künsel* belongs to this class of teachings. This cycle of teachings is based on guru sadhana. When I received the lineage of the *Rinchen Terdzö* from the previous incarnation of Jamgön Kongtrül, the one immediately following Jamgön Kongtrül Lodrö Thaye, one day he told me,

"During my lifetime, I have performed the *drubchen* (the "one-week sadhana" on *Barchey Künsel*) three times. Every single time there was some very special miraculous sign.

"The first time we performed the drubchen, the main *torma* on the shrine started to leak nectar, not just a little bit, but enough that it overflowed the shrine and drenched the floor all the way out to the main entryway. People were tasting it and saying it had a very special flavor that was sweet yet strong and potent, incomparable with anything else in this world. The second time I performed the drubchen, the *kapala,* the "skull cup" containing *amrita,* started to boil, and it continued to boil throughout the rest of the drubchen. The third time I performed the drubchen, we were preparing *mendrub,* "sacred medicine," at the same time. The fragrance issuing from the fermentation of the mendrub was very remarkable, unlike anything people had ever smelled in this world. The scent of it spread as far as Thrangu Rinpoche's monastery, a distance of four day's walk. People from that monastery asked where the fragrance came from. In my whole life, I have never witnessed signs as amazing as the ones during those three times." This could also be due to the combination of the profound terma teaching and such an extremely great master.

When great masters are practicing a fresh terma, in the beginning there are always great blessings, because the "vapor from the dakinis' breath" has not yet had time to evaporate from the terma. In this way, terma teachings with a short lineage have a particularly great blessing and effect for those who practice them.

There are four versions of the primary guru sadhana of the *Barchey Künsel:* the extensive version, the *Trinley Gyepa;* the medium-sized edition, the *Trinley Dringpo;* the condensed medium-length version, which is like its essence, the *Trinley Nyingpo;* and the extremely short *Concise*

Daily Practice. That doesn't mean something is lacking or lost when being condensed—it becomes even more precious, just as butter is the essential extract of milk.

In the mandala circle of this practice, Guru Rinpoche is surrounded by twelve emanations of himself that are inseparable from twelve different yidams. The inseparability of the yidam and guru aspects is called the "twelve manifestations." Additionally, above Guru Rinpoche's head is Amitayus, representing dharmakaya. Beneath Amitayus is Avalokiteshvara, representing sambhogakaya. Guru Rinpoche is the *nirmanakaya* representation. In the four cardinal and intermediate directions, four and eight emanations appear respectively—twelve emanations altogether. At the four gates, in the four directions, are the four gatekeepers. These are the deities included within this mandala.

It is said that the tantric scriptures of Mahayoga are included within the scriptures of Anu Yoga; and the scriptures of Anu Yoga are included within the oral instructions of Ati Yoga. All of these are included within the sadhana scriptures, which are included within your own application.

In this particular context, all the different classes of deities are embodied within the twelve manifestations of Guru Rinpoche, such as the eight herukas, the *mamos,* the peaceful and wrathful deities, Yamantaka, as well as Kilaya and Gongdü. These indispensable yidams in the Nyingma tradition are called *Ka, Gong,* and *Phur*, which represent Kabgye *(Eight Heruka Sadhanas),* Gongdü (Lama Gongdü, mind embodiment of the gurus), and Phurba (Vajra Kilaya).

In the *Tukdrub Barchey Künsel,* these twelve manifestations correspond to various emanations of Guru Rinpoche. Gyalwey Dungdzin is Padma Gyalpo. Mawey Senge is Manjushri. Kyechok Tsülzang is Jambhala. Dükyi Shechen is Dorje Phurba. Dzamling Gyenchok is Vishuddha Heruka. Pema Jungney is Urgyen Dorje Chang. Kyepar Phakpey Rigdzin is Guru Rinpoche taming the dakas, dakinis, and spirits. Dzutrül Tuchen is Dorje Drollö. Dorje Draktsal is Guru Drakpo and Pema Heruka. Kalden Drendzey is all eight herukas together, especially Palchen Heruka. Raksha Tötreng is Vajrapani. Dechen Gyalpo is Gongdü and Chakrasamvara.

In the past, when Guru Rinpoche did the practices of Kabgye, Gongdü, Phurba, and all the other yidams, he and the yidams became inseparable. Thus the blessings became greater, the accomplishments became swifter, and the practice became superior to any other. This is why the blessings are greater and the accomplishment swifter in the *Barchey Künsel* than in the other termas of Chokgyur Lingpa. For this practice, no obstacles can arise. The oral instructions of the great tertön himself say that if a practitioner can perfect the preliminary practices according to the *Barchey Künsel*, no obstacles will arise for that practitioner. This is the promise that was passed down to my own teacher.

What was the actual moment of discovering this terma? Chokgyur Lingpa and Jamyang Khyentse went to a place called *Da-Nying Khala Rong-Go*. Between the cliffs and the place where the terma was unearthed is the great Tsangpo River (Brahmaputra). The cliff overlooking the site is extremely steep.

Chokgyur Lingpa and Jamyang Khyentse, with their large entourages, arrived on the precipice overlooking the Tsangpo River. Chokgyur Lingpa pointed to the opposite shore and said, "On the other side, at the white rocks, there is a terma that I must take out." His attendants said, "Yes, but it will take at least a day to walk there. First you have to climb all the way down this cliff, find a place to ford the river, and then walk back up to the actual site on the other shore. That must be at least a day's hike." Chokgyur Lingpa said, "No, no, no! It won't take long at all. There is one very easy way to reach there." Saying this, he unfolded his shawl and using it as "wings," he simply flew through the air to the other side of the river. Landing there, he took the terma out. Returning, he simply walked across the water itself and climbed up on the opposite shore. All the people who witnessed this were utterly amazed and felt he truly possessed miraculous powers. Tertöns are people like this.

Guru Rinpoche practice is extremely important, because Guru Rinpoche, the Lotus-Born One, is not just a legendary figure from some old story of the past. He is an actual person who continuously carries out spontaneous activities, not only by sending emanations of himself into this world as tertöns, so there is always a fresh, unimpaired teaching that people can practice, but also because Guru Rinpoche's spiritual influence and blessings are unceasing. If we can practice this sadhana, it will be very beneficial.

It's best, of course, if we can do the actual practice in an intense way, according to the three versions of the sadhana, but next best is to perform the even shorter version—just one and a half pages in length—called the *Concise Daily Practice Manual*, or *Gyüngyi Köljang*. If we don't find time to do even this, we should at least say the six-line supplication to

Guru Rinpoche that starts out *Düsum sangye, Guru Rinpoche*, meaning Buddhas of the three times, Guru Rinpoche, and so forth. Each day, we should also say at least one *mala* of the Vajra Guru mantra. This will be extremely beneficial for our own development, because Guru Rinpoche, being miraculously born, is totally unharmed by gods, demons, or humans. Moreover, he manifested in such a way as to be the resplendent subjugator of appearance and existence, meaning of all worlds and beings. Therefore, the practice of Guru Rinpoche and the recitation of his mantra dispel all obstacles and accomplish all harmonious circumstances.

REMOVING OBSTACLES

Orgyen Topgyal Rinpoche

Lamey Tukdrub Barchey Künsel is the most profound terma of the universal monarchs, Chokgyur Dechen Lingpa and Jamyang Khyentse Wangpo. There are many different sections of this teaching: the main part and the secondary teachings associated with this cycle. As it is said, "First, you need to hear the history in order to bring about confidence in the teachings. Next, you receive empowerment in order to ripen your mindstream. Then you receive the instructions and follow them in order to achieve liberation." In accordance with this quotation, I will first tell a little bit about the history of these teachings, in order for everyone to gain confidence and trust in their authenticity. In the land of the Aryas, in India, there were no dissimilarities in terms of the different sets of teachings. When the teachings were later brought to Tibet, distinctions arose between the Nyingma, the old school, and the Sarma, the new school. The *Tukdrub Barchey Künsel* is part of the Nyingma teachings.

Within the Nyingma tradition, there are three sets of teachings: the long lineage of the oral instructions of the *Kama*, the short lineage of the profound terma, and the extremely short lineage of pure visions. *Tukdrub Barchey Künsel* belongs to the profound teachings of terma. There are different kinds of termas: earth treasures, mind treasures, treasures revealed through remembrance, and treasures revealed through a rediscovered terma. This is an earth terma, which Chokgyur Lingpa discovered as a yellow scroll in *Da-Nying Khala Rong-Go,* when he was twenty-five-years old. Jamyang Khyentse Wangpo also revealed these teachings as a mind terma, called *Tukdrub Deshek Dupa*, which he considered to be almost the same in terms of both words and meaning as the earth terma of *Tukdrub Barchey Künsel;* so he then decided to bring those two termas together.

These teachings originally came about as follows: The precious master Padmasambhava was residing at Samye in Central Tibet, invited by the Dharma King Trisong Deütsen. One day, in the turquoise-covered chamber of one of the temples, Padmasambhava sat with nine of his closest disciples: the king; his three sons (the three princes); the consort appointed by the vajra command, the dakini Yeshe Tsogyal; the great master Vairotsana, whose realization was equal to that of Padmasambhava himself; the monk Namkhai Nyingpo; and the Ngakpas Dorje Dudjom and Nubchen Sang-gye Yeshe. Together, they supplicated him many times, offered a mandala, and made other offerings. Wholeheartedly and earnestly, they asked these questions: "When there are hindrances and obstacles for enlightenment, at this time and in future times, what are the methods to dispel these obstacles? When the hindrances are cleared, how does one reach attainment? What are the ways for that to happen?"

The Precious Master replied: "Right now, at present and in future generations, there will be countless varieties of obstacles for enlightenment and attainment on the path. The one single method that suffices for clearing away all obstacles and hindrances is to call upon your guru— from the core of your heart. That itself will remove every type of obstacle. Once hindrances are cleared away, attainment is reached, right at that moment." In short, it's exceedingly important to supplicate your guru.

This could be one of the most important sentences Padmasambhava has said. It is found in the first volume of *Barchey Künsel* and in the text called *Sheldam Nyingjang,* the essence manual of all instructions. It says to call upon the guru, one's personal guru, who shows the path to enlightenment. One's personal guru may have every virtue equal to all buddhas of the three times; still, in terms of kindness, one's personal guru is kinder than all other buddhas. Due to the power of incredible aspirations and merit made by a buddha in the past, another buddha manifests, awakening to true and complete enlightenment and teaching the 84,000 sections of the Dharma. In our aeon, the Buddha Shakyamuni has done so, but we did not have the fortune to meet him and receive his teachings.

For us, our individual root guru is the person who shows what to adopt, what to avoid, and how to follow a true path. Having a root guru is the same as a blind person getting an eye operation and then being able to see. Therefore, the person who shows us the path in an authentic way, the master who teaches the Dharma, is our personal root guru, our primary teacher. That kindness has no equal. To appreciate that with respect and trust from the core of one's heart, from the marrow of one's bones, is exactly what is needed. Without that trust and devotion, the plant of progress in the Dharma is, one can say, rotten from the root.

These days, many teachers give us teachings, empowerments, and advice. It's fine to have many teachers, and it shows earnestness and sincerity in finding and understanding the Dharma. However, we need to have one particular person who opens up and clarifies the path, saying *that* is the way to go. We need to have a personal teacher and to know who that is. This is not a simple matter. It takes a lot of combined merit and noble wishes from many, many lifetimes to be able to connect with one person and have that trust and devotion. We shouldn't think it's easy.

When you look at the life stories of past masters, often you see that after having done a lot practice, yidam practice for example, he or she may have had a vision of the wisdom deity, who makes a prediction that such-and-such person is their root guru. Meeting such a person transforms one's experience completely, and that is one of the sure signs of having found the personal root guru.

For example, in the Nyingma tradition, Prahevajra's root guru was Vajrasattva, and Manjushrimitra's root guru was Prahevajra, and so forth. Each of these had very clear indications pointing to his or her primary master. So this is how we have one after the other in an unbroken lineage. In the Kagyü lineage, we have lists of masters: Vajradhara, Tilopa, Naropa, Marpa, Milarepa, and so forth. We can count them, one after the other; they are called the Golden Rosary of the Kagyü masters. When you read their biographies, you will understand. For example, Naropa was already a great, learned master, a pandita, when he had a vision of a dakini who told him he must meet Tilopa, in order to attain the supreme siddhi of Mahamudra. Naropa set out to find him, and after finding Tilopa, he was forced to undergo many very difficult trials. At the end, he attained realization of the supreme accomplishment of Mahamudra. In all of these biographies you see that the Kagyü lineage masters found one outstanding person who was their unique, personal master. Read their biographies, think about them, and gain some understanding of this point.

According to the tantras, there are four different kinds of gurus: the guru from whom one receives empowerment, the guru who explains the meaning of the tantras, the guru who gives oral transmission, and so forth. These are counted in different ways, according to the degree or profundity of kindness, whether it's a triple, double, or singular kindness. But the root guru who introduces us to the view of Mahamudra or Dzogchen, bringing us face-to-face with our mind's nature—not only pointing out the state of pure knowing, but also infusing our being completely with the blessings to realize and recognize the true state of Mahamudra or Dzogchen—that is called the extraordinary root guru. That kindness is inconceivably great. When someone who is completely caught within the web of emotions, ignorance, and karma is shown, in one instant, the awakened state of all buddhas, which can halt and end *samsara*, how can there be any greater kindness given? If we have stayed in a dark dungeon for countless aeons, and then a person comes and switches on the light, dispelling all the darkness in a single moment, how amazing! In essence, we are brought face-to-face with our own nature, the dharmakaya nature of all buddhas. What greater kindness could there possibly be? If one has a root guru like that, great! If one doesn't, make sure to get one, because without such a guru, there is no way to be enlightened.

According to the sutras, the guru is a spiritual friend or guide, who shows us what to do and what not to do, so we can progress. But according to the Mantrayana or Vajrayana, empowerment is the entrance door to practicing the tantras. Of the four empowerments, the most important is the fourth, which empowers us so the play of pure knowing ripens. Without having a guru to point this out, so we can recognize this basic nature, there is no way to practice Vajrayana.

Here in this text, Padmasambhava says, "When a person wants to practice the Dharma in an authentic and true way, he or she needs to follow a guru. When following a guru, trust, real trust from the core of one's heart, from the marrow of one's bones, is of utmost importance; otherwise, the root of Dharma practice has rotted." What does it mean for a root to be rotten? It means something is wrong, like when the seed of a flower or plant becomes spoiled, preventing growth. No petals, leaves, or plant will come out of it. The Three Precious Ones are present as the root guru, so without a root guru something really important is missing. Moreover, the guru is the root of blessings, so without a guru and devotion to a guru, there will be no blessings and no inspiration. Whether we have trust or not depends upon our mind; but without having a true object of trust, a person we have properly identified and in whom we place our trust, there is absolutely no way to attain enlightenment.

The lama is the root of blessings, the yidam is the root of accomplishments, and the dakinis and dharma protectors are the roots of activities. Those are the Three Roots. Actually the Three Roots are all gathered into the lama. The title of this practice refers to the lama, indicating that this is a practice to accomplish the lama. If we are able to merge our mind with the wisdom mind of the lama, then we are accomplishing the lama, Guru Rinpoche. If we are actually able to accomplish the indivisibility of our own mind with the wisdom mind of the lama, then we are accomplishing Guru Rinpoche. If not, we are not accomplishing the lama.

If one has already found a genuine master, then Padmasambhava's advice to supplicate one's guru becomes relevant. The precious master Padmasambhava appeared in Tibet and taught his primary twenty-five disciples. He empowered them to appear at various intervals in the future, manifesting, for example, as the one hundred major treasure-revealers. But understand that all of them are indivisible from Padmasambhava; they are the magical web, the play of his wisdom mind, without exception.

Padmasambhava is Buddha, and Buddha is dharmakaya. Dharmakaya permeates, or is present as, the nature of mind of every single being in a constant, spontaneously present, and all-pervasive way. Thus, firmly resolve that your personal root guru is indivisible from the Precious Master Padmasambhava. Your personal root guru is none other than the dharmakaya of all buddhas. Having understood this, call upon Padmasambhava from the core of your heart with complete surrender. He says there is no deeper advice than supplication. This is the intent of all sutras and tantras. You can supplicate in many ways, but the condensed essence of all supplication is calling upon your root guru. To clear away all hindrances and gain every accomplishment, there is one supreme method, which is calling upon your root guru. Padmasambhava has personally said there is no deeper advice than that.

There are many obstacles and blockages as well as methods to overcome them. All mistaken experiences are a hindrance, but once you understand that every thought-state is your own display, there is no hindrance whatsoever. If you don't understand this, there are many obstacles. For a person who wants to practice the Dharma in an authentic way, it is possible to diagnose exactly what's wrong—the outer hindrances, the imbalances of the four elements, the imbalances in this illusory body and in the subtle channels and energies, and the hindrances created by fixating on duality and deluded thinking. Just being overcome by obstacles and leaving it like that is absolutely not all right. We need to identify exactly what's wrong, and Padmasambhava, who is omniscient, made categories for all the obstacles and hindrances.

Now, let's get back to the rest of the history of this cycle, the *Tukdrub Barchey Künsel*. After listening to Guru Rinpoche's advice for overcoming obstacles, heartfelt supplication to the guru, his three main students, King Trisong Deütsen, Yeshe Tsogyal, and Prince Murub Tseypo, reflected on his words. They came to realize Avalokiteshvara is the main deity associated with Tibet and Guru Rinpoche is the chief lama associated karmically with Tibet. As for themselves, they had no other refuge, no other lama than Guru Rinpoche. They asked him to give an actual means of accomplishment, a way to be able to really eliminate obstacles. Guru Rinpoche agreed. Placing his left hand on the head of Yeshe Tsogyal, his right hand on the head of King Trisong Deütsen, and his forehead on the forehead of Prince Murub Tseypo, he brought forth from the vast expanse of his dharmakaya wisdom mind the prayer called *Sampa Lhündrub*.

Then they told Guru Rinpoche this was an extraordinary prayer that all his students would recite, but they still requested him to give an actual sadhana, an application, to eliminate obstacles. Guru Rinpoche agreed, and he manifested the *Tukdrub Barchey Künsel* mandala. Padmasambhava is the main deity, as the nirmanakaya *Nangsi Zilnön*. Above him is the sambhogakaya Avalokiteshvara, and above him is the dharmakaya Amitabha or Amitayus, together with the twelve manifestations of Guru Rinpoche, the four gate keepers, and the dakas and dakinis in union. Guru Rinpoche displayed the mandala and gave this teaching, complete with the root tantra, as well as the sadhanas and the different texts for accomplishing the activities through this teaching.

Later these teachings were transmitted to his disciples, who practiced them and, in this way, removed all obstacles and attained accomplishment. Yeshe Tsogyal wrote down the teachings. Twelve years after Guru Rinpoche left Tibet, she hid this terma in the cave of *Da-Nying Khala Rong-Go,* according to Guru Rinpoche's prophecy. King Trisong Deütsen's middle son, Murub Tseypo, made very deep and noble wishes, which, combined with Guru Rinpoche's blessings, enabled him to appear as Chokgyur Dechen Lingpa and reveal this terma. He kept this terma secret for eight years, just practicing it himself. At the same time, King Trisong Deütsen incarnated as the great master Jamyang Khyentse Wangpo. These two together brought forth this terma treasure of incredible blessing and swift results, known as *Lamey Tukdrub Barchey Künsel.* With the help of Jamgön Kongtrül, an incarnation of the translator

Vairotsana, these teachings were spread throughout Tibet and are now present up to this day.

Lamey Tukdrub Barchey Künsel is the guru's heart practice that clears away all hindrances, thus actualizing the siddhis. To combine everything in essence and clear hindrances and obstacles, supplicate the root guru. Outer hindrances, caused by the eight or sixteen types of threats, can be removed by calling upon the root guru. All the hindrances inside the subtle channels and energies, which result from mistaken use of the structured channels, the moving energies, and the blissful essences, can be cleared away by calling upon one's root guru. Defilements can also be cleansed by supplicating one's root guru. On a secret level, deluded thinking, the multitude of different thoughts that well up, can be purified as well by calling upon one's root guru.

This is a short explanation that hits the point. In order to apply this deep method, one needs to be a person of higher capacity, someone who has identified and has trust in a root guru—not just lip service, platitudes, or other superficial forms of trust, but a deep willingness from the core of one's heart to see the root guru as the Buddha in person. Having this trust, one is able to feel complete devotion and surrender, seeing whatever the guru does as perfect and whatever he or she says as excellent. If one is that kind of disciple, able to call upon the root guru out of deep yearning and devotion, with or without words, from the basic seed of one's mind, completely surrendering from the core of one's being to the root guru—that is enough. But if one isn't, and one needs more of a detailed way of going about removing obstacles, then one should supplicate the four additional deities in this cycle, Arya Tara, Achala, Mewa Tsekpa, and Dorje Bechön, to clear away outer, inner, secret, and innermost obstacles. For each of these deities, there is an empowerment, a sadhana, pith instructions on how to practice, activities to carry out, and so forth—many details.

(clockwise from top left): Dorje Bechön, Miyowa, Mewa Tsekpa, Tara

THE QUINTESSENCE OF WISDOM OPENNESS ፧

Padmasambhava

Emerging from samadhi, Padmakara taught this root yoga,
the source of all mandalas: ፧

Having obtained the supreme freedoms and riches, and being
    weary of impermanence,፧
With intense renunciation, endeavor in accepting and rejecting
    what concerns cause and effect.፧
Those possessing faith and compassion,፧
Who wish to attain the supreme and common siddhis in this very
    life,፧
Should ripen their being through empowerment and, with totally
    pure samaya,፧
Take refuge, the root of the path,፧
As well as generate the twofold bodhichitta, the essence of the
    path.፧
All evil deeds and obscurations, the conditions opposing
    experiences and realization፧
Of Vajrayana, the ultimate part of the path,፧
Should be purified through the profound practice of Vajrasattva.፧
In order to perfect the positive conditions, the accumulation of
    merit and wisdom,፧
Offer the mandalas of the ocean-like realms of the three kayas.፧
In particular, apply the key points of the essence of all the paths,፧
The guru yoga of devotion:፧
Amid an ocean of offering clouds in the sky before me,፧
Upon the lion throne and layered lotus, sun, and moon,፧
Is Orgyen Tötreng Tsal, the embodiment of all objects of refuge.፧
He has one face and two arms and is wrathfully smiling and
    glowing with resplendent light.፧

He wears the lotus crown, secret dress, gown, Dharma robes, and
    brocade cloak.
Holding a vajra in his right hand and a skull with a vase in his left,
He embraces the secret mudra in the hidden form of a khatvanga.
With his two feet in the reveling posture, he is within a sphere of
    five-colored rainbow light.
He sends out cloud banks of the all-encompassing Three Roots.
All that appears and exists is the essence of the glorious guru.

Perform the external practice in the manner of supplication
And the inner practice in the manner of recitation.
Afterward, receive the four empowerments and dissolve Guru
    Rinpoche into yourself.
In the luminous state of your mind inseparable from the guru,
Experience one-pointedly the secret, ultimate guru.

Through the practice of the great emptiness, the space of suchness,
Where all the relative and ultimate dharmas
Are the great supreme dharmakaya of the inseparable two truths,
You will realize death as the natural state of luminosity.
Through the practice of the all-illuminating samadhi,
In the illusory manner of nonconceptual compassion,
Toward unrealized sentient beings pervading space,
The bardo will appear as the forms of the deities of the Magical
    Net.

Particularly, in order to purify the process of taking birth,
Practice the development stage, which ends clinging to ordinary
    experience:

Visualize as perfected in instantaneous recollection in order to
    purify miraculous birth,
And visualize through the emanation and absorption of the seed
    syllable in order to purify birth by warmth.
Visualize the seed syllable, attributes, and bodily form in order to
    purify womb birth,
And visualize the cause and effect heruka in order to purify egg
    birth.
In all cases, visualize the mandala of the base and the based,
And the faces, arms, and attributes in total completeness.

First, in order to train gradually in this,§
Visualize yourself in the form of the single mudra§
With vivid features, like a rainbow.§
At best, regard it as the natural great absolute;§
As the next best, envision the distinct general and specific features;§
At least, plant the stake of unchanging concentration.§
Place an image with all the characteristics before you§
And focus your mind, eyes, and *prana* one-pointedly upon it.§
When a vivid presence appears, abandon the defects of drowsiness
    and agitation,§
Rest in the state where the form of the deity is the unity of
    appearance and emptiness,§
And the experience will arise, in which the turbulence of thoughts
    has subsided.§

Sometimes rest, bringing consciousness to its natural state.§
Sometimes transform the expression of your concentration into
    many different things.§
In each session, bring the clear appearance of the deity to
    perfection.§
In each session, plant the great stake of the essence mantra.§
In each session, rest in the same taste of the deity and your mind.§
In each session, accomplish the magical display of emanating and
    absorbing rays of light.§
At all times, keep the pride of being inseparable from the deity.§
Since the path illustrates the unity of ground and fruition,§
Practice the total purity that stops the clinging to ordinary
    experience.§
In between sessions, mend the samayas with feast gatherings and
    tormas.§
Bring all that appears and exists onto the path§
As the essence of the magical deity, mantra, and great wisdom.§

If you practice one-pointedly in this way,§
The experiences of movement, attainment, habituation, steadiness,
    and perfection will arise,§
And you will actually meet with the form possessing the threefold
    vividness.§

You will accomplish the truth of speech and a changeless mind.⁑

Next, fix your mind on the entire mandala circle,⁑
And when you have gradually attained its vivid presence,⁑
Emanate groups of buddha families filling the sky.⁑

Through the samadhi of the Magical Net⁑
Of the Vidyadhara power-wielders, and appearance and existence
    as manifest ground,⁑
And by means of group practice in an assembly,⁑
The highest siddhi will be accomplished.⁑
With the perfect place, time, teacher, retinue, and articles,⁑
Correctly perform the "rite of the land"⁑
And practice the sadhanas of outer, inner, and secret retreat.⁑

Erect the sign mandala as the support for concentration,⁑
A vivid and complete image adorned with ornaments.⁑
Visualize yourself and the whole retinue, the self-existing mandala
    deities,
As inseparable means and knowledge.⁑

By the light rays of Approach and Full Approach,⁑
Purify the outer world into the Lotus Net Realm.⁑
By the emanation and absorption of the light rays of
    Accomplishment,⁑
Transform all the inner inhabitants into the forms of the Magical
    Net of the Vidyadharas.⁑
Purify your being by the Great Accomplishment.⁑
Then, through the vivid presence of the deity forms and the rays of
    the mantra,⁑
And through the samadhi of bliss and emptiness and the practices
    of uniting and freeing,⁑
When completing six, twelve, or eighteen months,⁑
As the outer signs, you will actually have a vision of the deity,⁑
The mandala will emit light, and the nectar in the vase will boil.⁑
The skull cup will tremble, and the butter lamp will ignite by
    itself.⁑
As the inner signs, your body, speech, and mind will be blissful;
    your prana and awareness will be clear;⁑

And your perception of all the dharmas of fixation and grasping
   will be illusory.ᢀ
As the secret signs, your mind will be changeless in one-pointed
   samadhi,ᢀ
And the assembly of deities will be perfected within you.ᢀ

Since at this time you will have realized the supreme siddhi,ᢀ
You can display various miracles of the one taste of appearances
   and mind.ᢀ
Even without changing your body, your mind will initially
   accomplishᢀ
The Vidyadhara of Full Maturation in the form of a deity.ᢀ
You will attain the mastery of life, the vajra body,ᢀ
And by means of the supreme family of the great mudra of the five
   aspects,ᢀ
You will perfect the ten bhumis and realize the great regency,ᢀ
The Vidyadhara of Spontaneous Accomplishment.ᢀ

The intent of recitation, the auxiliary of the development stage,ᢀ
Has four visualizations of Approach and Accomplishment.ᢀ
First, upon the moon in your heart center,ᢀ
Within the center of the five-pronged golden vajra,ᢀ
Is the letter HRIH upon a moon, glowing like a flame.ᢀ
The mantra garland surrounding itᢀ
Is self-resounding and revolves continuously.ᢀ
To fix your mind on this, like the moon with a garland of stars,ᢀ
Is called the intent of Approach invoking the mind of the deity.ᢀ

The mantra garland emanating from there emerges through your
   mouthᢀ
And enters through the mouth of the wisdom being before you.ᢀ
Passing through the bodily form and the navel lotus,ᢀ
It enters your navel and revolves as before.ᢀ
Light rays and essences gather in your heart bindu.ᢀ
Imagine that the wisdom of great bliss is stabilizedᢀ
And that all the siddhis are mastered.ᢀ
This concentration, like the wheel of a firebrand,ᢀ
Is the intent of the Full Approach to the deity.ᢀ

This can also be exchanged with the form of the consort, your own
  radiance,

Or with any of the different emanation visualizations

In order to invoke the surrounding assembly of deities.

By the light rays emanating from the mantra,

Offering clouds make offerings to the noble ones and gather the
  blessings back into you.

The obscurations are purified, the accumulations are perfected, and
  you have obtained the empowerments and siddhis.

As they emanate again, the karmas and disturbing emotions of the
  beings of the three realms are purified.

Emanating and absorbing, like the emissaries of the king,

Is the intent of mastering the Accomplishment of siddhis.

At this time, the outer world is the vajra realm of Akanishtha.

Appearances are deities, and all the animate and inanimate sounds
  are mantras.

Thoughts are the display of nondual wisdom.

During this, reciting in the great state of appearance and existence
  as manifest ground,

This practice, like a beehive broken open,

Is the intent of the Great Accomplishment of siddhis.

You should apply these four intents of vajra recitation

Chiefly to the practices of the single form, the elaborate form,

The group, and the gathering.

The next practice should be entered when the vivid presence of the
  former is perfected.

However, through the intent of these instructions of mine, Self-
  Born Lotus,

The way of practicing the recitation intents of Approach and
  Accomplishment,

Combined into one in a single sitting session,

Has been taught in order to swiftly produce blessings and signs.

Through the internal way of profound HUNG recitation,

Clinging to the appearances of the development stage stops and the
  power of awareness increases.

Through the secret and most profound method of the prana
     recitation of great bliss,
Samadhi is stabilized and pliancy is attained.

As to the ultimate practice of dissolution into luminosity,
By HUNG hung hung, the world and its inhabitants, along with
     your body,
Gradually dissolve into the seed syllable, the letter HRIH.
This again dissolves into the innate state of nonconceptual
     luminosity.

Where the past has ceased and the future has not yet arisen,
In the unimpeded state of present wakefulness,
Rest in the manner of mind looking into mind.
No matter what thoughts may arise at this time,
They are all the display of the single mind essence.
As the nature of space is unchanging,
You will realize the all-pervasive mind essence to be changeless.
This is the Great Perfection, the ultimate of all vehicles,
The unexcelled meaning of the self-existing Mind Section.

Whoever practices this ultimate yoga
Will have limitless secret signs and virtues.
The great power of experience and realization will gradually be
     perfected,
And they will attain the wisdom of the Ever-Excellent Padma.
By then uttering PHAT phat phat,
Perceive yourself and the world with its inhabitants as the mandala
     circle.
Within the state of the unity of the development and completion,
Further increase the two accumulations of merit and wisdom.

This essence of the ocean of tantras and oral instructions
Is complete and concise and has immense blessings.
It is easy to practice and is the path to enlightenment in one
     lifetime.
It contains the key points in the intent of the *Magical Net of the
     Vidyadharas*
And of the *Direct Vision of the Ever-Excellent Mind Essence,*
Which I have gathered as the vital blood in my heart.

I, the great Self-Born Padma, have taught it᠄

For the benefit of the present king, his sons, and my disciples᠄

And for the benefit of qualified beings in the future.᠄

Future generations, do not let this nectar dissipate, but collect this
   essence᠄

And accomplish the supreme and common siddhis!᠄

My children, practice continuously!᠄

Practitioners of knowledge mantras, never be apart from
   development and recitation!᠄

Yogis, bring your realization to encompass dharmadhatu!᠄

Samaya, seal, seal, seal.

Having expounded this most affectionate instruction, pouring out from
the treasury of his realization, he entered the all-magnetizing samadhi.᠄

This was the fourth chapter from the Wish-Fulfilling Essence Manual
of Oral Instructions, *on the Quintessence of Wisdom Openness, the root
samadhi, which is the source of all mandalas.*᠄

NOTES ON ARRANGEMENT OF THE LITURGY FOR THE DETAILED PRACTICE OF THE APPROACH, ACCOMPLISHMENT, AND ACTIVITIES OF TUKDRUB BARCHEY KÜNSEL

Jamyang Khyentse Wangpo

Some people wishing to engage in extensive practice of the approach, accomplishment, and activities of *Tukdrub* may not have initially found time to complete the preliminaries in the usual allotment of time, such as one year. In that case, chant 10,000 of refuge, as much as you can of arousing bodhichitta, 10,000 of the Hundred Syllables, and 10,000 of either the long or short mandala offering. It is excellent if you can do 10,000 prostrations combined with the same number of the short supplication of the outer practice of guru yoga. If you can, also recite about 1,000 of *Barchey Lamsel*. Chant four times 100,000 of the Vajra Guru mantra for the inner practice. At the end of the session, do the secret practice of sustaining the realization.

After having fully completed all the preliminaries in this way, arrange the *amrita, rakta*, torma, and the seven enjoyments for the recitation practice of the main part. In the dawn session—from among the four sessions—do the full preliminaries and recitation of the main part, according to the liturgy of the *Medium Practice Manual*, the *Trinley Dringpo*. Do the *Extensive Practice Manual*, the *Trinley Gyepa*, in the late morning session; the *Medium Practice Manual* in the afternoon session; and the *Extensive Practice Manual* at the end of that session, following it through the feast down to the verses of auspiciousness. It is permissible to omit the invocation, covenant, *Tenma* offerings, and the horse dance every day, but definitely perform them on the tenth day and so forth. Before the feast, or otherwise before the residual offering, also do the petition offering to the *Five Tseringma Sisters,* the teaching guardians, up to the praises, as well as the torma offering to *Kharak Khyung Tsünma,* the treasure guardian. If you don't do the mending prayers, mending of disharmony rituals, or the *Tenma* petition on a daily basis, perform them on special days, such as the tenth. In particular, make extensive mending prayers on the eighth.

In the evening session, perform the *Medium Practice Manual.* Whether you are following the *Medium Practice Manual* or the *Concise Daily Practice Manual,* open up the recitation mansion saying, Bhrung vishva vishuddhe hrih hung phat jah at the end of the praises.

At the point of recitation-invocation in the *Extensive Practice Manual,* invoke with the words, "Boundless Light and your assembly of deities, manifest from dharmadhatu…" Chant the elaborate visualization for recitation. For the *Medium Practice Manual,* just follow the text; for the other two, combine it with them.

When concluding a session at the time of doing the life recitation, do as much as you can of the Seven Syllables, Vajra Guru, and Tötreng Tsal mantras as well as the Harinisa mantra, following the *Medium Practice Manual*; also chant the Vowels and Consonants and the Essence of Causation mantras. As indicated by this, when doing the Seven Syllables and so forth, simply maintain the continuity of the preceding and following recitations.

If you follow the *Extensive Practice Manual,* say, "Wisdom deities, I invite you, please come…" Make the praises saying, "Om. Wisdom of the Bliss-Gone Recite the *Barchey Lamsel* supplication and confess faults with "Om. Entire assembly of vidyadhara mandala deities…" Saying, Om ah hung svaha…, toss the flower of awareness and dissolve the wisdom beings in front into you; then stabilize that with the Hundred Syllables. Saying, "Hung. In unborn emptiness…", perform the dissolution and emergence down to the verses of auspiciousness.

If you follow the *Medium Practice Manual,* proceed through the Vowels and Consonants and Essence of Causation mantras as above. Make the Thousand-Point offering, saying, "Gathering of wisdom deities…" At the end of the *Barchey Lamsel* supplication, confess faults with the Hundred Syllables. Saying, Jah hung bam hoh, imagine that the wisdom beings in front dissolve into you, stabilize with the Hundred Syllables, dissolve with the triple hung, and continue through to the utterance of auspiciousness in the general way.

In this order, chant eleven times 100,000 of the Amarani mantra; for a two-month duration, chant four times 100,000. Recite ten, seven, or four times 100,000 for the Seven Syllables, according to what is possible, as in the general manner. Be sure to do a full twelve times 100,000 of the Vajra Guru mantra as well as the amending number.

Following that, if you can integrate the accomplishment, the detailed way is to do this according to the system of the Great Accomplishment liturgy. If you cannot do that, perform the elaborate planting of the poles of the great kings and engage in the accomplishment. If you have to interrupt in the middle, it will be fine at this point to do the accomplishment practice in an abbreviated manner, along with the activity applications. Thus, combining this with the key points for visualization according to the *Medium Practice Manual*, recite four times 100,000 Tötreng Tsal mantras and 10,000 Harinisa mantras.

It is good if you can perform the fire ritual of amendment; if not, chant the Hundred Syllables at the end of the session for a few days. Finish retreat after performing 100 *ganachakras*, mending and confession prayers to the dharmapalas, and thanksgiving offerings.

If you are engaging in the accomplishment practice, get the details elsewhere. It is fine to plant the poles of the great kings at the time of the preliminaries; otherwise, follow the general system.

It is best if you can begin the recitation practice in the afternoon during the waning moon with auspicious astrology; plant the poles of the great kings at that time. When finishing, elaborately perform the ritual for receiving the siddhis at the end of the dawn session on a day with auspicious astrology during the waxing moon; then come out as the sun is rising.

You can learn about what to avoid, adopt, and so forth while in retreat from the general recitation manuals.

This was composed by Khyentse Wangpo. May it be virtuous.

(top) King Trisong Deutsen; (above) Vairochana

A SEED OF THE GREAT SAL TREE

A Concise Composition of Notes on the Approach and
Accomplishment for Lamey Tukdrub Barchey Künsel,
The Guru's Heart Practice, Dispeller of All Obstacles

Jamgön Kongtrül

The thought of you dispels all obstacles
And when supplicated, you bestow the two siddhis.
Lord Guru, embodiment of all buddhas,
Accept me throughout all my lives.

I will now, in accord with my master's words,
Compose an application of the Approach and Accomplishment
For this unique buried treasure,
The wondrous essence of one-billion guru sadhanas.

Generally, for the basic descriptions of how to practice this, take the third
chapter taught in the *Sheldam Nyingjang* as the basis and apply it, following your teacher's oral advice in the extensive, medium, or concise version (*Trinley Nyingpo*), whichever is appropriate, and in accordance with
the situation, in terms of place, time, and type of person.

Whether you begin the practice of development or completion, first
perform the general preliminaries of the fourfold mind training and the
four special preliminaries.

For the main part, according to the specifications of Terchen Chokgyur Lingpa, take *Sheldam Nyingjang* as the basis and first practice
dharmakaya Amitayus, followed by sambhogakaya Great Compassionate One, combined with the *Lotus Magical Net*. After that, practice the
nirmanakaya aspect combined with the extensive or medium version,
whichever is suitable, and complete the set numbers of individual recitations for approach and accomplishment. Following that, it is necessary
to perform successively the specific approach recitations, by combining

the twelve manifestations with *Trinley Nyingpo,* and to complete the four activities and the four ancillary practices as well as the practice of the teaching guardians.

According to the directions of the omniscient master, Padma Ösel Do-Ngak Lingpa (Jamyang Khyentse Wangpo): Perform the single mudra according to the *Gyüngyi Köljang,* the *Concise Daily Practice Manual,* as the beginning of the main part for the approach; perform the condensed outer mandala of *Trinley Nyingpo,* the *Yoga of Essential Activity,* for the full approach; do the *Trinley Dringpo,* the *Medium Practice Manual,* for the accomplishment; and perform *Trinley Gyepa,* the *Extensive Practice Manual,* together with *Dzapkyi Köljang,* the *Recitation Manual,* and so forth in a detailed way for the great accomplishment. The samadhis (concentrations) and visualizations for recitation of these should conform with the third chapter of the root text (*Sheldam Nyingjang*). Having properly performed the four aspects of approach and accomplishment, he taught that one should then perform the "specific practices," such as those for dharmakaya, sambhogakaya, and so forth, whichever are suitable.

There is no difference between following either of these two sets of directions, since they are both lords of these profound teachings. Nevertheless, in harmony with the methods of both great treasure masters, I will structure what they have taught on the way of performing the approach and accomplishment recitations, by means of only the *Leyjang, Practice Manual, (Trinley Dringpo).* I will describe it in a way that is easy to apply and in conformity with the present day's general practitioners of number recitations. This structure has two parts: the extensive and the concise ways.

THE EXTENSIVE WAY

It is essential to first have completed the mind training of the general preliminaries, such as the difficult-to-find freedoms and riches, and so forth. If you have not practiced them, they can be linked to the special preliminaries in this following way:

Train your mind in the difficult-to-find freedoms and riches, thinking, "I will engage myself in taking refuge, the basis of all means for utilizing these freedoms and riches!" With this thought, visualize the objects of refuge. The chief figure is your own master as Nangsi Zilnön, the glorious subjugator of all that appears and exists, surrounded by the masters of the lineage. Before him are the yidams. To his right is the nirmanakaya Buddha. Behind him is the Dharma. To his left is the Sangha. All around him you imagine the dakinis, dharma protectors, and wealth gods.

While understanding the general way of taking refuge and so forth, take refuge 100,000 times together with the amending number. It will be most excellent if you can make 100,000 prostrations, either at this point or at the time of the following Seven Branches.

After that, inspire yourself with the thought of impermanence, thinking, "In this short life, when the time of death lies uncertain, I will develop the two kinds of bodhichitta, the essence of all means for utilizing the freedoms and riches. I will mount the steed of the awakened heart and possess the confidence of moving through increasing levels of happiness!" Carried along by this thought, recite 100,000 each for the aspiration, the gathering of accumulation, and the application. This is the extensive way of developing bodhichitta. The medium way is to do a suitable number, such as 10,000 of each. The short way is to do 10,000 or such of just the bodhichitta of aspiration, since the application is essentially included within that.

No matter where one may take rebirth after dying, one's experience has the nature of suffering, the root of which lies in the truth of origin, which consists of karma and disturbing emotions. While understanding that reducing this suffering depends on purifying your misdeeds and failings, which are produced by the disturbing emotions, be sure to complete 100,000 Hundred Syllable mantras as well as the amending number, in accordance with what is taught about the meditation and recitation of Vajrasattva. Also, recite the Six Syllables as much as you can.

Following that, reflect on the way in which the results of actions ripen. With the intention to quickly create an immense accumulation of virtue, visualize the field of accumulation, as at the time of taking refuge, and complete 100,000 of the extensive mandala offerings; alternately, perform 10,000 of the extensive offering and a full 100,000 of the short offering taught in the context of the Tara practice: "OM AH HUNG. The three realms, worlds, and beings..." until "RATNA MANDALA PUJA HOH."

Next, consider the benefits of liberation, knowing that the ultimate path of obtaining it depends on receiving the master's blessings. So, while intent on engaging in the guru yoga of devotion, first visualize the support for practicing in the external way of supplication and complete a number, such as 10,000 or 1,000 of the supplication *Barchey Lamsel, Clearing Obstacles on the Path,* and a full 100,000 of the short *Düsum Sangye* supplication. In addition, at the beginning of the session, count a suitable number of *Barchey Lamsel,* such as twenty-one or seven times, followed by the short supplication. For practicing in the inner way of approach, recite the Vajra Guru mantra—at best 10,000,000 times, or next best twelve times 100,000, or at least four times 100,000. For the innermost practice of sustaining the wisdom mind, rest for a long time in composure at the end of all sessions.

Furthermore, from taking refuge up until the guru yoga, make the specific practice you are doing the main part of the session and complete one full set of preliminaries in each session. The *Seed of Supreme Enlightenment,* composed by the Lord Guru Khyentse Rinpoche, clarifies the way to chant these practices.

If you are interested in doing a short set of preliminaries for a program of approach and accomplishment recitations, it is initially good if you can do a corresponding number of prostrations together with taking refuge 10,000 times. For the bodhisattva resolve, do as many as you can. Perform 10,000 of the Hundred Syllables and 10,000 of either the long or short mandala offerings, whichever is suitable. For the outer practice of the guru yoga, complete 10,000 of the short supplications and, if you can, about 1,000 of the *Barchey Lamsel* as well. For the inner practice, do four times 100,000 of Vajra Guru and perform the innermost practice of sustaining the wisdom mind at the end of all sessions.

Having completed all the preliminaries in an excellent way, prepare the approach of the main part, by arranging representations of Guru Rinpoche's body, speech, and mind in front of you, using whatever you have. Place before that the *Shining Jewel Torma,* with amrita on its right and rakta on its left sides. Set out the seven enjoyments in front of the torma.

To the right of the amrita, place the torma of the teaching guardian, *Tseringma,* upon the central bulb of a white torma with four petals, with one pellet in each of the four directions. The white torma is surrounded by pills in the intermediate spaces and has a white staff. To the left of the rakta, place the torma of the treasure guardian, *Kharak Khyung Tsünma,* a triangular red torma with ornaments, surrounded by pellets.

Also arrange the *kartor* (white torma); *gektor* (obstructor's torma); feast articles; tormas for the covenant, the *Tenmas*; and so forth—all that is needed for the *Practice Manuals.*

Begin with the afternoon session on an auspicious date. On the occasion of an approach and accomplishment recitation, you should chiefly perform the *Medium Practice Manual* and the *Concise Daily Practice Manual*; perform the *Extensive Practice Manual* when doing a drubchen. Here, begin with the supplications, such as the *Seven Lines,* and perform the *Trinley Dringpo*, the *Medium Practice Manual.*

When throwing the gektor outside, plant the poles and draw the boundary lines of protection. Perform the preliminary phases and the main part from the visualization of the deities up through the praises. Open up the recitation mansion and do the invocation for the recitation. At the end of completing a certain set of recitations, repeat the offerings and praises. Chant the supplication *Barchey Lamsel.* Apologize for faults, receive the empowerments, and dissolve the recitation mansion. Perform either the extensive or short torma offering for the guardians *Tseringma* and *Kharak Khyung Tsünma.* Offer a feast together with the mending. Keep the residual offering (*lhagma*) "imprisoned," without sending it out, until you finish the approach-accomplishment recitation. You may also wait until you finish retreat to perform the covenant and give the *Tenma* tormas. At the end, make a thanksgiving with offerings, praises, and apology for faults. Request the feast guests to remain perpetually in the shrine objects. Perform the dissolution and emergence of the mandala of self-visualization. Do the dedication, aspiration, and utterance of auspiciousness.

During the evening session, perform refuge, bodhichitta, and the Seven Branches. Visualize the protection circle as done earlier; if not possible, do the *Trinley Nyingpo,* which will suffice. At the point of expelling the obstructors, instead of saying, "Take this torma," say, "Don't remain in this place." At the end of the praises, open the recitation mansion and so forth, as before. When finishing the session, make offerings and recite the praises, supplication, and apology for faults. Dissolve the recitation mansion and perform the dissolution and emergence of the self-visualization. Make dedication, aspiration, and utterance of auspiciousness. Thereafter, engage in the yoga of sleep.

At dawn, perform the yoga of waking up, the blessing of your voice, and so forth; do the *Trinley Nyingpo.* Perform the *Trinley Dringpo* in both the morning and afternoon sessions. For the evening session, it is more convenient to just do the *Trinley Nyingpo,* yet it is permissible to arrange this session according to your own liking. Make the torma offering to the teaching guardians each day without a break. As for the feast offering, it is permissible to do it only on auspicious days, such as the tenth and so forth, if you cannot make it daily.

When beginning and finishing the retreat, it is important to include profound and extensive mending and apology chants.

When performing the sadhana in this fashion, start with the dharmakaya recitation, Boundless Life; the set number for this recitation is eleven times 100,000. Prior to completing this number, make that alone the principal recitation in the main part of your session. At the end of the session, recite about 100 of each of all the others.

After completing the specified number of recitations of the first mantra, continue to recite it about 100 times at the beginning of each session. For the main part of the session, recite ten or seven times 100,000 of the Seven Syllables of sambhogakaya.

Having completed the sambhogakaya recitation, recite some of both dharmakaya and sambhogakaya at the beginning of each session. In the main part, recite the essence of nirmanakaya, the Vajra Guru mantra, at best forty-eight times 100,000; if you cannot, make sure to complete a full twelve times 100,000.

Following this, for the combined practice, recite four times 100,000 of Tötreng Tsal. At this point, it is very important to chant it seven or twenty-one times at the beginning of the session, applying whichever tune you know.

After that, for reciting the activity application, it is taught that one should recite one-tenth as much as the approach recitation; so recite a little more than 10,000. Completing this recitation along with the extras for each mantra is the extensive way of reciting based on the *Practice Manuals*.

THE CONCISE WAY

If you wish to establish a connection with this practice within a month's time, use one day for reciting the preliminaries, refuge, bodhichitta, and the Seven Branches; one day for Vajrasattva; one day for the mandala offering; one day for supplication; and one day for the recitation of the inner practice of the guru yoga.

Having completed these five days, use *Trinley Dringpo* on the first and last days of the main practice. For the principal part, based on *Trin-*

ley Nyingpo, use seven days for reciting Amarani and seven days for the Seven Syllables. Recite four times 100,000 of the Vajra Guru mantra. Use three days for reciting Tötreng Tsal mantra and about one day for the activity application. This way will also be right.

Whether you practice in the extensive or short way, complete the set numbers of recitations and, when drawing close to finishing retreat, recite as many of the Hundred Syllables as you can at the end of each session. The evening before the final morning, change the offerings for new ones and elaborately arrange whatever feast articles you have. At the dawn session the next morning, follow the root text of the *Practice Manual (Trinley Dringpo)* and recite as much as you can. Make offerings and praises, *Barchey Lamsel* supplications, and apologies for faults in a more extensive way.

At the break of dawn, invoke the siddhis with the lines from *Trinley Gyepa*, the *Extensive Practice Manual*. Touch the torma visualized as the deities to your three places, do the visualization for receiving the siddhis, and enjoy some of the torma. Receive the empowerments and dissolve the recitation mansion. After that, perform 100 feast and mending chants as a thanksgiving. If you cannot do this, still make an elaborate feast offering, with a mending apology.

Place all the residual offerings gathered earlier outside. Make a torma offering to the teaching guardians, invoke their heart-samaya, give the covenant and *Tenma* offerings, and complete it with the horse dance. Then make a thanksgiving, offerings, praises, apologies for faults, and so forth, as before. Make elaborate dedications and aspirations in the extraordinary Mahayana way and utterances of auspiciousness in the general way.

If you mend the number of recitations with a fire offering, do the pacifying fire offerings in a number equal to one-tenth of the approach recitations. If you cannot do that, you should be sure to complete one-tenth of the set number of each of the recitations from the earlier occasions of doing the approach.

The visualization for recitation described in the *Medium Practice Manual (Trinley Dringpo)* is only like a seed. The details should be done according to the *Dzapkyi Köljang*, the *Recitation Manual*. In other words, perform both dharmakaya and sambhogakaya recitations as clearly described in the root text. For the nirmanakaya, first visualize a moon disc in your heart center, upon which there is a five-pronged golden vajra. In its center, upon a moon disc, is the radiant white letter HRIH.

Around it, the white, self-resounding garland of the Vajra Guru mantra circles uninterruptedly in a clockwise direction. To focus your mind on that, like the moon with a garland of stars, is the intent of the approach, invoking the mind of the deity.

A second mantra garland then streams forth uninterruptedly from the first one, coming out through your mouth. It enters into the mouth of the wisdom being in front of you. It passes through the bodily figure and comes out through the navel. Entering your own navel, it circles around your heart center as before. The clear essence of light rays gathers within the bindu of your heart and hereby stabilizes the wisdom of great bliss and brings mastery over the two kinds of siddhis. To imagine this, like the wheel of a firebrand, is the intent of the close approach of oneself to the deity.

Boundless rays of light then stream forth from the mantra circle. They permeate all the infinite buddha realms, becoming cloud banks of outer, inner, and secret offerings to please the Three Roots, the victorious ones, and their offspring. All the blessings of their three secrets are then gathered back. They dissolve into you, purifying the two obscurations; perfecting the two accumulations; and bestowing all the empowerments, blessings, and siddhis. Again rays of light stream forth. They touch all the sentient beings of the three realms, purifying their obscurations of karma and disturbing emotions along with their habitual tendencies. Imagining this, like sending out the king's emissaries, is the intent of mastering the accomplishment of siddhis.

At the conclusion, the outer vessel-like world is the vajra realm of Akanishtha; all that appears as the inner content-like beings are mandala deities; all animate voices and inanimate sounds are the spontaneous tones of mantras; and all thinking is the play of the great self-existing wakefulness. Thus, to recite within the continuity of appearance and existence, as being the great manifest ground, known as the yoga that is like a bee hive breaking open, is the intent of the great accomplishment, the actualization of the siddhis.

According to the tantric system, these four described aspects of recitation intent are chiefly applied to the single mudra form, the elaborate mudra form, and the accomplishment of the group gathering. It has been taught that one gradually engages in each of them after achieving the vivid presence of samadhi in the previous one. However, here I have described the intent of the oral instructions of Guru Rinpoche, which is to combine the fourfold recitation intent of approach and accomplishment into one single sitting, since that is taught to be the profound key point for the quick occurrence of the signs of blessings and siddhis.

In this way, you can fully complete the recitations for approach and accomplishment. The way of benefiting others, by accepting them through the elaborate, medium, or condensed empowerments, is clarified elsewhere.

The way of accomplishment in a group assembly, according to the *Siddhi Vase Practice,* a treasure revealed at *Blazing Light Rock* in upper Go, is described in an appendix to the practice discussed here. So, instead of performing that, if you combine it with the *Root Heart Practice* and so forth, the analogy will be like putting a goat's head on a sheep.

Furthermore, you can learn the key points of the development stage, what to avoid or adopt during retreat practice, from the rudimentary scriptures and from the general presentations of approach and accomplishment. Here I have not elaborated on these for fear of involving too many details.

> *Although this vajra verse supplication had appeared in the past,*
> *Its sadhana has formerly not been widely known.*
> *Having newly appeared by the power of it being the right time,*
> *It is complete and concise, a treasure teaching that exceeds all*
> *others.*

> *I wrote this in order to show the direction for the practice of all*
> *fortunate ones,*
> *Who, after discerning the reason, have acquired confident trust.*
> *And so, may the correct practice of the meaning of the text*
> *expanded here*
> *Be like the sun spreading light everywhere.*

Although I could have expanded upon this in great detail, due to fully possessing the excellent fortune of the ripening and liberating instructions from both of the two great treasure masters, the lords of this profound teaching, I, Padma Garwang Lodrö Thaye, merely aiming to write a convenient practice for beginners, composed this at the practice place of the third *Devikoti*, the Tsari-Like Jewel Rock.

May virtuous goodness increase.

THE PRACTICE MANUAL FOR THE RECITATION OF APPROACH AND ACCOMPLISHMENT:

According to The Guru's Heart Practice, Dispeller of All Obstacles:

Dzapkyi Köljang

The Practice Manual for the Recitation of Approach and Accomplishment, the *Dzapkyi Köljang,* and the text *Opening of the Mansion of Recitation (dza pra khang dbye ba),* also called *Gzhi Bstod,* are like skeletons of the practice that are interwoven at appropriate places. Additionally, verses from the *Barchey Lamsel* are inserted as a supplication and an offering prayer. Sometimes merely one line and the etcetera sign reference these. In the past, the practitioner was expected to know most of these verses by heart or at least be capable of flipping back and forth very quickly between the two primary parts. For the sake of ease, for both us modern-day yogis and the reader, I have combined them all together in the way they are chanted. It helps to get a clearer idea of the meaning, even though it falls short of strict purity.

Please excuse any breaches.

—*Marcia Dechen Wangmo*

ༀ༔རྒྱུད་ཁྲོས་ཞི་ཏྲི་ཧྲཱིཿ

I, Padma Tötreng, ༔
Am the embodiment of the ocean of the Three Roots. ༔
Like the infinite mandala circles, ༔
Which arise from and dissolve back into space, ༔
I manifest mantras, mudras, ༔
And various kinds of inconceivable activities, ༔
In every possible way, for those who need to be tamed. ༔
The meaning and words of the wisdom essence, ༔
Of the especially profound tantra sections, ༔
Known as Vidyadhara Mayajala, ༔
Are unfailing and have swift blessings ༔
For helping the devoted to accomplish siddhi. ༔
Having resolved this essence of the most profound heart practice, ༔
Through ascertaining the oral instructions, ༔
I now teach the magical wheel of the visualizations for reciting ༔
The Approach, Accomplishment, and Activities ༔
Of the inner practice of Barchey Künsel, ༔
For the benefit of the qualified king and my present disciples, ༔
As well as for those of future generations. ༔
Samaya. ༔

To accomplish this, first there is the threefold approach, ༔
Benefiting self and other separately and mutually. ༔
First, chiefly for the benefit of self, ༔
There is the gathering of the blessings and siddhis ༔
And the practice of vidyadhara life, ༔
By means of the Lord of the Family. ༔
Spin the magical wheel of visualization in this way: ༔

HUNG HRIH! ༔
Lord of the Family, Amitayus, manifest from space. ༔
Uttering the sounds of recitation, I invoke you. ༔
From the core of your heart-samaya, please come! ༔
With apparent and empty bodily forms, you fill the billionfold
    universe. ༔
With resounding and empty mantra tones of speech, you roar like
    thunder. ༔

With the aware and empty space of mind, you rest in the state of
   luminosity.ༀ
All the deities, delighting in the dance of bliss,ༀ
Invoke the mantras with effortless vajra songs.ༀ
The liberating life force of wisdom endows your mindༀ
Until attaining clarity, I will endeavor in visualization and
   recitation.ༀ
Until I reach perfection, please don't forsake your intentions!ༀ
Do not forget me; the time for your great heart-samaya has come!ༀ
On this very seat, let me perfect the fourfold Approach and
   Accomplishment,ༀ
And make me realize the lord of the mandala.ༀ

From the HRIH in the heart center of Lord Amitayus, the lord of
   the family above my head,ༀ
Rays of light radiate throughout the ten directions,ༀ
Restoring my life and vitality, which have been cut, damaged, or
   dwindled away.ༀ
Externally, the essences of the universe's elements of earth, water,
   fire, and wind,ༀ
Internally, the life, merit, and power of its inhabitants, the beings of
   the three realms,ༀ
And innermostly, the wisdom qualities of knowledge, compassion,
   and abilityༀ
Of all the victorious ones and their sons,ༀ
Are all summoned back in the form of five-colored nectar,ༀ
Which enters the vase he holds in his hand, where it melts and
   boils.ༀ
Passing down through the top of my head, it fills my entire body.ༀ
The four obscurations are purified, the empowerments and siddhis
   are obtained,ༀ
And the vajra life of immortal great bliss is accomplished.ༀ

Thinking this, recite:

OM AMARANI DZIWANTIYE SOHAༀ

At times, make offerings and praises:⚶

Offering Prayer

Assembly of wisdom deities, I invite you. Please come!⚶
I offer you outer, inner, and secret offerings.⚶
I praise your body, speech, mind, qualities, and activities.⚶
I confess careless transgressions and errors.⚶
Maha amrita balingta rakta khahi⚶

Thus, play music and, after each cycle of one-thousand mantras, repeat the offerings and praises.

With your palms joined, say:

Hrih!⚶
From the amazing, excellent, abundant realm of Great Bliss,⚶
Perfectly arranged, immeasurable palace,⚶
All buddhas of the three times,⚶
The essence of the dharmakaya,⚶
The vividness of all wisdom appearances,˙
The lord of all the victorious ones, Amitayus,⚶
Master and lady, son and queen,⚶
With all of your assembled retinues,⚶
With your compassion, bestow your blessings upon me.⚶
With your love, guide me and others on the path.⚶
With your realization, grant me the siddhis.⚶
With your powers, dispel my obstacles and those of others.⚶
Clear the outer obstacles externally.⚶
Clear the inner obstacles internally.⚶
Clear the secret obstacles into space.⚶
Respectfully, I bow down and take refuge in you.⚶
Om amarani dziwantiye soha⚶
By that reflection,
Supplicate in this way.

Recite four or twelve times one hundred thousand

To meet the deity in actuality,

Hear his voice, and find attainment in samadhi.

Or when these occur in vivid visions,

Or when, finally, in dreams, the sun and moon rise,

Recognize the signs of accomplishment of body, speech, and mind.

To drink nectar, to have crops ripen,

To see a great river overflow, and so forth,

These are omens that you will accomplish immortality.

At that time, you should receive the siddhis.

Samaya.

By means of the noble Tamer of Beings,

For the benefit of others, envisage these steps of concentration,

Which shake the six realms from their depths:

HUNG HRIH!

Tamer of Beings, Great Compassionate One, manifest from space.

Uttering the sounds of recitation, I invoke you.

From the core of your heart-samaya, please come!

With apparent and empty bodily forms, you fill the billionfold universe.

With resounding and empty mantra tones of speech, you roar like thunder.

With the aware and empty space of mind, you rest in the state of luminosity.

All the deities, delighting in the dance of bliss,

Invoke the mantras with effortless vajra songs.

The liberating life force of wisdom endows your mind.

Until attaining clarity, I will endeavor in visualization and recitation.

Until I reach perfection, please don't forsake your intentions!

Do not forget me; the time for your great heart-samaya has come!

On this very seat, let me perfect the fourfold Approach and Accomplishment,

And make me realize the lord of the mandala.

In the heart center of the noble Tamer of Beings, upon a lotus and moon,

The brilliant white letter HRIH glows with light,
Adorned by the Six Syllable mantra on the six petals surrounding
   it.
By the power of invoking with the vajra-melody recitation, the six
   realms are purified:

From HUNG, the essence of the mirror-like wisdom,
Deep blue rays of light stream forth to the hell realms,
Purifying the misery of heat and cold resulting from aggression.
The world and its inhabitants become the noble Vajra Realm.

OM MANI PEME HUNG HRIH

From ME, the essence of the wisdom of equality,
Yellow rays of light stream forth to the realm of *pretas,*
Purifying the misery of hunger and thirst resulting from greed.
The world and its inhabitants become the noble Ratna Realm.

OM MANI PEME HUNG HRIH

From PAD, the essence of dharmadhatu wisdom,
White rays of light stream forth to the realm of animals,
Purifying the misery of stupidity and muteness resulting from
   ignorance.
The world and its inhabitants become the noble Sugata Realm.

OM MANI PEME HUNG HRIH

From NI, the essence of discriminating wisdom,
Red rays of light stream forth to the realm of human beings,
Purifying the misery of bustle and poverty resulting from desire.
The world and its inhabitants become the noble Lotus Realm.

OM MANI PEME HUNG HRIH

From MA, the essence of the all-accomplishing wisdom,
Green rays of light stream forth to the world of *asuras,*
Purifying the misery of fighting and strife resulting from envy.
The world and its inhabitants become the noble Karma Realm.

OM MANI PEME HUNG HRIH

From OM, the essence of the wisdom of luminosity,
Brilliant white rays of light stream forth to the world of the gods,
Purifying the misery of transmigration and falling resulting from
  arrogance.
The world and its inhabitants become the noble All-Embodying
  Realm.

OM MANI PEME HUNG HRIH

From HRIH, the essence of undivided wisdom,
Boundless rays of light radiate, filling all of space,
Purifying the karmas, kleshas, and sufferings of beings equal to the
  sky in number.
Thus everything becomes the noble realm of the Tamer of Beings.

OM MANI PEME HUNG HRIH

All sights are the forms of the Great Compassionate One;
All sounds are the song of the Six Syllable mantra;
All thoughts are the continuity of indivisible emptiness and
  compassion.
The activity of shaking *samsara* from its depths is perfected.

OM MANI PEME HUNG HRIH

Offering Prayer

Assembly of wisdom deities, I invite you. Please come!
I offer you outer, inner, and secret offerings.
I praise your body, speech, mind, qualities, and activities.
I confess careless transgressions and errors.
MAHA AMRITA BALINGTA RAKTA KHAHI

HRIH!
From the Mount Potala Buddhafield in the eastern direction,
The great awakened palace,
All buddhas of the three times,
The essence of the sambhokakaya
Glorious Lotus Dance Master,
Lord Avalokiteshvara, protector of beings,
The bodhisattvas and bodhisattmas of the good kalpa,

And the retinue of all the vidyadharas,⸖

With your compassion, bestow your blessings upon me.⸖

With your love, guide me and others on the path.⸖

With your realization, grant me the siddhis.⸖

With your powers, dispel my obstacles and those of others.⸖

Clear the outer obstacles externally.⸖

Clear the inner obstacles internally.⸖

Clear the secret obstacles into space.⸖

Respectfully, I bow down and take refuge in you.⸖

OM MANI PEME HUNG HRIH⸖

Through practicing one-pointedly in this way,⸖

By ten million you will accomplish all the activities.⸖

At that time, the signs of accomplishment will be,⸖

In actuality, in vision, or in dreams, though without fixation,⸖

To meet the Noble One,⸖

To feel effortlessly altruistic and compassionate,⸖

To dream that pus, blood, and filth pour down,⸖

To take a bath and put on white garments,⸖

To fly through the sky and travel upon water,⸖

To deliver many beings from dreadful places, and so forth.⸖

These and other signs of virtue⸖

*Should be known as omens of purified obscurations and benefit
    for others.⸖*

Samaya.⸖

As for the recitation for self and others without duality,⸖

By means of the main figure of the mandala,⸖

Give rise to all the various visualizations⸖

Of deity, mantra, and all aspects.⸖

HUNG HRIH!⸖

Supreme Chief of the Mandala, Guru, manifest from space.⸖

Uttering the sounds of recitation, I invoke you.⸖

From the core of your heart-samaya, please come!⸖

With apparent and empty bodily forms, you fill the billionfold
    universe.⸖

With resounding and empty mantra tones of speech, you roar like
    thunder.⸖

With the aware and empty space of mind, you rest in the state of luminosity.༔
All the deities, delighting in the dance of bliss,༔
Invoke the mantras with effortless vajra songs.༔
The liberating life force of wisdom endows your mind.༔
Until attaining clarity, I will endeavor in visualization and recitation.༔
Until I reach perfection, please don't forsake your intentions!༔
Do not forget me; the time for your great heart-samaya has come!༔
On this very seat, let me perfect the fourfold Approach and Accomplishment,༔
And make me realize the lord of the mandala.༔

In my heart center, as the Guru Embodying All Families,༔
Within the central sphere of a five-pronged golden vajra,༔
Is the white letter HRIH, the spiritual life force, upon a moon disc.༔
Surrounding it, the radiant white mantra chain revolves clockwise.༔
The strings of five-colored rays of light radiate immensely,༔
Making offerings to the victorious ones and their sons abiding in all realms of the ten directions,༔
And gathering back the blessings and siddhis of body, speech, and mind.༔
Radiating again, they fill the universe and all inhabitants of the three realms,༔
Thus purifying the clinging to ordinary experience together with its continuation.༔
In the external world, as the realm of the Lotus Net,༔
All beings manifest as the forms of the Guru Embodying All Families.༔
The resounding yet empty sound of the vajra mantra fills all of space.༔
Self-liberated thoughts are the adornment of the space of luminosity.༔
Self and others without duality, like the moon in water or like rainbows,༔
Are perfected in the single mandala of appearance and existence as manifest ground.༔

Recite within the state of indivisible space and awareness:

OM AH HUNG BENZA GURU PEMA SIDDHI HUNG

Offering Prayer

Assembly of wisdom deities, I invite you. Please come!
I offer you outer, inner, and secret offerings.
I praise your body, speech, mind, qualities, and activities.
I confess careless transgressions and errors.
MAHA AMRITA BALINGTA RAKTA KHAHI

HUNG HRIH!
From the Glorious Buddhafield of Chamara to the southwest,
The palace of lotus light,
All the buddhas of the three times,
The essence of the nirmanakaya,
Glorious Lotus-Born Buddha,
Subjugator of appearance and existence, Tötreng Tsal,
Yidams, dakas, and dakinis,
Surrounded by an ocean of dharma protectors,
With your compassion, bestow your blessings upon me.
With your love, guide me and others on the path.
With your realization, grant me the siddhis.
With your powers, dispel my obstacles and those of others.
Clear the outer obstacles externally.
Clear the inner obstacles internally.
Clear the secret obstacles into space.
Respectfully, I bow down and take refuge in you.
OM AH HUNG BENZA GURU PEMA SIDDHI HUNG

With OM at the beginning and hung at the end,
The ten vajra syllables in between
Are the root mantra embodying all the vidyadharas.
By reciting them twelve hundred thousand times, you will attain
*   siddhi.*
At that time, the signs of accomplishment will be,
In actuality, in vision, or in dreams, though without fixation,
To meet him face-to-face or hear his voice, to feel great bliss blaze forth,

To attain powers, to have experience and realization increase,
To witness dakas and dakinis gather,
To hear the sounds of song and dance, music and chanting,
To behold a rain of flowers fall, to be enveloped in exquisite fragrance,
To have the great resplendence of wisdom descend, and so forth.
These are explained as the omens of blessing and siddhi.
Samaya.

The yogi who has already mastered the Approach
Should practice the general and specific Accomplishment.
First, in the outer way, practice the Accomplishment
Of all the mandala figures:

HUNG HRIH!
Divinities of Vidyadhara Gurus, manifest from space.
Uttering the sounds of recitation, I invoke you.
From the core of your heart-samaya, please come!
With apparent and empty bodily forms, you fill the billionfold
    universe.
With resounding and empty mantra tones of speech, you roar like
    thunder.
With the aware and empty space of mind, you rest in the state of
    luminosity.
All the deities, delighting in the dance of bliss,
Invoke the mantras with effortless vajra songs.
The liberating life force of wisdom endows your mind.
Until attaining clarity, I will endeavor in visualization and
    recitation.
Until I reach perfection, please don't forsake your intentions!
Do not forget me; the time for your great heart-samaya has come!
On this very seat, let me perfect the fourfold Approach and
    Accomplishment,
And make me realize the lord of the mandala.

From myself and the entire assembly of mandala deities,
Body replicas stream forth, filling the sky.
They perform vajra dances and proclaim the tremendous sounds of
    mantra.
Their minds are the blissful experience of changeless luminosity.

Offering clouds of qualities gather throughout all realms of the ten
  directions,
Pleasing all the victorious ones and their sons with unconditioned
  bliss.
The limitless activities of deeds to tame beings
Completely purify the two obscurations of all beings of the three
  realms.
By receiving empowerments from the nectar of bodhichitta,
Everyone manifests in the forms of the deities of the Three Roots.
These wisdom mandala deities of indivisible appearance and
  emptiness
Are present as the groups of the infinite web of magical creations.
OM AH HUNG BENZA GURU PEMA TÖTRENG TSAL BENZA SAMAYA DZA
SIDDHI PALA HUNG AH

In the inner way, perform the profound HUNG practice:

Fivefold HUNG syllables from the letter HUNG in the heart centers
Of myself and all the mandala figures
Roar their thunderous self-sound,
Pervading the entire phenomenal world.
They make offerings to the victorious ones, gather back siddhis,
And purify all beings' karmas and *kleshas,*
Especially their clinging to ordinary experience.
The main figure and the entire retinue sing the song of HUNG.
Through this vajra melody,
The experience of the wisdom of great bliss blazes forth,
And the supreme empowerment of awareness expression is
  attained.

Imagining this, chant:

HUNG HUNG HUNG HUNG HUNG

For the innermost, perform the prana and great bliss recitation.
Assuming the body posture, expel the stale breath.
Linking HUNG to the exhalation, inhalation, and retention,
Recite one-pointedly without distraction.

The mantra chain emerges from the spiritual life force,

The essence of great bliss.
It enters through the mouth of the self-radiant consort
And appears blissfully from the lotus.
Passing through the pathway of the vajra jewel,
It circles, like a spinning firebrand,
Making the experience of wisdom blaze forth.
In this blissful state, plant the stake of undistracted concentration.

Offering Prayer

Assembly of wisdom deities, I invite you. Please come!
I offer you outer, inner, and secret offerings.
I praise your body, speech, mind, qualities, and activities.
I confess careless transgressions and errors.
MAHA AMRITA BALINGTA RAKTA KHAHI

OM AH HUNG BENZA GURU PEMA SIDDHI HUNG
Dharmakaya Amitabha, I supplicate you![1]
Sambhogakaya Great Compassionate One, I supplicate you!
Nirmanakaya Padmakara, I supplicate you!
My Guru, wonderful nirmanakaya,
You were born in the land of India, where you studied and
    contemplated.
Journeying in person to Tibet, you tamed the demonic forces
Residing in the land of Orgyen, accomplishing the benefit of
    beings.
With your compassion, bestow your blessings upon me.
With your love, guide me and others on the path.
With your realization, grant me the siddhis.
With your powers, dispel my obstacles and those of others.
Clear the outer obstacles externally.
Clear the inner obstacles internally.
Clear the secret obstacles into space.
Respectfully, I bow down and take refuge in you.
OM AH HUNG BENZA GURU PEMA TÖTRENG TSAL BENZA SAMAYA DZA
    SIDDHI PHALA HUNG AH

---

1 *Barchey Lamsel,* verse 1

Between sessions, practice according to the outer way:
Perform the mudras and dance movements
And sing the songs of chanting and recitation.
By exerting yourself in this way for three weeks,
The great resplendence of body will descend into your body,
Majestic brilliance will glow forth, and great bliss will dawn.
Through receiving the empowerment of speech in your speech,
You will possess powers and accomplish the words of truth.
Through perfecting the power of mind in your mind,
You will become proficient in subtle samadhis.
By merely directing oneself to the favorable coincidence,
The yogi observing these signs
Will accomplish all the stages of the activities.
Samaya.

As to the specific individual accomplishments:
With the pride of the chief vidyadhara,
Who is yourself inseparable from the three kayas,
Apply the key points for each
Of the magical wheels of the particular visualizations
And envision the various displays of samadhi
Within the Magical Net of Wisdom,
Which is one manifesting in the form of many.

HUNG HRIH!

Vidyadhara Gyalwey Dungtsob, manifest from space.

Uttering the sounds of recitation, I invoke you.

From the core of your heart-samaya, please come!

With apparent and empty bodily forms, you fill the billionfold universe.

With resounding and empty mantra tones of speech, you roar like thunder.

With the aware and empty space of mind, you rest in the state of luminosity.

All the deities, delighting in the dance of bliss,

Invoke the mantras with effortless vajra songs.

The liberating life force of wisdom endows your mind.

Until attaining clarity, I will endeavor in visualization and recitation.

Until I reach perfection, please don't forsake your intentions!⸙

Do not forget me; the time for your great heart-samaya has come!⸙

On this very seat, let me perfect the fourfold Approach and
　　Accomplishment,⸙

And make me realize the lord of the mandala.⸙

Hung!⸙

In the eastern direction of the mandala, upon a lotus seat,⸙

In the heart center of Vidyadhara Gyalwey Dungtsob⸙

Is the letter HRIH upon a moon disc, encircled by the mantra chain.⸙

The radiating light gathers all the perfections of existence and
　　peace⸙

In the forms of the auspicious signs and substances of the seven
　　royal attributes⸙

And of spheres of five-colored rainbow light.⸙

By dissolving into me, a brilliant, vast splendor blazes forth,⸙

And I become the great lord of all of samsara and nirvana.⸙

OM AH HUNG BENZA GURU PEMA RADZA A NRI TRI DZA DZA SARVA
　　SIDDHI PHALA HUNG⸙

Offering Prayer

Assembly of wisdom deities, I invite you. Please come!⸙

I offer you outer, inner, and secret offerings.⸙

I praise your body, speech, mind, qualities, and activities.⸙

I confess careless transgressions and errors.⸙

MAHA AMRITA BALINGTA RAKTA KHAHI⸙

When seeing the wonder of bodily forms,⸙[2]

Your right hand makes the mudra of the sword,⸙

And your left hand makes the summoning mudra,⸙

With gaping mouth, bared fangs, and upward gaze.⸙

Gyalwey Dungdzin, Lord of Beings,⸙

With your compassion, bestow your blessings upon me.⸙

With your love, guide me and others on the path.⸙

With your realization, grant me the siddhis.⸙

---

2 *Barchey Lamsel,* verse 2

DISPELLER OF OBSTACLES

With your powers, dispel my obstacles and those of others.�095
Clear the outer obstacles externally.�095
Clear the inner obstacles internally.�095
Clear the secret obstacles into space.�095
Respectfully, I bow down and take refuge in you.�095
OM AH HUNG BENZA GURU PEMA RADZA A NRI TRI DZA DZA SARVA
SIDDHI PHALA HUNG�095

HUNG HRIH!�095
Vidyadhara Mawey Senge, manifest from space.�095
Uttering the sounds of recitation, I invoke you.�095
From the core of your heart-samaya, please come!�095
With apparent and empty bodily forms, you fill the billionfold
    universe.�095
With resounding and empty mantra tones of speech, you roar like
    thunder.�095
With the aware and empty space of mind, you rest in the state of
    luminosity.�095
All the deities, delighting in the dance of bliss,�095
Invoke the mantras with effortless vajra songs.�095
The liberating life force of wisdom endows your mind.�095
Until attaining clarity, I will endeavor in visualization and
    recitation.�095
Until I reach perfection, please don't forsake your intentions!�095
Do not forget me; the time for your great heart-samaya has come!�095
On this very seat, let me perfect the fourfold Approach and
    Accomplishment,�095
And make me realize the lord of the mandala.�095

HUNG!�095
In the southern direction of the mandala, upon a lotus seat,�095
In the heart center of Vidyadhara Mawey Senge,�095
Is the letter HRIH upon a moon disc, encircled by the mantra chain.�095
The radiating light clears away the darkness of ignorance in all
    beings.�095
The wisdom of all the victorious ones and their sons,�095
And the intelligence of the noble *shravakas* and *pratyekabuddhas,*
    and of ordinary beings,�095
Is gathered back in the form of light and dissolves into me.�095

The illumination of knowledge and wisdom is fully bloomed.

Om ah hung benza guru pema prajna jnana sarva siddhi hung

Offering Prayer

Assembly of wisdom deities, I invite you. Please come!
I offer you outer, inner, and secret offerings.
I praise your body, speech, mind, qualities, and activities.
I confess careless transgressions and errors.

Maha amrita balingta rakta khahi

When bestowing the precious, sacred teachings,[3]
Your radiant body is endowed with a luminous complexion.
Your right hand holds the scriptures of the Tripitaka,
And your left hand holds the volumes of Kilaya.
You comprehend all the profound teachings.
Pandita of Yangleshö,
With your compassion, bestow your blessings upon me.
With your love, guide me and others on the path.
With your realization, grant me the siddhis.
With your powers, dispel my obstacles and those of others.
Clear the outer obstacles externally.
Clear the inner obstacles internally.
Clear the secret obstacles into space.
Respectfully, I bow down and take refuge in you.

Om ah hung benza guru pema prajna jnana sarva siddhi hung

Hung Hrih!
Vidyadhara Padmasambhava, manifest from space.
Uttering the sounds of recitation, I invoke you.
From the core of your heart-samaya, please come!
With apparent and empty bodily forms, you fill the billionfold
    universe.
With resounding and empty mantra tones of speech, you roar like
    thunder.
With the aware and empty space of mind, you rest in the state of
    luminosity.

---

3 *Barchey Lamsel,* verse 3

All the deities, delighting in the dance of bliss,⸎
Invoke the mantras with effortless vajra songs.⸎
The liberating life force of wisdom endows your mind.⸎
Until attaining clarity, I will endeavor in visualization and
    recitation.⸎
Until I reach perfection, please don't forsake your intentions!⸎
Do not forget me; the time for your great heart-samaya has come!⸎
On this very seat, let me perfect the fourfold Approach and
    Accomplishment,⸎
And make me realize the lord of the mandala.⸎

Hung!⸎
In the western direction of the mandala, upon a lotus seat,⸎
In the heart center of Vidyadhara Padmasambhava,⸎
Is the letter HRIH upon a moon disc, encircled by the mantra chain.⸎
The radiating light dispels all degenerations of the world and its
    inhabitants.⸎
An immense rain of desirable things showers down from the cloud
    of wisdom.⸎
The splendor and wealth of existence and peace is vastly increased.⸎
By all the essences and elixirs dissolving into me,⸎
I attain the siddhi of holding the sky treasury.⸎
Om ah hung benza guru pema sambhawa sarva siddhi hung⸎

Offering Prayer

Assembly of wisdom deities, I invite you. Please come!⸎
I offer you outer, inner, and secret offerings.⸎
I praise your body, speech, mind, qualities, and activities.⸎
I confess careless transgressions and errors.⸎
Maha amrita balingta rakta khahi⸎

When binding the vow holders under oath,⸎[4]
At the beautiful and immaculate supreme place⸎
On the borderline of India and Tibet,⸎
You bestowed your blessing at the moment of arrival,⸎
At that mountain endowed with enveloping fragrance,⸎

---

4 *Barchey Lamsel,* verse 4

Where even in winter, lotus flowers bloom⁞
And a spring of enlightenment, with nectar-like water flows.⁞
In this supreme and blissful place,⁞
Kyechok Tsülzang, dressed in the robes of the Dharma,⁞
Your right hand holding a nine-spoked vajra,⁞
And your left hand holding a jewelled casket⁞
Filled with rakta nectar,⁞
You bound under oath the dakinis and vow holders.⁞
Seeing the yidam face-to-face, you accomplished the siddhis.⁞
With your compassion, bestow your blessings upon me.⁞
With your love, guide me and others on the path.⁞
With your realization, grant me the siddhis.⁞
With your powers, dispel my obstacles and those of others.⁞
Clear the outer obstacles externally.⁞
Clear the inner obstacles internally.⁞
Clear the secret obstacles into space.⁞
Respectfully, I bow down and take refuge in you.⁞
OM AH HUNG BENZA GURU PEMA SAMBHAWA SARVA SIDDHI HUNG⁞

HUNG HRIH!⁞
Vidyadhara Dükyi Shechen, manifest from space.⁞
Uttering the sounds of recitation, I invoke you.⁞
From the core of your heart-samaya, please come!⁞
With apparent and empty bodily forms, you fill the billionfold
    universe.⁞
With resounding and empty mantra tones of speech, you roar like
    thunder.⁞
With the aware and empty space of mind, you rest in the state of
    luminosity.⁞
All the deities, delighting in the dance of bliss,⁞
Invoke the mantras with effortless vajra songs.⁞
The liberating life force of wisdom endows your mind.⁞
Until attaining clarity, I will endeavor in visualization and
    recitation.⁞
Until I reach perfection, please don't forsake your intentions!⁞
Do not forget me; the time for your great heart-samaya has come!⁞
On this very seat, let me perfect the fourfold Approach and
    Accomplishment,⁞

And make me realize the lord of the mandala.

HUNG!
In the northern direction of the mandala, upon a lotus seat,
In the heart center of Vidyadhara Dükyi Shechen,
Is the letter HUNG upon a sun disc, encircled by the mantra chain.
The radiating light fills the three-thousandfold universe,
As a rain of vajras, Kilayas, and weapons showers down with a
    great throng and flash.
It liberates the awareness of the hordes of *maras* into the
    dharmadhatu.
Having reduced their bodies to dust,
It is absorbed back, dissolving into me and blazing forth as an
    immense, majestic brilliance.
OM AH HUNG BENZA GURU PEMA KILI KILIYA SARVA BIGHANEN BAM
HUNG PE

Offering Prayer

Assembly of wisdom deities, I invite you. Please come!
I offer you outer, inner, and secret offerings.
I praise your body, speech, mind, qualities, and activities.
I confess careless transgressions and errors.
MAHA AMRITA BALINGTA RAKTA KHAHI

When establishing the doctrine of the victorious ones,[5]
You performed the sadhana in the Slate Mountain Forest,
Throwing your recitation dagger into the sky's expanse.
With the vajra mudra, you caught and rolled it.
As you wielded it, you flung it into the Sandalwood Forest.
The fire blazed and dried up its lake.
Instantly, you burned away the whole land of the *tirthikas,*
And you crushed the dark *yakshas* to dust.
Matchless Dükyi Shechen,
With your compassion, bestow your blessings upon me.
With your love, guide me and others on the path.

---

5 *Barchey Lamsel,* verse 5

With your realization, grant me the siddhis.⚬

With your powers, dispel my obstacles and those of others.⚬

Clear the outer obstacles externally.⚬

Clear the inner obstacles internally.⚬

Clear the secret obstacles into space.⚬

Respectfully, I bow down and take refuge in you.⚬

OM AH HUNG BENZA GURU PEMA KILI KILIYA SARVA BIGHANEN BAM
   HUNG PE⚬

HUNG HRIH!⚬

Vidyadhara Dzamling Gyenchok, manifest from space.⚬

Uttering the sounds of recitation, I invoke you.⚬

From the core of your heart-samaya, please come!⚬

With apparent and empty bodily forms, you fill the billionfold
   universe.⚬

With resounding and empty mantra tones of speech, you roar like
   thunder.⚬

With the aware and empty space of mind, you rest in the state of
   luminosity.⚬

All the deities, delighting in the dance of bliss,⚬

Invoke the mantras with effortless vajra songs.⚬

The liberating life force of wisdom endows your mind.⚬

Until attaining clarity, I will endeavor in visualization and
   recitation.⚬

Until I reach perfection, please don't forsake your intentions!⚬

Do not forget me; the time for your great heart-samaya has come!⚬

On this very seat, let me perfect the fourfold Approach and
   Accomplishment,⚬

And make me realize the lord of the mandala.⚬

HUNG!⚬

In the eastern direction, upon the glowing spoke of the jewel,⚬

In the heart center of Vidyadhara Dzamling Gyenchok,⚬

Is the letter HUNG upon a sun disc, encircled by the mantra chain.⚬

As the vajra sparks, the radiating rays of light⚬

Destroy the *drekpas* and purify the fixation on a real phenomenal
   realm.⚬

By gathering back, the light dissolves into me, and in blessing me,⚬

Self-cognizance is perfected into the mind of Mahaguru.⚬

The five poisons are self-liberated, and mastery over the wisdoms is
  attained.
Om rulu rulu hung jo hung
Offering Prayer
Assembly of wisdom deities, I invite you. Please come!
I offer you outer, inner, and secret offerings.
I praise your body, speech, mind, qualities, and activities.
I confess careless transgressions and errors.
MAHA AMRITA BALINGTA RAKTA KHAHI

When you subjugated the rakshasas,[6]
As a young boy in nirmanakaya attire,
You displayed a wonderous form of goodness,
With magnificent color, even teeth, and beautiful, golden hair.
Like a youth of sixteen years,
Wearing all kinds of jewel ornaments,
Your right hand grips a bronze phurba,
Subjugating maras and rakshasas.
Your left hand holds a teak phurba,
Granting protection to your devoted sons and daughters.
Wearing an iron phurba around your neck,
You are indivisible from the yidam deity.
Dzamling Gyenchok, nondual nirmanakaya,
With your compassion, bestow your blessings upon me.
With your love, guide me and others on the path.
With your realization, grant me the siddhis.
With your powers, dispel my obstacles and those of others.
Clear the outer obstacles externally.
Clear the inner obstacles internally.
Clear the secret obstacles into space.
Respectfully, I bow down and take refuge in you.
OM RULU RULU HUNG JO HUNG HUNG

HUNG HRIH!
Vidyadhara Pema Jungney, manifest from space.
Uttering the sounds of recitation, I invoke you.
From the core of your heart-samaya, please come!

6 *Barchey Lamsel,* verse 6

With apparent and empty bodily forms, you fill the billionfold universe.⸸

With resounding and empty mantra tones of speech, you roar like thunder.⸸

With the aware and empty space of mind, you rest in the state of luminosity.⸸

All the deities, delighting in the dance of bliss,⸸

Invoke the mantras with effortless vajra songs.⸸

The liberating life force of wisdom endows your mind.⸸

Until attaining clarity, I will endeavor in visualization and recitation.⸸

Until I reach perfection, please don't forsake your intentions!⸸

Do not forget me; the time for your great heart-samaya has come!⸸

On this very seat, let me perfect the fourfold Approach and Accomplishment,⸸

And make me realize the lord of the mandala.⸸

Hung!⸸

In the southern direction, upon the glowing spoke of the jewel,⸸

In the heart center of Vidyadhara Pema Jungney,⸸

Is the letter HRIH upon a moon disc, encircled by the mantra chain.⸸

The radiating light rays, reveling in bliss and emptiness,⸸

Make offerings to all the *jinas* and purify the two obscurations of beings.⸸

From the three places of all beings appearing and existing as the Three Roots deities,⸸

Bodily forms, mantra chains, and attributes fall like rain.⸸

By dissolving into me, the wisdoms are increased.⸸

Om ah hung benza guru pema tötreng tsal benza samaya dza siddhi phala hung ah⸸

Offering Prayer

Assembly of wisdom deities, I invite you. Please come!⸸

I offer you outer, inner, and secret offerings.⸸

I praise your body, speech, mind, qualities, and activities.⸸

I confess careless transgressions and errors.⸸

Maha amrita balingta rakta khahi⸸

When you decided to go to Dreyul, land of phantoms,[37]
A fiery inferno spreading upon the valley's earth
Became a lake the width of an arrow shot.
There, on a lotus blossom, you appeared, cool and refreshed.
Within the lotus, you displayed your realization
And won the name of Padmasambhava, Lotus Born.
You appeared as the perfect Buddha in person.
O Wondrous Nirmanakaya, such as this,
With your compassion, bestow your blessings upon me.
With your love, guide me and others on the path.
With your realization, grant me the siddhis.
With your powers, dispel my obstacles and those of others.
Clear the outer obstacles externally.
Clear the inner obstacles internally.
Clear the secret obstacles into space.
Respectfully, I bow down and take refuge in you.
OM AH HUNG BENZA GURU PEMA TÖTRENG TSAL BENZA SAMAYA DZA
SIDDHI PHALA HUNG AH

HUNG HRIH!
Vidyadhara Khyepar Phakpa, manifest from space.
Uttering the sounds of recitation, I invoke you.
From the core of your heart-samaya, please come!
With apparent and empty bodily forms, you fill the billionfold
    universe.
With resounding and empty mantra tones of speech, you roar like
    thunder.
With the aware and empty space of mind, you rest in the state of
    luminosity.
All the deities, delighting in the dance of bliss,
Invoke the mantras with effortless vajra songs.
The liberating life force of wisdom endows your mind.
Until attaining clarity, I will endeavor in visualization and
    recitation.
Until I reach perfection, please don't forsake your intentions!
Do not forget me; the time for your great heart-samaya has come!

---

7 *Barchey Lamsel,* verse 7

On this very seat, let me perfect the fourfold Approach and
    Accomplishment,
And make me realize the lord of the mandala.

Hung!
In the western direction, upon the glowing spoke of the jewel,
In the heart center of Vidyadhara Khyepar Phakpa,
Is the letter HRIH upon a moon disc, encircled by the mantra chain.
The light rays radiate into the ten directions with boundless
    resplendence,
Invoking the minds of the gurus, yidams, and dakinis.
The hosts of dharma protectors and guardians are enjoined to act,
And the armies of elemental forces of the phenomenal world are
    subdued and destroyed.
By gathering back and dissolving into me, power and strength
    blaze forth.
OM AH HUNG BENZA MAHA GURU SARVA SIDDHI HUNG
Offering Prayer
Assembly of wisdom deities, I invite you. Please come!
I offer you outer, inner, and secret offerings.
I praise your body, speech, mind, qualities, and activities.
I confess careless transgressions and errors.
MAHA AMRITA BALINGTA RAKTA KHAHI

When you shone as the sun of Tibet,[8]
Glorious guide of devoted beings,
You displayed all forms necessary to tame beings according to their
    needs.
At the Khala Pass in Tsang,
You bound the *dralha genyen* under oath.
In the valley of Tsawe Tsashö,
You bound twenty-one arrogant genyen of the gods under oath.
In Mangyul at Jamtrin,
You bestowed siddhis on the four bhikshus.
O supreme Khyepar Phakpa Rigdzin,
With your compassion, bestow your blessings upon me.
With your love, guide me and others on the path.

---

8 *Barchey Lamsel,* verse 8

With your realization, grant me the siddhis.⁀

With your powers, dispel my obstacles and those of others.⁀

Clear the outer obstacles externally.⁀

Clear the inner obstacles internally.⁀

Clear the secret obstacles into space.⁀

Respectfully, I bow down and take refuge in you.⁀

OM AH HUNG BENZA MAHA GURU SARVA SIDDHI HUNG⁀

HUNG HRIH!⁀

Vidyadhara Dzutrül Tuchen, manifest from space.⁀

Uttering the sounds of recitation, I invoke you.⁀

From the core of your heart-samaya, please come!⁀

With apparent and empty bodily forms, you fill the billionfold
     universe.⁀

With resounding and empty mantra tones of speech, you roar like
     thunder.⁀

With the aware and empty space of mind, you rest in the state of
     luminosity.⁀

All the deities, delighting in the dance of bliss,⁀

Invoke the mantras with effortless vajra songs.⁀

The liberating life force of wisdom endows your mind.⁀

Until attaining clarity, I will endeavor in visualization and
     recitation.⁀

Until I reach perfection, please don't forsake your intentions!⁀

Do not forget me; the time for your great heart-samaya has come!⁀

On this very seat, let me perfect the fourfold Approach and
     Accomplishment,⁀

And make me realize the lord of the mandala.⁀

HUNG!⁀

In the northern direction, upon the glowing spoke of the jewel,⁀

In the heart center of Vidyadhara Dzutrül Tuchen,⁀

Is the letter HUNG upon a sun disc, encircled by the mantra chain.⁀

Light rays and a mass of fire spread in the ten directions.⁀

The sound of HUNG roars throughout the three worlds.⁀

The hordes of samaya corruptors and elemental forces are reduced
     to dust,⁀

And all obstacle-demons are liberated into the space of primordial
     purity.⁀

By gathering back and dissolving into me, the power of awareness
is increased.ᵒ̐

Oᴍ ᴀʜ ʜᴜɴɢ ʙᴇɴᴢᴀ ɢᴜʀᴜ ᴅᴏʀᴊᴇ ᴅʀᴏᴡᴏʟö ʟᴏᴋᴀ sᴀʀᴠᴀ sɪᴅᴅʜɪ ʜᴜɴɢᴼ̐

Offering Prayer
Assembly of wisdom deities, I invite you. Please come!ᵒ̐
I offer you outer, inner, and secret offerings.ᵒ̐
I praise your body, speech, mind, qualities, and activities.ᵒ̐
I confess careless transgressions and errors.ᵒ̐

Mᴀʜᴀ ᴀᴍʀɪᴛᴀ ʙᴀʟɪɴɢᴛᴀ ʀᴀᴋᴛᴀ ᴋʜᴀʜɪᴼ̐

On the glorious plain of Palmotang,ᵒ̐⁹
You bound the twelve *Tenma* goddesses under oath.ᵒ̐
Up on the Khala Pass in Central Tibet,ᵒ̐
You bound the Fleshless White Glacier under oath.ᵒ̐
Before Damshö Lhabüi Nying,ᵒ̐
You bound Thangla Yarshyü under oath.ᵒ̐
At the very summit of Hepori,ᵒ̐
You bound all the devas and rakshasas under oath.ᵒ̐
Of these great gods and demons,ᵒ̐
Some offered the core of their life force,ᵒ̐
Some undertook to guard the teachings,ᵒ̐
And some took the pledge to be your servants.ᵒ̐
Mighty Dzutrül Tuchen,ᵒ̐
With your compassion, bestow your blessings upon me.ᵒ̐
With your love, guide me and others on the path.ᵒ̐
With your realization, grant me the siddhis.ᵒ̐
With your powers, dispel my obstacles and those of others.ᵒ̐
Clear the outer obstacles externally.ᵒ̐
Clear the inner obstacles internally.ᵒ̐
Clear the secret obstacles into space.ᵒ̐
Respectfully, I bow down and take refuge in you.ᵒ̐

Oᴍ ᴀʜ ʜᴜɴɢ ʙᴇɴᴢᴀ ɢᴜʀᴜ ᴅᴏʀᴊᴇ ᴅʀᴏᴡᴏʟö ʟᴏᴋᴀ sᴀʀᴠᴀ sɪᴅᴅʜɪ ʜᴜɴɢᴼ̐

Hᴜɴɢ Hʀɪʜ!ᵒ̐
Vidyadhara Dorje Draktsal, manifest from space.ᵒ̐
Uttering the sounds of recitation, I invoke you.ᵒ̐

---

9 *Barchey Lamsel,* verse 9

DISPELLER OF OBSTACLES

From the core of your heart-samaya, please come!

With apparent and empty bodily forms, you fill the billionfold universe.

With resounding and empty mantra tones of speech, you roar like thunder.

With the aware and empty space of mind, you rest in the state of luminosity.

All the deities, delighting in the dance of bliss,

Invoke the mantras with effortless vajra songs.

The liberating life force of wisdom endows your mind.

Until attaining clarity, I will endeavor in visualization and recitation.

Until I reach perfection, please don't forsake your intentions!

Do not forget me; the time for your great heart-samaya has come!

On this very seat, let me perfect the fourfold Approach and Accomplishment,

And make me realize the lord of the mandala.

Hung!

In the southeastern direction, upon the glowing spoke of the jewel,

In the heart center of Vidyadhara Dorje Draktsal,

Is the letter HUNG upon a sun disc, encircled by the mantra chain,

From which light rays, flames, iron scorpions,

And numerous wrathful yaksha kings blaze forth like a storm.

The haughty *rahulas, nagas,* and *gyalpos* are bound under oath,

And the *gongpo* spirits who ruin Tibet and Kham are reduced to dust.

By gathering back and dissolving into me, my greatness and might become matchless.

OM AH HUNG ARTSIK NIRTSIK NAMO BHAGAWATE HUNG HUNG PE A HUNG HUNG PE

Offering Prayer

Assembly of wisdom deities, I invite you. Please come!

I offer you outer, inner, and secret offerings.

I praise your body, speech, mind, qualities, and activities.

I confess careless transgressions and errors.

Maha amrita balingta rakta khahi⁸

When you established the doctrine of the sacred Dharma,⁸¹⁰
Like hoisting a banner of victory,⁸
Samye was spontaneously accomplished, without being erected,⁸
And you fulfilled the wishes of the king.⁸
You were endowed with the names of three great beings—⁸
One was Padmakara,⁸
One was Padmasambhava,⁸
And one was Lake-Born Vajra.⁸
Dorje Drakpo Tsal, we invoke you by your secret name.⁸
With your compassion, bestow your blessings upon me.⁸
With your love, guide me and others on the path.⁸
With your realization, grant me the siddhis.⁸
With your powers, dispel my obstacles and those of others.⁸
Clear the outer obstacles externally.⁸
Clear the inner obstacles internally.⁸
Clear the secret obstacles into space.⁸
Respectfully, I bow down and take refuge in you.⁸
Om ah hung artsik nirtsik namo bhagawate hung hung pe a
    hung hung pe⁸

Hung Hrih!⁸
Vidyadhara Kalden Drendsey, manifest from space.⁸
Uttering the sounds of recitation, I invoke you.⁸
From the core of your heart-samaya, please come!⁸
With apparent and empty bodily forms, you fill the billionfold
    universe.⁸
With resounding and empty mantra tones of speech, you roar like
    thunder.⁸
With the aware and empty space of mind, you rest in the state of
    luminosity.⁸
All the deities, delighting in the dance of bliss,⁸
Invoke the mantras with effortless vajra songs.⁸
The liberating life force of wisdom endows your mind.⁸
Until attaining clarity, I will endeavor in visualization and
    recitation.⁸

---

10 *Barchey Lamsel,* verse 10

Until I reach perfection, please don't forsake your intentions! ᛝ
Do not forget me; the time for your great heart-samaya has come! ᛝ
On this very seat, let me perfect the fourfold Approach and
    Accomplishment, ᛝ
And make me realize the lord of the mandala. ᛝ

Hung! ᛝ
In the southwestern direction, upon the glowing spoke of the
    jewel, ᛝ
In the heart center of Vidyadhara Kalden Drendze, ᛝ
Is the letter HUNG upon a sun disc, encircled by the mantra chain, ᛝ
From which light rays of great bliss ᛝ
And the adamantine mantra sound of resounding emptiness
    pervade all realms. ᛝ
The four activities, the eight major accomplishments, ᛝ
And all siddhis, such as the kayas and wisdoms, ᛝ
Gather back and dissolve into me, so I become the nature of the
    Great Glorious One. ᛝ
OM BENZA KRODHA MAHA SHRI HERUKA HUNG PE ᛝ

Offering Prayer

Assembly of wisdom deities, I invite you. Please come! ᛝ
I offer you outer, inner, and secret offerings. ᛝ
I praise your body, speech, mind, qualities, and activities. ᛝ
I confess careless transgressions and errors. ᛝ
MAHA AMRITA BALINGTA RAKTA KHAHI ᛝ

At Samye Chimphu, when practicing sadhana, ᛝ[11]
You repelled negative conditions and granted siddhis. ᛝ
You established the king and ministers on the path to liberation ᛝ
And caused the *Bön* doctrine, negativity in manifest form, to wane. ᛝ
You showed the precious, immaculate dharmakaya. ᛝ
Kalden Drendze you who takes the destined ones to buddhahood, ᛝ
With your compassion, bestow your blessings upon me. ᛝ
With your love, guide me and others on the path. ᛝ
With your realization, grant me the siddhis. ᛝ

---

11 *Barchey Lamsel,* verse 11

With your powers, dispel my obstacles and those of others.

Clear the outer obstacles externally.

Clear the inner obstacles internally.

Clear the secret obstacles into space.

Respectfully, I bow down and take refuge in you.

Oᴍ ʙᴇɴᴢᴀ ᴋʀᴏᴅʜᴀ ᴍᴀʜᴀ sʜʀɪ ʜᴇʀᴜᴋᴀ ʜᴜɴɢ ᴘᴇ

Hᴜɴɢ Hʀɪʜ!

Vidyadhara Raksha Tötreng, manifest from space.

Uttering the sounds of recitation, I invoke you.

From the core of your heart-samaya, please come!

With apparent and empty bodily forms, you fill the billionfold
universe.

With resounding and empty mantra tones of speech, you roar like
thunder.

With the aware and empty space of mind, you rest in the state of
luminosity.

All the deities, delighting in the dance of bliss,

Invoke the mantras with effortless vajra songs.

The liberating life force of wisdom endows your mind.

Until attaining clarity, I will endeavor in visualization and
recitation.

Until I reach perfection, please don't forsake your intentions!

Do not forget me; the time for your great heart-samaya has come!

On this very seat, let me perfect the fourfold Approach and
Accomplishment,

And make me realize the lord of the mandala.

Hᴜɴɢ!

In the northwestern direction, upon the glowing spoke of the
jewel,

In the heart center of Vidyadhara Raksha Tötreng,

Is the letter ʜᴜɴɢ upon a sun disc, encircled by the mantra chain.

Light rays, a mass of fire, *garuda* sparks,

Emanations, and re-emanations radiate to fill the world.

The eight classes of *drekpas* of the three realms are enjoined to
service.

The hosts of samaya violators and elemental forces are reduced to
dust.

Everything is the play of awareness, the unimpeded state of
     primordial purity.
By gathering back and dissolving into me, my power and strength
     become matchless.
OM BENZA TSENDA SARVA DUSHTEN HUNG PE

Offering Prayer

Assembly of wisdom deities, I invite you. Please come!
I offer you outer, inner, and secret offerings.
I praise your body, speech, mind, qualities, and activities.
I confess careless transgressions and errors.
MAHA AMRITA BALINGTA RAKTA KHAHI

When you left for the land of Orgyen[12]
To subjugate the rakshasas,
Your great qualities surpassed all human beings,
And your actions were wonderful and amazing.
Mighty one with power and miracles,
With your compassion, bestow your blessings upon me.
With your love, guide me and others on the path.
With your realization, grant me the siddhis.
With your powers, dispel my obstacles and those of others.
Clear the outer obstacles externally.
Clear the inner obstacles internally.
Clear the secret obstacles into space.
Respectfully, I bow down and take refuge in you.
OM BENZA TSENDA SARVA DUSHTEN HUNG PE

HUNG HRIH!
Vidyadhara Padmavajra, manifest from space.
Uttering the sounds of recitation, I invoke you.
From the core of your heart-samaya, please come!
With apparent and empty bodily forms, you fill the billionfold
     universe.
With resounding and empty mantra tones of speech, you roar like
     thunder.

---

12 *Barchey Lamsel,* verse 12

With the aware and empty space of mind, you rest in the state of
luminosity.⟟
All the deities, delighting in the dance of bliss,⟟
Invoke the mantras with effortless vajra songs.⟟
The liberating life force of wisdom endows your mind.⟟
Until attaining clarity, I will endeavor in visualization and
recitation.⟟
Until I reach perfection, please don't forsake your intentions!⟟
Do not forget me; the time for your great heart-samaya has come!⟟
On this very seat, let me perfect the fourfold Approach and
Accomplishment,⟟
And make me realize the lord of the mandala.⟟

Hung! ⟟
In the northeastern direction, upon the glowing spoke of the
jewel,⟟
In the heart center of Vidyadhara Padmavajra,⟟
Is the letter HRIH upon a moon disc, encircled by the mantra
garland.⟟
The light rays of great bliss radiating from it⟟
Dissolve into me and the whole assembly of mandala deities.⟟
The experience of bliss and emptiness blazes forth, and we unite
with the self-radiant consort.⟟
The sounds and light rays of the bliss of union⟟
Invite the buddhas and their sons, who enter my mouth,⟟
Pass through my bodily form, and melt into light in my heart
center.⟟
Again this blesses my being and flows into the space of the consort,⟟
Becoming self-replicated sons performing the deeds of the
buddhas.⟟
Gathering back, they dissolve into me and the supreme siddhi is
attained.⟟
OM AH HUNG MAHA GURU PEMA BENZA DHUNGA GHAYE NAMA SOHA⟟

Offering Prayer

Assembly of wisdom deities, I invite you. Please come!⟟
I offer you outer, inner, and secret offerings.⟟

I praise your body, speech, mind, qualities, and activities.
I confess careless transgressions and errors.
MAHA AMRITA BALINGTA RAKTA KHAHI

Possessing enlightened body, speech, and mind, you are the
Glorious Guide of Beings,[13]
Having disgarded all obscurations, you perceive the three realms
vividly.
Having achieved the supreme siddhi, the supreme body of great
bliss,
You surely dispel the obstacles to attaining enlightenment.
With your compassion, bestow your blessings upon me.
With your love, guide me and others on the path.
With your realization, grant me the siddhis.
With your powers, dispel my obstacles and those of others.
Clear the outer obstacles externally.
Clear the inner obstacles internally.
Clear the secret obstacles into space.
Respectfully, I bow down and take refuge in you.
OM AH HUNG MAHA GURU PEMA BENZA DHUNGA GHAYE NAMA SOHA

For the recitation intent of all of these,
Place mantra garlands in the heart centers of both
Yourself, the samaya mandala,
And the deities of the wisdom mandala in front.
The light radiating from you invokes the ones visualized in front.
The light radiating and absorbing from them,
Accomplishes the siddhis, as explained.
At the end, they dissolve into your heart center.
When you practice this kind of yoga fully,
With a clear visualization,
You will directly perceive the mandala circle,
Hear the sounds of the vajra mantras,
And achieve the signs of yogic discipline.
At least, there is no doubt that in dreams
You will get all the signs described above
And receive the indications

---

13 *Barchey Lamsel,* verse 13

Of accomplishing all the various activities.

As to the number, recite four hundred thousand

Of whichever activity mantra you chiefly focus on.

In general, you should verbally recite it one-tenth

As much as the root mantra.

Samaya.

When you have invoked the heart-samayas through Approach,

And are endowed with the capacity

Of achieving whichever siddhis you may desire through
    Accomplishment,

You should achieve them through the stages of the four activity
    applications.

First, when practicing the pacifying activity,

Face east at dawn.

In the sattva *posture recite the chanting tune*

In a gentle, quiet, and relaxed way.

For the visualization of the emanation-absorption of the samadhi,

Together with a peaceful and clear frame of mind, imagine that:

From myself and all the mandala deities in front,

Nectar-like light rays stream forth

Invoking the minds of the Vajra Daka and Dakini.

The white rays of light radiating from them

Permeate the entire billionfold world system.

Sickness, evil forces, misdeeds, veils, and curses,

The eight and sixteen fears, and so forth,

All discordant factors, are completely pacified.

By gathering back and dissolving into me,

All the pacifying activities are accomplished.

Attach this at the end of the root mantra:

Ha benza dakini ra benza gingkara om shantim kuru soha

At times, emanate and absorb bodily forms,

Mantra garlands, and attributes.

Thus, by exerting yourself in the specifics for single sessions,

Within a certain number of weeks and days,

In actuality, disharmony is pacified
And you achieve the true speech that benefits others.
In dreams, you bathe and wear new clothes,
And you go beyond fearful places, and so forth.
These are taught to be the signs of having accomplished the pacifying
   activity.
Samaya.

When practicing the activity of increasing favorable conditions,
Face south at sunrise.
In the reveling posture, recite the chanting tune
In a melodious, slow, and dignified way.
Together with a magnificent and awe-inspiring frame of mind, imagine
   that:

From myself and all the mandala deities in front,
Light rays stream forth, like a rising sun,
Invoking the minds of the Ratna Daka and Dakini.
The yellow rays of light radiating from them,
Permeate the entire billionfold world system.
Life span, merit, splendor, and wealth,
Strength, fame, wisdom, goodness, and so forth,
All favorable conditions, are fully increased.
By gathering back and dissolving into me,
All the increasing activities are accomplished.
RI RATNA DAKINI TSA RATNA GINGKARA DROOM PUSHTIM KURU OM

In actuality, favorable conditions are increased
And food, wealth, and enjoyments are effortlessly gathered.
In dreams, plants and trees spring up, rivers swell,
Many people gather, and so forth.
These are taught to be the signs of having accomplished the increasing
   activity.
Samaya.

When practicing the activity of magnetizing desirable things,
Face west in the evening.
In the lotus posture, recite the chanting tune
In a manner that is passionate and attached.
Together with a yearning and wishing frame of mind, imagine that:

From myself and all the mandala deities in front,⁞
Rays of light, the nature of passion, stream forth⁞
Invoking the minds of the Padma Daka and Dakini.⁞
The red rays of light radiating from them⁞
Permeate the entire billionfold world system.⁞
Powerful gods, humans, and yakshas,⁞
Food, wealth, enjoyments, dominion, and so forth,⁞
All desirable things, are brought under control.⁞
By gathering back and dissolving into me,⁞
All the magnetizing activities are accomplished.⁞
Ni pema dakini hri pema gingkara hrih washam kuru ho⁞
In actuality, food, wealth, and women are gathered,⁞
And you are able to change the perception of others effortlessly.⁞
In dreams, you ride on the sun and moon,⁞
Drink up an ocean, traverse the four continents, and so forth.⁞
These are taught to be the signs of having accomplished the magnetizing
    activity.⁞
Samaya.⁞

When practicing the wrathful activity of annihilating,⁞
Face north at dusk.⁞
In the fierce posture, recite the chanting tune,⁞
Like the showering of a great hailstorm.⁞
Together with a ferocious and violent frame of mind, imagine that:⁞

From myself and all the mandala deities in front,⁞
Violent, sparking rays of light stream forth⁞
Invoking the minds of the Karma Daka and Dakini.⁞
The dark blue rays of light radiating from them⁞
Permeate the entire billionfold world system.⁞
The ten objects to be liberated and the seven transgressors,⁞
The samaya violators, elemental forces, evil spirits, obstructors, and
    so forth,⁞
All vicious spirits, are annihilated.⁞
By gathering back and dissolving into me,⁞
All the wrathful activities are accomplished.⁞
Sa KARMA DAKINI YA KARMA GINGKARA HUNG MARAYA PE⁞

In actuality, the enemies of the doctrine pass away
And omens appear indicating the haughty spirits are subdued.
In dreams, lakes dry up, rocks crumble,
You kill vicious animals, and so forth.
These are taught to be the signs of having accomplished the wrathful
  activity.
Samaya.

Then, for the supreme activity application,
The practice of the group gathering,
Practice correctly,
According to the elaborate sadhana section of the Kadü.
Having completed the four aspects of Approach and Accomplishment,
At dusk, invoke the minds of the deities.
At midnight, receive the siddhi of liberating.
At dawn, take union onto the path.
By means of such yogas,
You will attain the four vidyadhara levels in this lifetime.

EMA, this wonderful and amazing path
Is the journey taken by the jinas of the three times.
Samaya. Seal. Seal. Seal.

For the specific individual practices
Of each of the twelve power-wielding vidyadharas,
Place him in the position of the chief figure
And place the chief figure in his position.
Follow the order of the activities to any suitable extent,
And condense Approach and Accomplishment into one.
By maintaining the yogas, practice this path
For quickly achieving whichever siddhi you desire.
Samaya. Seal. Seal. Seal.

The entire Lamey Tukdrub,
Like the essence of my heart-blood,
Is my innermost heart practice.
I, Padma, have now completely taught
This most profound intent of visualizations
To the king, father, and son.

And, lovingly considering the future suffering

Of the destitute Tibetan people,

Tsogyal, commit this to writing

And conceal it as a precious essence of earth.

Many signs will indicate when the time for its disciples has come:

Everywhere throughout India, Nepal, and Tibet

Outer and inner fighting and strife will occur repeatedly.

There will be a sudden outbreak of plague for human beings and
  cattle.

The assemblies of the great beings upholding the doctrine

Will fall subject to sudden obstacles,

Or with their minds influenced by demonic forces,

They will behave in all kinds of improper ways.

At that time, this profound instruction

Will benefit all central countries in general

And Tibet in particular.

It will then greatly extend the duration of the teachings of the Buddha.

Thus, he spoke.

I, Tsogyal, wrote down exactly what he had spoken and concealed it as
  a secret, supreme treasure. Samaya. Seal, seal, seal.

This is a genuine secret of the profound treasures of the emanation of Prince Damdzin, the undisputed and timely incarnated great treasure-revealer Orgyen Dechen Lingpa.

QUESTIONS ON DZAPKYI KÖLJANG

Lama Putsi Pema Tashi

STUDENT: Are the seed syllables in the deities' heart centers the same color as their bodies?

LAMA: Here, we are talking about the twelve manifestations. The seed syllables in their heart centers always correspond to their body colors. The peaceful manifestations always have a HRIH, and the wrathful ones all have a HUNG. In the case of the peaceful deities, the seed syllable HRIH stands on a moon disc. In the case of the wrathful ones, the seed syllable HUNG always stands on a sun disc.

STUDENT: Is Dechen Gyalpo wrathful or peaceful?

LAMA: Dechen Gyalpo is semi-peaceful and semi-wrathful. He has a HRIH in his heart center.

STUDENT: Regarding Gyalwey Dungdzin, what does *brilliant splendor* mean?

LAMA: This phrase has something to do with being dignified. You can see that powerful people have some special bearing or brilliance about them. A beggar doesn't have that. Usually, this phrase is used to describe deities who engage in magnetizing activity or taking-charge activity. When certain people speak, other people always say, "Yes, yes, all right" to whatever they say. It is this kind of quality.

In this case, the deity is called Gyalwey Dungdzin, but as one of the eight aspects of Guru Rinpoche, he is called Pema Gyalpo. Even though he is white here, a strong red hue shines forth from within. That light takes control over all of samsara and nirvana, magnetizing or gathering back all the splendor of samsara, which is merit, longevity, power, and so forth. It also gathers back the omniscient wisdom and all the enlightened qualities of nirvana. We should imagine that all of these appear in the form of the eight auspicious articles and emblems, the seven royal possessions, and bindus of five-colored rainbow light. All this dissolves into you. Through this, your demeanor of power and dignity blazes forth tremendously. Everything is perfected. The mantra says PADMA RAJA, which refers to Pema Gyalpo.

STUDENT: Please give a brief explanation of each of the twelve manifestations.

LAMA: Since this is primarily a guru sadhana, all the deities are the display of the wisdom of the guru's mind. There is no variation in quality, such as one being superior or inferior—there's no difference whatsoever. Many different forms appear because sentient beings have many different thoughts and emotions occur through the expression or display of dualistic mind. In the same way, all the various forms of deities, yidams, dakas, dakinis, and so forth are the natural expressions of the state of rigpa.

There are also many aspects and forms due to the different inclinations and karmic links of sentient beings. Even though there is no difference in quality, still there is a difference in the speed of accomplishment, depending upon the individual. For example, when you throw the flower of awareness into the mandala during an empowerment, it is said that if you practice the deity upon which the flower lands, accomplishment will be swifter than practicing any of the other deities. This deity is not superior, but it is more suitable to you. In one story, when Guru Rinpoche was giving the empowerment of *Kabgye*, Trisong Deütsen's flower fell in the center of the mandala of Chemchok Heruka. He then practiced that deity primarily. This is why there are so many deities. Gyalwey Dungdzin is more appropriate for magnetizing activity. If you want to accomplish supreme wisdom and knowledge, you should focus more on Mawey Senge. Kyechok Tsülzang is appropriate for increasing wealth. Each deity has its specific purpose. They are not in any way inferior to or different from Guru Rinpoche himself. They are all exactly the same but in a different form.

STUDENT: Regarding Kyechok Tsülzang, what do *essential extract* and *sky treasury* mean?

LAMA: The first words, *essential extract,* mean the "pure essence" that is extracted. When you steep tea leaves, you keep the drink containing the pure essence and throw away the leaves. They are not the essence. In the same way, here the pure essences of all of samsara and nirvana are extracted, like tea from tea leaves. This represents the splendor, wealth, and so forth that dissolves into you, rendering you the owner of the sky treasury. The sky treasury is inexhaustible, just like Bodhisattva Samantabhadra's boundless, inexhaustible offerings, which are like an infinite cloud bank spread throughout the sky. The sky is both infinitely immense and immaterial. So, *sky treasury* means both "inexhaustible" and "very vast" at the same time.

STUDENT: Regarding Dükyi Shechen, what does *shik-shik yom-yom* mean?

LAMA: *Shik-shik yom-yom* indicates that the rain of daggers and vajras fills up the entire billionfold universe, just like a great snowfall, a blizzard of snowflakes.

STUDENT: Regarding Dzamling Gyenchog, what does *drekpa* mean?

LAMA: A *drekpa* is an independent, enterprising evil spirit. There are different spirits called *tsen,* gyalpo, and so forth, who are not obeying the command of Guru Rinpoche. They are, in fact, eager to steal the life force of sentient beings and sometimes create obstacles for their life span.

STUDENT: Regarding Dzamling Gyenchog, what does *Self-cognizance is perfected into the mind of the Mahaguru* mean?

LAMA: Once all these drekpas have been cut down and terminated and the clinging to all that appears and exists as being real has been purified, then everything that was previously emanated returns back and dissolves into you. By being blessed in this way, your mind is perfected into being the mind of Guru Rinpoche. What does this mean? It means the five poisons have been self-liberated, and you have achieved mastery over wisdom. Among the different yidams, this form of Guru Rinpoche is the same as Yangdak (Vishuddha) Heruka.

STUDENT: Regarding Pema Jungne what does *reveling in bliss and emptiness* mean?

LAMA: *Reveling* here means the "indivisibility of bliss and emptiness." They are indivisible.

STUDENT: Regarding Pema Jungne, what does *What appears and exists as the Three-Roots deities* mean?

LAMA: *Nangsi,* or *appearance and existence,* is an abbreviation of *appearance,* which is the "vessel of the world," and *existence,* which is the "contents, or sentient beings," within this container. From the very beginning, the world and beings are actually the Three Roots. The world is a pure bud- dhafield, and all sentient beings in their pure form are the deities of the Three Roots. When we receive the vase empowerment, the samaya is to regard all that appears and exists as the all-encompassing purity, a pure land with deities.

From the three places of all beings, who appear as deities, a shower of attributes rains down upon you and increases the wisdom. The word *play* here, or *display,* is the same as when we watch a movie. Everything that appears on the movie screen is a "magical display." All kinds of things occur, but they are all illusory. In this case, the display is the "indivisibility of bliss and emptiness."

Display can also mean "enjoying" or "enjoyment," such as the five sense pleasures. The eye faculty enjoys or partakes in visual forms. The ear faculty enjoys sound. It's the same way with the other sense faculties. In some remote dialects, *display* is also the honorific form of the verb "to beat."

STUDENT: Regarding Khyepar Phakpa Rigdzin, are *jungpos* and *drekpas* the same?

LAMA: Yes, they are the same.

STUDENT: Regarding Dzultrül Tuchen, what does *the power of awareness is increased* mean?

LAMA: It means the quality of experience and realization blazes forth; here, it literally means "to grow, expand, or increase." It's like a baby chick, which doesn't look like much; you can easily step on it. But when it grows up, it becomes a magnificent rooster, with beautiful feathers and so forth. Also, when the power of rigpa expands and strengthens, the power of experience and realization blazes forth. That is the mean- ing here. In the beginning, when you have not recognized the state of rigpa, this doesn't happen. But once you recognize and train in rigpa, its strength enlarges and expands.

STUDENT: Regarding Rigdzin Dorje Draktsal, who or what is a *Yaksha Wrathful King?*

LAMA: Dorje Draktsal has five armor deities on his body: Yamantaka is in the forehead; Hayagriva is in the throat; Vajrapani is in the heart; Tröma Nagmo is in the navel; and the fifth, Trogyal Yaksha Mebar, is in the secret place. This is how Guru Drakpo looks. Tröma Nagmo is a black form of Vajra Yogini. When he sends out these deities, they clean up the whole world completely and subjugate all the different kinds of troublemaker spirits. His name is Trogyal Yaksha Mebar. *Mebar* means "blazing with intense heat." It is like a flame that immediately obliterates a tiny insect that flies toward it. In the same way, these emanations, especially the fifth, Trogyal Yaksha Mebar, fill up the world and completely destroy all that needs to be destroyed. Guru Drakpo is the form Guru Rinpoche assumed when he subjugated all the drekpas and local spirits of Tibet and bound them under oath. All forms of Guru Drakpo have these five deities in their five places.

STUDENT: Are the activities of Dorje Drolö and Dorje Draktsal the same?

LAMA: Yes. The practice we have here is the unified mandala of the entire cycle of the *Barchey Künsel,* in which all the deities are present together in a single mandala. But each of the twelve manifestations has its own individual practice with its own sadhana, from beginning to end. These correspond to the separate chapters within the *Sheldam Nyingjang* scriptures. For example, the first of the twelve manifestations, Gyalwey Dungdzin, who gathers or takes control over the entire threefold existence, is surrounded by the four dakinis of the four families, who travel to the realms of the gods, the nagas, the human beings, and so forth, gathering back all the wealth and enjoyments. They hold different implements in their hands.

The *Eight Sadhana Teachings,* the *Drubpa Kabgye*, has a mandala of nine deities with Chemchok Heruka in the center and Yamantaka, Hayagriva, Amritakundali, and Vajra Kilaya in the four directions. In the four intermediate directions, it has the *Mamo,* the *Dra-ngak,* and the *Rigdzin* as the ninth.[14] All together, they are called the *Palgu,* or the Nine Glorious Ones. They are practiced together in a single mandala, yet they can also be practiced individually. For example, if you do Yamantaka alone, it is called the "individual practice from the *Eight Sadhana Teachings.*" You can also practice Hayagriva or Vajra Kilaya alone. In the same

---

14 Only eight are listed here.

way here, in the mandala of *Barchey Künsel*, the deities are practiced as a group in one mandala, but if you focus on one specific activity, you can just practice a single deity. For example, Kyechog can be practiced in order to increase wealth. This means visualizing a form that Guru Rinpoche has deliberately taken in order to accomplish a specific purpose.

STUDENT: Regarding Kalden Drendzey, what does *adamantine mantra sound of resounding emptiness* mean?

LAMA: Everything one sees is the unity of appearance and emptiness. Everything one hears is audible yet empty. Whatever one thinks or feels is the unity of awareness and emptiness. This is how things really are.

The vajra mantra resounds throughout all worlds. Our normal voice is not necessarily the vajra mantra. It is just ordinary speech. But still, it is empty yet resounding. This means that whatever is heard, whatever resounds, is empty of self-nature and possesses no substantial entity. This is the meaning of indivisibly audible yet empty.

STUDENT: Regarding Kalden Drendzey, what are the eight major accomplishments?

LAMA: There is a list of eight, but there are actually just two types, the eight general siddhis and the eight supreme siddhis. In the *Exposition of the Three Levels of Precepts, Domsum Namngey*, you can find the list.

STUDENT: Regarding Raksha Tötreng, what does *Everything is the play of awareness, the unimpeded state of primordial purity* mean?

LAMA: *Everything* here means that whatever occurs within the mind, such as the different emotions, thoughts, and so forth, is the expression of awareness. It is none other than primordial purity, which is the state of emptiness totally devoid of constructs.

The quality of buddha nature is that it has always been pure from the very beginning. It has always been utterly pure, and this is called "primordial purity." The corresponding deity among the eight aspects of Guru Rinpoche is Senge Dradrok.

STUDENT: When you do the practice, do you visualize yourself as Raksha Tötreng with another Raksha Tötreng in front of you?

LAMA: The visualization in front of you is always the same as your self-visualization. You invoke the front visualization with rays of light, and from the front visualization, the rays are emanated and reabsorbed, accomplishing the all-encompassing activities, regardless of your focus.

STUDENT: Regarding the gatekeepers in the east and pacifying activity, what is the *sattva posture?*

LAMA: *(He demonstrates)* The knees are not touching the ground. The vajra posture is Buddha Shakyamuni's pose. When practicing the vajra leaps among the yogic exercises, one also lands in the vajra posture.

STUDENT: Do you append the Harinisa mantra to the end of the Tötreng Tsal mantra?

LAMA: Yes. In the *Trinley Nyingpo* and the *Trinley Dringpo,* the mantras of the four dakas and dakinis are said together as one and appended to the end of the Tötreng Tsal mantra. But here in the *Trinley Gyepa,* with the mantras from the *Dzapkyi Köljang,* the mantras are said one family at a time. At the end of the Tötreng Tsal mantra, you would add: HA BENZA DAKINI RA BENZA GINGKARA...and so forth.

STUDENT: After that it says, *sometimes you emanate bodily forms.* Does that refer back to the dakas and dakinis emanating out or to Guru Rinpoche?

LAMA: As we said before, when the text says *at times*, this means we can alternate what we think of when we cannot keep everything in mind all at once. Sometimes we imagine the rays of light streaming out and returning. Sometimes we rest in the state where our mind and the deity's mind are indivisible. We can focus alternately on the bodily forms, the mantra garlands, and the attributes. You can focus according to your preference.

STUDENT: Regarding the southern gatekeepers and increasing activity, what is the *reveling posture?*

LAMA: It is the playful posture of the king. When Guru Rinpoche sits with his right leg slightly extended, he's in the reveling posture.

STUDENT: Regarding the western gatekeepers and magnetizing activity, what time is evening?

LAMA: It is at dusk, when it gets dark. Each general aspect of the four activities—pacifying, increasing, magnetizing, and subjugating—has its own method of application, focus, and most effective time of day and direction. This is a general teaching for all practices. For pacifying activity, face east and practice at dawn; for increasing activity, face south at sunrise. Magnetizing activity is most effective when practiced at dusk. The terminating activity is performed at midnight. According to Tibetan astrology, the twenty-four hours of the day are divided into two-hour periods matching the twelve animals. In this way, there are six periods of day and six periods of night. The first period is between dawn and sunrise, the second period is between sunrise and the heat of the sun, the third is midday, the fourth is afternoon, the fifth is late afternoon, and the sixth is evening. The last period, at 6:00 PM or 7:00 PM, is the time for magnetizing activity to be practiced.[15]

STUDENT: Aren't dawn and sunrise synonymous?

TRANSLATOR: Dawn is when there is light in the sky, and sunrise is when you can actually see the sun. There is a list from Dharamsala, India, showing exactly when it's most effective to eat certain Tibetan medicines. It depends on when you were born and who you are.

STUDENT: The text refers to *group practice*. Does that refer to a Great Accomplishment practice (*drubchen*)? What is the practice of the *Kadü*? I don't understand this whole section of text beginning with *take the siddhis at dawn, terminate at midnight*...

LAMA: In the *Concise Daily Practice Manual*, the *Gyüngyi Köljang*, the words *then, for the supreme activity, which is the sadhana of the group gathering* refer to performing a *drubchen,* where many yogis and yoginis gather to practice together.

There are two kinds of yogis and yoginis: those who are fully ripened disciples and those who try to imitate fully ripened disciples. A fully ripened disciple has undergone the training in approach and accomplishment, perfected the recitations, and reached accomplishment in this.

---

15 Here's the list that breaks up the twenty-four hours into twelve different periods. *Daybreak* is 5:00AM–7:00AM. *Early morning* is 7:00AM–9:00AM. *Mid morning* is 9:00AM–11:00AM. *Noon* is 11:00AM–1:00PM *Early afternoon,* is 1:00PM–3:00PM. *Late afternoon* is 3:00PM–5:00PM. *Sunset* is 5:00PM–7:00PM. *Early evening* is 7:00PM–9:00PM. *Late evening* is 9:00PM–11:00PM. *Midnight* is 11:00PM–1:00AM. *Dark of the night* is 1:00AM–3:00AM. *Pre-dawn* is 3:00AM–5:00AM. These times tell when to eat the medicine, depending upon which animal you are.

When a whole group of such people assemble, they can engage in the supreme activity, not just the general activity of pacifying, increasing, and so forth.

The supreme activity of a group sadhana mirrors the style of the *Kadü*, or the "assemblage of teachings," an extensive sadhana. Yarje Orgyen Lingpa revealed the main terma, but Chokgyur Lingpa also had a version, and you can follow either one. The *Kadü* gathers different teachings together in a single mandala. To practice this correctly, after completing the four aspects of approach and accomplishment, invoke the samaya of the deities in the evening and receive the siddhis of liberation at midnight. At dawn, practice the "path of union." At this point, just before the conclusion of the drubchen, accomplished disciples practice the third empowerment with a consort. This only applies to accomplished disciples, not imitators. Through this kind of yoga and practice, you will accomplish the four vidyadhara levels—maturation, longevity, Mahamudra, and spontaneous accomplishment—in this lifetime.

What is the difference between being a "ripened disciple" and an "imitator" of one? The word for *imitation* means "mask." For example, during a lama dance, the dancers don the mask of a deity and pretend to be that deity. Here, even if you are not fully accomplished, you will attain the four vidyadhara levels in this lifetime, if you adhere to this practice perfectly. This is the meaning here.

The way to enter Vajrayana is through receiving empowerment. When receiving empowerment, we obtain the samayas of the vidyadharas. When receiving the vase, secret, wisdom-knowledge, and word empowerments, we receive the empowerment precepts of Vajrayana. What are those exactly? They are none other than the commitment to do the practices connected with the four empowerments.

The practice connected with the first empowerment, the vase empowerment, is to train in seeing the world—beings, sounds, thought activity, and so forth—as a pure display of deities, mantra, and samadhi. To engage in this properly, you train in the practice of the vase empowerment until reaching perfection—until you actually see things as they already are: the world as a pure buddhafield; all beings as male and female deities, dakas, and dakinis; all sounds as mantra; all thought activity as wisdom. Having trained again and again in the development stage until you stabilize this view, perceiving this way all the time, you can then request the secret empowerment.

The secret empowerment is conferred by means of the bodhichitta of the guru and consort. Once you have received the secret empowerment, you begin the practices connected with the inner path of Vajrayana, which has three aspects: preparation, main part, and conclusion. One's body is endowed with the skillful means of using another's body. The third and fourth empowerments have the two aspects of "wisdom as example" and "wisdom as the meaning." The latter refers to "ultimate wisdom," not the symbolic wisdom.

The first of the inner practices connected to the secret empowerment is training in the *nadis, pranas,* and *bindus* in order to gain mastery. The most important is to be able to control the flow of bindus, especially to reverse the flow. This is a very important point. Prior to attaining this mastery, you do not engage in consort practice. Such practice only comes after you have gained the ability to control the bindus. When you have achieved this, by means of training in the channels, mastering the different breathing exercises, and controlling the bindus, you can then request the third empowerment, called the "wisdom-knowledge empowerment." This refers to training in the wisdom that unites bliss and emptiness, which is also called "symbolic wisdom." Once you accomplish that, you are given the fourth empowerment, which is identical with the third empowerment in essence—but only in essence. It is the real, or "ultimate wisdom," of the unity of bliss and emptiness, totally free from all constructs and as vast as space.

This is the progressive journey through the practices connected with the four empowerments. This journey, which brings one to the state of complete enlightenment, corresponds exactly to the normal Sutra path of the five paths and ten bhumis. The distance traveled is the same, but the speed is different. Taking the Sutra path is like walking overland, for example, to Bodhgaya, while taking the Vajrayana path is like flying there. You cover the same distance, but it is much faster. It is said that the Vajrayana path is like an optical illusion, in which you instantly traverse what would otherwise take a tremendously long time. It's the same as looking down at the ground from an airplane; you can see that you are covering the distance, but in a few seconds you have gone very far.

According to Mahayoga, the Vajrayana path is divided into the four vidyadhara levels. The first, the vidyadhara level of maturation, corresponds to arriving at the "heat and summit" aspects of the Path of Joining. The second, the vidyadhara level of longevity, corresponds to arriving at the first bhumi. The third, the vidyadhara level of Maha-mudra, or the "great symbol," corresponds to the next nine bhumis. The fourth, the vidyadhara level of spontaneous perfection, corresponds to the very end of the stream of the ten bhumis.

Concerning the first, the vidyadhara level of maturation, the body we have right now is mature because it is a result of past karma. Our previous karmic deeds compelled our consciousness to take the form of the human body we now possess. It is the form of the ripening, or maturation, of past karma. If one reaches the vidyadhara level of maturation, it is said that the mind matures into the form of the deity, while keeping the body that is the maturation of karma. So, we still look like a human being, but our consciousness has matured into the deity. Therefore, at the very moment of death, the human body is left behind, while the mind becomes the deity. Just as a baby *garuda* bird, when hatching from its egg, is immediately able to fly, the practitioner who has reached the first vidyadhara level immediately goes to a pure land in the form of a deity, at the time of death.

Prince Damzin

THE SHORT NOTES FOR PERFORMING THE APPROACH, ACCOMPLISHMENT, AND ACTIVITIES

Homage to Guru Rinpoche,
Possessor of the Threefold Kindness.

Chokgyur Lingpa

Having obtained the supreme freedoms and riches; being inspired by the thoughts of impermanence, weariness, and renunciation; and desiring to attain buddhahood within this lifetime, you should receive the empowerments and keep the samayas. Then, at the time of an auspicious constellation during the waxing moon, make as many general confessions as you can, sweep your dwelling place, sprinkle cleansing water, and burn incense. Place on the western wall either a painted or sculpted image of Urgyen Rinpoche. Upon a ledge covered in cloth in front of it, arrange amrita, rakta, torma, and the seven enjoyments. Draw a *swastika* with white chalk under your seat and attach some of your master's hair above you. Thus, make the auspicious coincidence for being able to complete the practice, reduce sickness, and increase vitality. If you have a perfect practice box, you should also use it; otherwise, this much will do. Furthermore, gather the vajra, bell, *damaru*, frankincense, mustard seeds, tossing grains, poles, and the preliminary tormas.

Following that, sit down on a comfortable seat, supplicate your master, and expel the stale breath. Present the local lord with the white torma. Then, in the presence of the embodiment of all the objects of refuge, in the sky before you—your root guru inseparable from Urgyen Rinpoche—think: "I and all beings take refuge in you. Practicing this profound path, I will attain the state of the Trikaya Guru within this very lifetime, for the sake of my mothers, all sentient beings!" Arousing bodhichitta in this way, dissolve the field of refuge into yourself.

Visualizing yourself as red Hayagriva holding a lotus and skull cup, emanate RAM YAM KAM from your heart center to burn, scatter, and purify the torma. Imagine that from DHRUNG appears a jewel vessel, within which OM AH HUNG emanate an ocean of nectar with sense pleasures. The light from your heart center summons all the obstructors and presents them with a satisfying offering. Afterward, order them to disperse on your command. Dispel the remaining ones with tiny wrathful ones holding skull clubs and fire lassos. Toss out the gektor, scatter charmed substances, and burn frankincense. Place the pole at your entrance with Shri Hayagriva in charge and close the outer and inner passageways. If someone needs to come in, include him or her in your visualization. Then gather back all the tiny wrathful ones to create the protection consisting of the vajra foundation, enclosure, dome, and mass of fire.

Hosts of Trikaya Guru deities arrive like a swirling blizzard and dissolve into you, your dwelling place, articles, and surroundings. Hereby your body becomes the enlightened body, your speech the enlightened speech, your mind the enlightened mind, your dwelling place a pure realm and celestial palace, your companions male and female deities, and your food and drink wisdom nectar. While not conceptualizing the offering articles, you are perceiving their essence as wisdom nectar. They take the form, nonetheless, of a torma emanating the five sense pleasures; a skull cup filled with nectar, which condenses the extracts of samsara and nirvana; and a skull cup filled with rakta, which is the nature of bliss. Moreover, imagine that offering goddesses multiply to fill the sky. These were the preliminary steps.

For the main part, meditate on the yoga of all phenomena being great emptiness. Within the state of the yoga of the magic-like compassion for all the sentient beings who have not realized this emptiness, your awareness, the union of emptiness and compassion, takes the form of a white HRIH. Rays of light radiate from the letter HRIH, purifying the world and beings. As the light rays gather back, the dark blue source of dharmas appears, as wide as space. Within it, there also appears the green vajra cross of wind, the white circle of water, the yellow square of earth, Mount Meru with its sides reflecting these respective colors, and the blazing triangle of fire. At the center of all this, surrounded by the eight great charnel grounds and situated upon the anthers of a thousand-petaled lotus, lies a pure land replete with perfect features.

Within it, there is a vajra cross with twelve spokes reflecting the respective directional colors: those pointing east are blue, and so forth. Its hub is a white square of precious substance, upon which rests the palace. The palace has five layers of walls, in one of two arrangements. In the first configuration, the palace's interior, made entirely of white crystal, is surrounded by another layer of walls, made respectively of sapphire in the east, gold in the south, ruby in the west, and emerald in the north. This arrangement progresses clockwise, with each additional ring of walls maintaining this color orientation and sequence. In the second constellation, progressing from innermost outward, the five layers of walls are respectively made of crystal, emerald, ruby, gold, and sapphire.

A red "platform of delights" adorned with offering goddesses runs along the base of the walls. A yellow frieze and a white ledge supported by posts with hanging rain spouts runs along the top of the walls. Golden scarves and lattices hang over the gaps. Golden vases supporting parasols, pennants, victory banners, flags, and tail fans rest upon the ledge. Decorative peacock feathers and silken streamers hang downward. At each of the four entrances, there is an eightfold architrave supported by four pillars. Above these, there are thirteen dharma wheels topped by a parasol and flanked by deer.

Inside, the galleries surrounding the white square have the colors of their respective directions, blue to the east, and so on. Below the ledge but above the golden beam, there are eight pillars supporting a circular beam that holds twenty-eight rafters marked with the attributes of the family.

Above the circular beam, there is another fivefold wall, a frieze, and a ledge similar to the wall below. The beams on this level have a checkered pattern and support sixteen rafters covered with jeweled planks, which have three tiers and are in the shape of a stupa. A lotus atop a set of posts supports thirteen golden rings that run up along a life-pillar, consisting of an unchanging vajra inserted within a cross. At the pinnacle, lattices encircle a golden parasol. The lotus roof is adorned with shining jewels. The transparent palace shines with rays of light, and its proportions are unfathomable.

Inside this, there is a flat eight-sided jewel made of sapphire with shining jewels on its sides and lattice-work decorations. On top of it, there is a four-petalled lotus made of various gems, on the center of which is a seat consisting of a lion throne, lotus, sun, and moon. Lotuses with moon seats adorn the four sides of the principal lotus. Upon the jewel itself, there are the following directional seats: to the east, a lotus and sun seat; to the south and west, lotuses with moon seats; to the north and in the intermediate directions, seats with lotuses, suns, and haughty spirits (*drekpas*); and to the northeast, a three-layered lotus, sun, and moon seat. The four gates have lotuses with sun seats. In this way, the five elements have the nature of the five consorts, while the celestial palace has the nature of the five wisdoms. The thirty-seven factors of enlightenment are all present within these details.

Regarding the visualization of the deities who inhabit the mandala, the primary text depicts the three main figures clearly. At the top of the lotus tree growing behind the Guru, you should visualize the two Lords of the Family as described in the *Practice Manual*. At this point, the surrounding figures are merely a "felt visualization." If you want to understand the details, consult either the *Extensive* or *Medium Practice Manual*. Gyalwey Dungdzin can either be standing or seated, as you prefer. The inner manifestations all have differing accoutrements. Gyalwey Dungdzin is Pema Gyalpo; moreover, other manuals, such as the *Güjang*, describe him as having a king's attire and a crown inlaid with white skulls and jewels. Mawey Senge has a yellow pandita hat and a jewelled top knot. Kyechok Tsülzang has a red lotus crown with five folds inlaid with shining jewels. Dükyi Shechen has a blue lotus crown with folds adorned with five dry skulls, and so on. In this way, they have many different accoutrements. However, here you should visualize according to the *Extensive Practice Manual*. This assembly of deities is pure, as the nature of your own aggregates, elements, and sense factors; it is the magical net, uniting means and knowledge. All of the deities have OM AH HUNG in their three places, as they are inseparable from the body, speech, and mind of the victorious ones. Having primordially perfected the empowerments of the five wisdoms, the crowns of their heads are marked with the five seed syllables. The main figure, Guru Rinpoche, has an *ushnisha* with a tiara of five gems on the crown of his head.

The rays of light streaming forth from the HRIH in your heart center invite the mandala of the support and the supported, or simply the supported deities. Do whichever is convenient, but dissolve it indivisibly with the samaya mandala.

From the heart center of the main figure, a version of you as the *karma-sattva* emerges, with one face, two arms, divine dress, and sublime ornaments—all in a variety of desirable colors. From its heart center and palms, offering goddesses with the seven enjoyments, amrita, rakta, and torma emanate and make offerings. Imagine that the deities drink the rakta without any remainder, thus emptying samsara. Receive the siddhis with the remaining nectar and dissolve the offering goddesses into the deity, which then in turn dissolves into you, in a process of creation and return.

For the secret offering, delight all the sugatas with the bodhichitta that comes from union with the corresponding consorts. Perform the union and liberation by liberating deluded samsaric thoughts into luminosity. For the "thatness" offering, allow the spontaneously present wisdom to rest in the space of primordial purity.

Make praises by emanating numerous beings, such as Vajra Varahi and the rest of the five dakinis, as well as Brahma, Shakra, and the universal monarchs, who then make praises with melodious songs and music before dissolving back into you.

In the context of the approach recitation, the recitation mansion is not divided. You visualize yourself in the form of the guru. In the heart center of both Lords of the Family, there is a syllable HRIH—white and red respectively—upon a moon disc. Rays of light radiate from these, gathering the nectar of longevity into the vase, which then overflows and pours down onto the crown of your head, without having to pass through the body of Avalokiteshvara.

At the time of the accomplishment practice, offering clouds emanate from the light rays of your body, pleasing the victorious ones throughout the directions and times, while bodily forms filling space emit light rays that purify beings' obscurations. Do this while linking HUNG to the breath's coming, going, and remaining. As a beginner training in the triple HUNG, this is sufficient—you do not need to visualize either a countless amount of HUNGs or the shape of the HUNG. The four classes of dakas perform the activities with the rays of light from bodily forms resembling themselves.

Perform the visualization for the recitation offering as above. No matter which of the six recitations you focus on, recite and meditate a little on all the others. Or, as is taught in the other manuals, at the time of benefiting oneself, practice only Amitayus and apply the same to the others in their context. This is also completely in accordance with scripture. For daily recitation, you should carry out the recitation and meditation of each of the six parts in full. In that context, as it is taught:

> Every session, bring out the deity's vivid appearance in fullness.
> Every session, plant the great stake of the essence mantra.
> Every session, rest in the one taste of your mind and the deity.
> Every session, practice the magical displays of projecting and
>   absorbing light rays.

Always take pride in being no different from the deity. After that, if you are doing the feast offering as a concluding activity, neatly arrange feast tormas, meat, and wine. Sprinkle them with clean water and purify them with RAM YAM KAM. From the state of emptiness, the five meats and the five nectars melt within the *bhandha* vessel, as you summon and dissolve the wisdom nectar of the three syllables into the samaya nectar. Visualize as when opening up the recitation mansion; if you have not already opened it, invite the field of accumulation. The goddesses of sense pleasures offer the first part of the feast. Make mending and apologies with the nectar of the second part. For the last part, even if you don't perform the visualization for liberation, proffer to the mouth the flesh and blood—the essence of enemies and obstructors—without any remainder. Make offerings to the body mandala, by enjoying the feast, while you visualize yourself as the deity. Then, the bodhichitta of Hayagriva and consort on your tongue—as OM AH HUNG—dissolves into the residuals, cleansing impurities and consecrating them with wisdom nectar. Magnetize all the guests for the residuals and imagine that they partake of it and fulfill the activities.

If you are not performing the feast, let the world and beings melt into light at the end of the recitation-praises and dissolve into the mandala, which in turn dissolves into the HRIH in your heart center. Then rest evenly without holding even that in mind. At that point, rest in shamatha—totally empty and without any thinking whatsoever, letting everything be as it is. Whenever thoughts arise, let them be free, naturally subsiding and dissolving, just as raindrops fall on a lake. Meditate like that for some time. When this leads to empty wakefulness dawning without fixation—free from there being someone observing something—that is the luminous view of Cutting Through, the realization of the Mind Section.

Then emerge as the deity again, vividly present in the form of the Guru, while visualizing OM AH HUNG in your three places and "donning the armor." In daily activities, regard appearances as being forms of deities, sounds heard as being mantras, and thoughts as being enlightened mind.

Think: "May the result of these virtues ripen right now to pacify adversities and gather favorable conditions, so we may be liberated into the space of luminosity through this very practice!" By the lines of auspiciousness of the Three Roots, aspire to accomplishing the benefit of yourself and others.

At the time of receiving the siddhis, set out the *Drangye* torma and skull cup with fine wine and sprinkle them with nectar. At the time of the dawn session, you may either open up the recitation mansion, or visualize the field of accumulation in front of you. In either case, let the rays of light radiating from the deities' three places dissolve into your own three places. You thereby obtain the siddhis of body, speech, and mind. Then, once more, light rays strike the articles, transforming them into nectar. By partaking of them, you obtain the supreme and common siddhis. Finally, let the assembly of deities dissolve into you; thereby generate the pride of being the nondual lord of the mandala. At the end of the verse for invoking the siddhis, which begins with *In the essence mandala, awakened mind,* it is sufficient to just chant the Guru Deva mantra and the verse that begins with *My nadis and* dhatus *are filled with the essence of nectar.* After that, perform the dissolution, emergence, utterance of auspiciousness, and aspirations. Gather the placards from the poles and come unhurriedly out of retreat. Leave all the practice articles in a remote place.

Beyond this, you can see the details of the celestial place and the elaborate teachings on the purification, ripening and perfection of the development stage, and so forth in the manual of Lama Mawey Senge, composed by Karmey Khenpo and written down exactly as I taught. The vital points for *Trinley Nyingpo,* which I have here stated in brief, were written at the request of Nangtsey Lama Rinpoche Kunga Chöwang; Ranyag Gyalsey Palden; the *Bön* lama Trigyalwa Yungdrung; the Geshe of Öndzong; the spiritual teachers of the Sakya and Kagyü monasteries of Nyindzong and Tridu; the more than one hundred *mantrikas* of Drichu Nyinsip, such as Palkhyim; as well as the hundreds of non-sectarian Sakya, Gelug, Kagyü, and *Bön* practitioners who have received the empowerments and reading transmissions of the New Treasures and who have practiced recitation for years in retreat. This was prepared as a celebration in response to the recent insistent requests of lamas, khenpos, and masters of Shendzong by Urgyen Chokgyur Dechen Lingpa during breaks in meditation at Tridu Ewam Chögar, while wandering through remote places in U and Tsang. It was composed on an auspicious day in one single sitting. The scribes were the retreat teacher Chögyal, who has mastered the five sciences, and Tsagang Lotsawa Rinchen Namgyal. May the virtue of composing this create the cause for all who encounter it to attain buddhahood in their very lifetime. Mangalam.

KEY POINTS OF PRACTICE

Tulku Urgyen Rinpoche

Concerning the question of exactly how to practice, when beginning, one cannot perfect the development stage practice without first having recognized awareness, rigpa. The development stage springs out of the samadhi of suchness, which means knowing the natural state as it is. Without this samadhi, the practitioner thinks, "This is emptiness!" and unavoidably fabricates it. It is better to rest in the state the guru has pointed out; that is the genuine suchness, the true and real awareness itself. In this way, one remains in the continuity of the practice. Otherwise, one practices a fake development stage. If we think, "All the sentient beings equal to the end of space are in nature empty and egoless, *mahashunyata*!" we are mentally fabricating emptiness. If we think, "Poor sentient beings who do not realize this emptiness!" we are fabricating compassion. These two thoughts are artificial versions of the samadhi of suchness and the samadhi of illumination, lacking recognition of one's mind essence. This is the development stage that most people practice.

When one recognizes awareness, however, one should rest without thinking it is "empty" or "not empty." That is the recognition of primordially pure, rootless, self-existing wakefulness—genuine suchness. When that happens, one spontaneously thinks, "Ah! Poor ones!" Just as water is wet and fire is hot, the natural expression of awareness is the flame-like heat of compassion. This awareness has unfabricated compassion as its nature; one spontaneously thinks, "Alas! Poor sentient beings, who do not realize the buddha mind as it is!" That is compassion, the samadhi of illumination.

All development stage practice is embraced by emptiness and compassion. In the Sutra teachings, emptiness is *prajna* (knowledge) and compassion is *upaya* (means). In the Mantra teachings, the samadhi of suchness is emptiness and the samadhi of illumination is compassion. Right now, as a beginner, these two appear to be false, but when really resting in awareness, in emptiness, the expression of this awareness spontaneously arises as compassion. These are the first two samadhis.

Within the unity of these two samadhis, emptiness and compassion, one must imagine the seed syllable. The spiritual life force or vital syllable of the deity, a white HRIH in the case of Guru Rinpoche in the *Tukdrub Barchey Künsel* practice, should be visualized like the moon or a star appearing in the expanse of space. This syllable then emanates the letter E for the mandala of space, then YAM, BAM, and so forth for the gradual layers of the elements of earth, water, fire, and wind. Upon these, one visualizes the letter SUM becoming Mount Sumeru on which the letter BHRUM becomes the celestial palace. So, these all appear one after the other.

To reiterate: first of all, from the space of dharmakaya comes sambhogakaya as the expression of compassion, then the nirmanakaya as the seed samadhi. The nirmanakaya is the emanation of emptiness and compassion; the letter is the meaning of nirmanakaya. On this basis, everything arises as development stage, and we visualize the external palace, with the internal inhabitants of deities.

First, the celestial palace arises with the lotus and moon seat inside. When that is complete, the white HRIH syllable descends from the seed samadhi. In some traditions, the syllable first becomes a hand emblem and then a bodily form. The hand emblem is the mental sign; the syllable is the verbal sign. Next, the visualized bodily form appears, with the hand emblem, the mental sign, in its heart center. Around this, the mantra chain, the essence mantra, circles.

Thus, in the *Tukdrub Barchey Künsel* practice, having first visualized the main figure, we then visualize the twelve emanations, which follow like the rays of light from the sun. After this, it is sufficient to remain unmoved from awareness, while practicing the development stage.

If you have grown accustomed to awareness, remain in the continuity of it, allowing the projection and dissolution of thoughts to arise as the development stage, like waves moving on the surface of water.

When the meditation manifests spontaneously within unmoving awareness, the expression of awareness arises as the development stage. In that way, the meditation is first class; then, as a matter of fact, development and completion stages are not separated. Remaining in awareness as the completion stage and letting the awareness-expression arise as the development stage, is the perfection of the development and completion stages as a unity.

If this is not possible, first cultivate emptiness, then compassion, followed by the visualization of the seed-syllable samadhi, wherein emptiness and compassion are united. Then the E YAM RAM BAM, and so forth are the layers of the five elements, upon which is the celestial palace. The seed syllable then descends and becomes the deity, and one visualizes oneself as the deity. Practice like this, one step after the other.

When one has not recognized mind-nature, the completion stage is scattered and the development stage practice resembles the building of a house. Without completion stage, the practitioner is like a man construct-ing a building. Thus, solely pursuing the development stage, if you are visualizing with attachment to substance and solidity, you should in the end methodically dissolve the visualization—the palace dissolves into the deity, the deity dissolves into the seed syllable, and the syllable dissolves into the *nada,* and then into emptiness. Thinking at last, "This is unborn and empty!" one completes the practice with emptiness. In such a case, that process of dissolving the visualization is called the completion stage.

Actually, first cultivate the development stage, then look at who is meditating. The recognition of the nature of the meditator is itself the completion stage. One cannot practice a perfect development stage with-out being introduced to awareness, to rigpa. When one truly recognizes awareness, the development stage practices do not interfere with aware-ness at all. What harm can be done to the state of awareness? All think-ing is empty, empty movement. The emptiness moves. How can there be any harm to the emptiness? It is like a child at play.

Again, it is quite permissible to simply imagine the five layers of ele-ments with the celestial palace, spontaneously manifest. You need not hold onto what you visualize. Just let go of the fixation and resolve your-self in the continuity of completion stage. Here you should resolve, and I mean resolve definitively, in the space of the three kayas.

In the Dzogchen teachings, we speak of differentiating the think-ing mind *(sem)* and awareness *(rigpa)*, resolving one's body, speech, and mind in the space of the three kayas. In short, this means that one's body, speech, and mind are the three vajras; they are resolved to be the essence of the three vajras. When one understands this mandala of the sponta-neously present nature, then all bodily appearances are the mandala of body, all resounding sounds are the mandala of speech, and all thought activity is the mandala of mind. One is not regarding something that is not and imagining it to be something that is. The absence of complexity is body, complete within awareness. The self-utterance of primordially pure emptiness is speech. That is resolving the space of speech. Thought activity as mind is awareness, untainted by defects, empty of both grasping and fixation. Untainted by outer grasping, uncorrupted by inner fixation, it is self-contained. Thus, thought activity is the vajra mind.

To differentiate the thinking mind and awareness, one must arrive solely in awareness. The thinking mind as the expression of awareness should be abandoned. When awareness is recognized, then the thinking mind is self-abandoned. Mind is changing, and awareness is unchanging. In this way, the two are differentiated. Look at the sky, which is unchanging, and the clouds, which are changeable; clouds are like the thinking mind and the space is like rigpa, awareness. The clouds change again and again, but space never changes. Awareness is both unceasing and unchanging.

In this way, the three vajras are complete and are resolved as vajra body, vajra speech, and vajra mind. The vajra body is uncompounded; the awareness is uncompounded. That is the nature of vajra body. It is not a formation or compound. The vajra speech is the unceasing sound. The vajra mind is the unobstructed mental activity, awareness. The obstructed, thinking mind is what ceases. Awareness does not cease. The mind first has one thought; when thinking of the next, the first thought has ceased. Awareness is unceasing and unlimited, beyond the conceptual mind of the three times, unmoving in the three times.

Empty essence, cognizant nature, and unlimited capacity—these three aspects are extremely profound. If the cognizance and the emptiness were limited, the limitation would result in only cognizance or only emptiness. That is not the case; the emptiness is cognizant, and the cognizance is empty. Moreover, neither limits the other, and that unobstructedness is itself the arising of the compassionate capacity.

The empty essence is dharmakaya, which is unconstructed, like space; the cognizant nature is sambhogakaya, which is intrinsic to space, like the sun and the moon. The unlimited capacity is like the image of the moon reflected on water. When the moon is reflected on the surface of the water, its image is not obstructed or limited. It appears naturally, except when there is no water. Likewise, the nirmanakaya works for the benefit of beings in an expansive and unrestricted way.

All three kayas are contained within awareness. When one has recognized that fact, one is said to have resolved it. Really, nothing is impossible once you recognize awareness. However, until recognition occurs, you will always have difficulties, no matter what you do—the perfect will not

DISPELLER OF OBSTACLES

come about, everything will remain imperfect or fake, and the development will also be unnatural. Therefore, one need not hold on to the cultivation of the development stage. To let the awareness-expression arise as development stage and then to remain within awareness is enough. One need not examine the awareness-expression at all.

Our present ordinary cultivation of the Vajrayana path is a short path, a method for purifying evil deeds, as in Mahayoga and Anu Yoga. In Ati Yoga, the development and completion stages are called Trekchö and Tögal, and they do not need to be produced. The development stage of Ati Yoga involves no development. All the deities are complete in the mind mandala of Ati Yoga. One cannot say that deities are nonexistent, because they do appear in the bardo.

Visualization is sufficient once in the beginning of the session. After that, let go and remain free from an object, free from a mental reference point. Visualize the whole thing vividly one time and then rest in the state of objectlessness. Alternating the practice, so one sometimes keeps an objective reference and sometimes not, will not cause any harm, but one doesn't need to alternate. Alternating between visualizing and resting does no harm, because thought occurrence is itself the expression of rigpa; when it arises as the visualization, this is fine.

Thoughts and visualization arise as the expression of rigpa, when one has attained some stability. Lacking stability, the expression becomes too forceful and the essence seems to get lost in that state. When the essence is "out of sight," not recognized, it is a defect that causes the development stage to increase discursive thoughts. On the other hand, when recognition of the essence is stabilized, the expression of rigpa within the state of the essence will appear vividly as the visualization of the development stage. Thus, the unobstructed expression of your awareness arises as the development state out of the primordially pure essence, the self-existing awareness, without moving away from this state for even an instant. *(Laughs)*

In our Guru Rinpoche practice, *Trinley Nyingpo*, after visualizing the deity, you proceed with the recitation of the various mantras. When reciting, you should try to recognize the essence of all thoughts as dharmakaya and be free from distraction.

This Guru Rinpoche practice first includes a recitation for Amitayus as the approach, then for Avalokiteshvara as the full approach, then for

Guru Rinpoche as the accomplishment, then for Tötreng Tsal as the intent of the great accomplishment. It ends with the Harinisa mantra, which fulfills the activities and is the application of the activities.

In another way, all aspects of approach and accomplishment can be completed within the recitation of a single mantra. The first of the four is the "moon with a garland of stars," where a garland of stars surrounds the syllable HRIH in Guru Rinpoche's heart center. Then, as the mantra starts to revolve, there is the second intent or visualization, which is called the "firebrand." These refer to approach and full approach, which are completed together in this practice. The "moon with the garland of stars" is generally considered the intent of the approach, and the "firebrand" is the intent of the full approach. These represent the first two of the four types of recitation intents, approach and full approach, which are here contained simply as approach.

The third, "the messenger of the king," begins with the emanation of light rays. Upwardly, one makes offerings to the mandala of the victorious ones; downwardly, the rays of light are the generosity, which purifies all the obscurations and negative karmas of sentient beings. This radiating upward and downward, while making offerings and purifying sentient beings, is called the intent of "the king's messenger," and it belongs to the third aspect of recitation, the accomplishment.

The fourth, the great accomplishment, includes all four of approach, full approach, accomplishment, and great accomplishment. At the time of pursuing the great accomplishment, there should be an individual for each of the deities in the practice. For example, for convocation of the peaceful and wrathful deities, one needs a hundred people for the hundred deities. Then such a practice can truly be called "great accomplishment."

In the practice of *Barchey Künsel,* the recitation of the Harinisa mantra fulfills the pacifying, enriching, magnetizing, and subjugating activities embodied by the four gate keepers. Each of the four types of activities has its own particular mantra for whatever action one has to complete. If one needs to magnetize, there is a magnetizing mantra; if one needs to subjugate, there is a subjugating mantra. Through the supreme mantra, which is the spontaneously accomplished activity, one can accomplish the supreme action. In this case, then, there are five activities: pacifying, enriching, magnetizing, subjugating, and the supreme activity, which is the spontaneously accomplished activity, the samadhi action of self-existing wakefulness.

In the *Barchey Künsel* sadhana, when practicing mantra recitation, one first visualizes the Buddha mandala of one's body, then practices the approach, accomplishment, and application of the activities simultaneously, like "bees swarming from the hive." One's body is visualized as the nature of deity, the deity's body; all sounds are of the nature of the deity's speech; all thoughts are of the nature of the deity's mind.

According to the Secret Mantra tradition of the Nyingmapa, sights have the nature of body, sounds have the nature of speech, and thoughts have the nature of mind. This is called the "triple application of sights, sounds, and awareness."

Yeshe Tsogyal

TEACHINGS ON TRINLEY NYINGPO

Orgyen Topgyal Rinpoche

INTRODUCTION

When listening to teachings, studying, and practicing, even if you are a seasoned practitioner, you should do so in order to bring all sentient beings to the state of true and complete enlightenment. Please keep that resolve in your mind as you read this.

Moreover, if you are studying Vajrayana, then you should not look at things in an ordinary way. Instead, you should see everything that appears and exists as all-encompassing purity. In other words, do not see the teacher as an ordinary human being, but as the dharmakaya Buddha, Vajradhara, Guru Rinpoche, or any other Buddha. Likewise, you, the student, should not think of yourself as merely being comprised of the five aggregates, the five elements, sense organs, and so on, but rather as having the divine nature of deities.

That's the traditional opening remark that a lama is supposed to make at the start of a sadhana teaching. At the beginning of *The Way of the Bodhisattva,* Shantideva states that he doesn't have any special virtues and is not very eloquent or poetic, so he has written in a frank, straightforward way. Here I will try to emulate his model. I have no pretense of composing great poetry or astounding you with my eloquence, but I will try to explain what I know. Don't expect to be shocked or overwhelmed either. Also, some masters may be able to liberate the students' mindstreams merely with the sound of their voices and the profundity of their instructions on development and completion stages. I doubt there is anyone like this alive anymore.

I came here for the purpose of teaching, but if the teaching is just like a lecture and there is no follow up with practice afterward, then, while you cannot say it's completely pointless, it's like going to the movies. You drive over there, pay for a ticket, watch the movie for a couple of hours, and then you go home. It was fun. Also, a lot of people these days go for the show of it, to see what the lama's going to talk about, what he or she is like. Then they drive home, and that was it. It is like going to last weekend's Reggae festival close by, where about 12,000 people got together to be entertained. Now I am going to try and make sure there's something valuable coming out of this. So when we listen, and also when it gets recorded and written down and somebody else sees it, there should be some benefit coming out of that.

I have been asked to begin with development and completion stages. It is pretty easy to explain, but the main point is to become practiced, to grow used to the meaning. It is best if one can combine development and completion stages together in one sadhana. All the tantras and scriptures, headed by the *Guhyagarbha Tantra,* explain Vajrayana in terms of development and completion stages.

In our tradition, the scripture, *Light of Wisdom*[1] *(Lamrim Yeshe Nyingpo),* explains the development stage in great detail. Also Jigmey Lingpa's *Staircase to Akanishtha Buddhafield* and a text by Paltrül Rinpoche are both exquisite. We have many teachings on the development stage, but unless you connect the teachings with a sadhana, they become disconnected from your practice; it seems like practice is one thing and the teachings are totally different. Therefore, you need to connect the teachings with the sadhana practice. Once you understand how to combine all the vital aspects of the sadhana into a very simple form, you can apply the same model to any sadhana you might practice. Here I will connect the instructions with the sadhana of Padmasambhava known as *Tukdrub Trinley Nyingpo.*

According to the terma tradition of Chokgyur Lingpa and Jamyang Khyentse, there are four levels of heart-practice or guru sadhanas: the outer is *Barchey Künsel*, the inner is *Sampa Lhündrub*, the secret is *Tsokye Nyingtig,* and the innermost secret is *Dorje Draktsal*. According to Chokgyur Lingpa's personal tradition, the primary or root practice is the *Gongpa Kündü*, *Embodiment of All Realization*; while the two subsidiary practices are *Barchey Künsel* and *Sampa Lhündrub.*

The *Trinley Nyingpo* belongs to *Barchey Künsel.* The root text of the *Barchey Künsel* is a scripture called *Sheldam Nyingjang, The Essence Manual of all Oral Instructions.* The *Barchey Künsel* cycle's structure is like the analogy of a precious vase.

Most termas explain that the qualities, virtues, and effects of their practice are great, but as explained in this terma, the benefits of practicing the *Barchey Künsel* are incredible. In the terma text, Padmasambhava states that anyone who hears or practices the teachings of *Tukdrub Barchey Künsel* will immediately be free of any misfortune and will avoid rebirth in the lower realms. "Wherever the *Barchey Künsel* is kept will be indivisible from the highest buddha realm known as Vajra Akanishtha, and the dakas and dakinis will swarm about, like gathering cloud banks. If that is not true, then I, Padmasambhava, will have lied to future generations," he says at the end of the terma text.

After Chokgyur Lingpa revealed the *Barchey Künsel* terma, he practiced it in secret for eight years, as I mentioned earlier. During this period, he wrote part of it down but did not pass it on to anyone, including the main holders of this terma lineage. After having realized the teaching, he first offered it to Jamyang Khyentse Wangpo, who was the destined holder of this lineage. A prediction about decoding the dakini script said the mother and child would meet together and establish the teachings. Only Jamyang Khyentse Wangpo was able to see all the writing that manifested from the yellow parchment. The "mother" refers to the yellow parchment script, and the "child" refers to what Chokgyur Lingpa had written down. So only Jamyang Khyentse Wangpo saw both the mother and child script. What they decoded is the "grandchild." It was said that the mother and child should then be allowed to disappear; therefore, they were eliminated.

Jamgön Kongtrül was then given the teachings. Due to these three practicing and propogating the *Barchey Künsel,* it became so widely spread that almost all masters had received the empowerments and practiced it.

From the original parchment, various root texts would appear, including the *Nyingjang, Yangjang, Yujang,* and *Güjang.* The *Yangjang* describes what and how the tertön himself should practice. The *Nyingjang* is the *Sheldam Nyingjang,* the large volume we have today. Apparently, there was also a *Yujang,* which means a turquoise manual, and a *Güjang,* a manual of necessities, but they seem to have been lost.

Today, we have the short instruction written down by Chokgyur Lingpa. As the years pass, personal instructions evaporate; they disappear. Chokgyur Lingpa's son, Wangchok Dorje, also received some personal instructions, but he died young and took those teachings with him. Nonetheless, though Chokgyur Lingpa was quite young when he revealed the *Barchey Künsel,* he did succeed in making it extremely complete. Many important points, subsidiary aspects, and so forth were written down, and the stream of its practice is still vibrant.

Fortunately, the lineage for *Tukdrub Barchey Künsel* is still alive and active; we should not let it die, but keep it vibrant through practice. Just having texts lying around is not that useful; they need to be put into practice. This particular text is being practiced here in western countries, as compared to other places. My commentary is backed up in writing by the extensive version of the sadhana, by the commentaries of Chokgyur Lingpa, Jamyang Khyentse, Kongtrül, and so forth. It brings all of that together, although I still haven't seen one commentary that puts it all together into one.

Misinterpretations can lead to doubts, so it is important to clarify the correct visualization for the development stage and make this available, not only for the present but also for the future. In this way, a lot of questions come up, and if correct teachings are given, recorded, and written down, then there is something for the future; otherwise, it just vanishes. Once the master dies, the knowledge is gone, like that. It is the same with a lot of other teachings. Unless the teachings are kept, they vanish with the master. These days, we only have the essence manual; we don't have the quintessence manual. It and another important manual both disappeared.

For development stage, the visualization of the deity is one of the more important points. When I explain, I will start with *the dharmakaya's basic space of suchness,* which is the samadhi of suchness, and the other samadhis. Therefore, this commentary is based on what can be definitively known from the extensive version of the sadhana, known as *Trinley Gyepa*, and from the commentaries by Chokgyur Lingpa, Jamyang Khyentse, and Jamgön Kongtrül. What we know today is about this much. And even if we were to run around and try to dig up things, we wouldn't find any more than what exists today. If you want to make up lies, you could, but what is straightforward and truthful is about this much. I will not make anything up and have only included what can be authenticated in the existing sources.

TITLE

Trinley Nyingpo, The Yoga of Essential Activity, from *Lamey Tukdrub Barchey Künsel, The Guru's Heart Practice, Dispeller of All Obstacles*

The sadhana of Guru Rinpoche from *Tukdrub Barchey Künsel* exists in four versions of varying length—the very extensive; the medium length; the essential, which is *Trinley Nyingpo*; and the concise version for daily practice, the *Gyüngyi Köljang. Trinley Nyingpo* means *Essence of Activity.* Just as the essential part of milk is contained in butter, the essential blessing of the elaborate, extensive form of the sadhana, the *Trinley Gyepa,* is condensed in the *Trinley Nyinpo.*

It is called "essence" (*nyingpo*) because people nowadays are often so busy they do not have time to do authentic practice. Therefore, Guru Rinpoche was asked to provide something concise yet complete, which would be easy to do and convenient to apply. So he condensed the teaching in this practice, and that's really appropriate. When I need to perform the feast offering with my monks on the tenth or twenty-fifth day of the month, we just wouldn't have time if we didn't have the "essential" size. Nevertheless, you shouldn't think that *Trinley Nyingpo* is lower quality just because it is short and condensed. On the contrary, the extensive version may go into more detail, but nothing is left out here. It is also more suitable as a daily practice, especially for westerners. This essence practice is therefore very important.

There's a famous saying: "In harmony with everyone, yet superior to them all." If one is not in tune with how everyone perceives and understands, then one doesn't really connect. But regardless of being in harmony with everyone, if there is nothing special at the same time, then what's the point? Then there's nothing interesting there. The *Trinley Nyingpo* is in harmony with all other teachings; yet at the same time, there's something extraordinary there. Also, you can combine the sadhana's instructions with some personal advice on how to go about it.

In addition, this practice includes Padmasambhava's personal advice on how to perform all the aspects of a Vajrayana ritual—when and how to use the drum, *damaru,* and bell; how to create the torma; and how to mingle development and completion stages. That, in itself, is something extraordinary.

At the beginning of the *Trinley Nyingpo*, there is a special seal to authenticate it as a terma by Padmasambhava. As you know, countries have a government seal for their important papers. In the same way, the seal here signifies the terma of Padmasambhava. *Trinley Nyingpo* is an earth treasure (*sa-ter*). There are seven major types of transmission, including earth treasure (*sa-ter*), mind treasure (*gong-ter*), and pure vision. Chokgyur Lingpa had all seven lines of transmission. He was destined to reveal one hundred different termas, but he only succeeded in revealing thirty-seven of them, of which the earth treasures, like the *Tukdrub Barchey Künsel,* were the more important ones. There is some debate among tertöns as to which is the most precious, the most profound. Jigmey Lingpa, for instance, felt that the mind treasure is the most special, and he was not too impressed by something that had been dug up from the ground. In the context of the *Nyingtik* lineage, he said that mind treasure—mind (*gong*) being the state of realization—means that the tertön's realization was indivisible from Padmasambhava's. This enables the tertön to decode or manifest the treasure; therefore, mind treasure is superior. On the other hand, the Fifth Dalai Lama's termas were in the form of revelations. He claimed that because the tertön receives the terma in person in a pure vision, it is superior. Others claim that receiving it from Padmasambhava's own mouth into their own ears is superior, making the hearing lineage the best. But Chokgyur Lingpa felt that the earth treasure was the best, because it could be authenticated. The yellow scrolls with the secret writing of the dakinis still exist as tangible proof; whereas, anybody can have a vision or inspiration.

The word *lamey* is an abbreviation of *lana mepa,* which literally means "highest" or "unsurpassed" and indicates that this scripture is very special.

Moreover, since the karmically destined yidam of Tibet is Avalokiteshvara and the karmically destined guru is Padmasambhava, the word *lama* or *guru* here refers to Guru Rinpoche, which is another name for Padmasambhava. When Padmasambhava came to Tibet, his main disciples were King Trisong Deütsen, the dakini Yeshe Tsogyal, and the great translator Vairotsana.

Among his other disciples were the twenty-five disciples, the nine heart sons, and so forth. To this very day, most of the great masters have been either direct emanations of Guru Rinpoche's mind or incarnations blessed through his influence. Padmasambhava himself said, "If you behold me, it is the same as beholding all buddhas. If you realize me, it is the same as realizing all buddhas."

In the Nyingma tradition, there are two main streams of transmission, the oral lineage and the treasure lineage, known respectively as Kama and Terma. The Three Roots are the guru, who is the root of blessings; the yidam, who is the root of accomplishments; and the dakini, who is the root of activities. Each of these then has a related sadhana, but the guru sadhana includes them all.

Guru sadhana here means that you should regard your own root guru to be indivisible from the mind of Padmasambhava. One's guru is seen as the blessings of Guru Rinpoche, and this is the real sense of the word *guru* here. That is the meaning of *heart practice,* through which we come to realize the mind of the guru.

The title also refers to *all obstacles.* Padmasambhava's close disciples asked if there were obstacles on the path to enlightenment. He replied, "Yes there are outer, inner, and innermost obstacles. There are countless obstacles and hindrances, and the one unexcelled way to remove them all is by supplicating your guru." As a matter of fact, when practicing the Dharma, any difficult or adverse circumstance is called an obstacle. The moment you overcome an obstacle is, in itself, an accomplishment. You can also understand it this way: Our basic nature, the buddha nature, or sugata-essence, is covered by temporary obscurations. When we remove or dispel these, the qualities intrinsic to the buddha nature become evident. That is called accomplishment, or *siddhi.* As supplicating one's guru is the best way to overcome these obstacles, the guru sadhana is an ideal way to attain accomplishment.

PREPARATION

Homage to the Guru, Trikaya Deity.
For the essence of accomplishing the Trikaya Guru,
Sit on a comfortable seat in a secluded place
And practice by means of preparation, main part, and conclusion.
Samaya.

The tertön wrote the first sentence, *Homage to the Guru, Trikaya Deity.* It means that all the deities of the three kayas are included in the sadhana as manifestations of Padmasambhava's mind. Therefore, by paying homage to the single form of Padmasambhava, one is paying homage to all of them. The word *deity* refers to the principal figure in the center, the twelve surrounding manifestations, and all the deities of the three kayas. The specific details on how to practice each of these deities is explained in the longer versions.

So to practice, one should *Sit on a comfortable seat in a secluded place.* This means a quiet, remote spot free of daily human activities, where ghosts do not roam at night; where there is no danger, such as from thieves, bandits, or wild animals; and where the masters of the past have practiced. Ideally, one's retreat should be blessed and pleasant.

A comfortable seat actually means a thick, wide cushion with a swastika design, either in chalk or *kusha* grass, underneath it. There are quite a few instructions about how to properly prepare a seat, but the most important point is that you should sit however you're most comfortable. If you need to sit for a long time, and you are uncomfortable, you will not be able to remain still. It does not say to sit on the bare ground, a high throne, chair, or anything else. It just says *sit on a comfortable seat,* whatever is comfortable for you personally. Most texts say you should sit facing west. Since Guru Rinpoche's pure land is to the west, then your seat should face in that direction.

One's practice, then, consists of preparation, main part, and conclusion. These three include all the important aspects of a sadhana. The preparation involves arranging the site, shrine, and so forth as well as reciting the verses for refuge, bodhichitta, protection circle, and so forth in the sadhana itself. The main part refers to the actual visualization of the development stage, and the conclusion includes the feast offering, dedication of merit, and so forth. The *Trinley Gyepa* has seven aspects for each of these three sections. The specific details for arranging a shrine are quite elaborate and should be learned from someone who knows how to do it properly. However, one important point is to have an image of Padmasambhava, which can be either a sculpture or painting. In front of that, you place the three main ingredients of amrita, rakta, and torma; the outer and inner offerings; and the feast articles. If you are practicing in a group, you should have various musical instruments; but if you are alone, then only a damaru (hand drum) and bell are required. You will also need a rosary.

Samaya means that this practice is not meant for people who are unsuitable.

Having prepared one's space and arranged the shrine, one sits down. After chanting suitable lineage prayers, one begins the sadhana itself, starting with refuge and bodhichitta:

REFUGE AND BODHICHITTA

NAMO:
I and all beings, equaling the sky in number,:
Take refuge in those who are the supreme refuge.:
Developing the bodhichitta of aspiration and application,:
I will accomplish the level of the Trikaya Guru.:

This verse is chanted three times. *Namo* means "homage." The first two lines of refuge are quite straightforward. At the beginning of refuge, imagine that rays of light emitting from your heart center call upon Guru Rinpoche, as the primary figure, and connect to the other objects of refuge, such as buddhas, bodhisattvas, masters of the lineage, and so forth, who are gathered like cloud banks around Guru Rinpoche. It is also perfectly fine to imagine the "single embodying jewel," meaning the chief figure, while keeping an awareness of all the other objects of refuge gathered, like cloud banks, around him. Then we chant the meaning for that. The visualization for taking refuge is explained in the *ngöndro* teachings, but, in brief, imagine that all sentient beings take refuge together with you at their head.

All beings means all sentient beings without exception, even the likes of Osama Bin Laden. We all take refuge in the Three Jewels on the outer level; in the Three Roots on the inner level; in the channels, essences, and energies on the secret level; and in the empty essence, the cognizant nature, and the unconfined capacity that manifests in the forms of the deities, according to the Dzogchen teachings.

To *take refuge* implies that from this moment until we attain complete buddhahood, these are the objects of refuge for us and all sentient beings.

In Vajrayana, it is important you understand the meaning of what you are chanting. Having witnessed our refuge vow, the objects of refuge emit rays of light in all directions. This light touches all sentient beings, removing their obscurations and negativities.

The next two lines encompass the bodhichitta of aspiration and application. The aspiration is simply the wish that we may resolve to attain enlightenment for the benefit of all sentient beings, as the buddhas and bodhisattvas have done. *Application* means that we will also actually apply ourselves to doing whatever is necessary to attain complete enlightenment. *Trikaya Guru* refers to the gurus of the three kayas. The dharmakaya guru is Amitayus, the sambhogakaya guru is Avalokiteshvara, and the nirmanakaya guru is Padmasambhava.

The *Trinley Gyepa* includes several extra lines for the bodhichitta of aspiration and application:

> Hoh꞉
> As all the victorious ones and their sons of the past
> Aroused their minds towards the unexcelled supreme
>   enlightenment,
> I too will accomplish buddhahood
> In order to benefit my mothers, all beings as numerous as space is
>   vast.

At the end of this, it is good to combine your breathing with the bodhichitta attitude. As you inhale, imagine you are inhaling all the disease and suffering of others, and then exhale rainbow light that purifies them of any obscurations and bathes them in happiness and joy.

The *Trinley Gyepa* also includes verses for the Seven Branches and four immeasurables. Though they are not explicitly mentioned here, the meaning of the Seven Branches is included later in the sadhana. We should, however, pause to contemplate the four immeasurables.

> By this merit, may all beings possess happiness.
> Freed from their suffering, may it ripen upon me instead.
> May they never part from the happiness devoid of misery,
> And may they abide in impartiality, the equal nature of all things.

DISPELLER OF OBSTACLES

GEKTOR — THE TORMA FOR THE OBSTRUCTORS

Then, all the objects of refuge, *the field of accumulation,* dissolve into you, after which you transform into the action deity, who in this case is the King of the Wrathful Ones, Hayagriva. He has one face and two arms, and on the top his head is a horse head. He has a club in one hand and a noose in the other. If you have a torma for the obstructors (*gektor*), then you should consecrate it with RAM YAM KHAM. From your heart center, countless small wrathful deities emanate, carrying hooks, nooses, lassos, bells, chains, and so forth. They capture any beings that seek to create obstacles for practitioners. As these obstructors are arrested and brought before you, you offer them the torma together with the mantra. And then you say, "From now on until all beings attain enlightenment, leave practitioners alone; go away, go home." Then say:

> HUNG HRIH!
> All demons, obstructors, and evil spritis of deluded duality
> Enjoy this torma and disperse to your own places.

Those who refuse are expelled with special wrathful means, such as commanding them with mantras, gestures, and mudras or piercing them with samadhi. This is called "giving the command."

The existence of *demons, obstructors and evils spirits* is dependent upon *deluded duality,* or the mistaken way of perceiving. As we maintain our ideas, which are dualistic in so many ways, then, according to our dualistic perception, *evil forces* do appear, and they can appear in an infinite variety of ways. Regardless, we say, "Take this torma with exquisite shape, smell, taste, texture, potency, and so forth. May it appear to you in whichever way you prefer. Take it and get out of here and don't make more interruptions for enlightenment." That's called the gektor, the obstructor's torma. If you don't have an obstructor's torma, you just say, "Do not remain here. Go to your own places."

The words and phrasing used in the *Trinley Gyepa* are just amazing:

> HUNG HRIH!
> Within the primordially pure mandala of all that appears and
> exists,

There are no names, such as dualistic fixation, obstructor, or
  deceiver.⁝
Yet, not realizing this, due to the dependency of momentary
  confusion,⁝
All you demons who prevent us from attaining enlightenment,⁝
Take this torma as payment for our debts⁝
And disperse leisurely to your respective dwellings.⁝

For me to realize the yoga of the wisdom form,⁝
In order to benefit all beings filling space,⁝
Including you, who is not beyond this space,⁝
Although distance does not exist for an altruistic mind,⁝
Due to the power of negative karma, you have no fortune⁝
To perceive this mandala; therefore, go elsewhere for a while.⁝

If you do not leave, the rain of vajra weapons⁝
Will completely reduce your body, speech, and mind to dust,⁝
All the way down to your seventh generation.⁝
Therefore, be gone right now.⁝

By my command, that of the great and mighty Sporting Steed,⁝
By the blessings of the precious Three Jewels,⁝
By the samadhis of the yidams of the Three Roots,⁝
By the perfect truth of dharmata,⁝
And by the unfailing coincidence of cause and effect,⁝
May the hordes of demons who disobey this command⁝
Be destroyed by the ferocious vajra display!⁝

You can actually attain complete enlightenment by just training in gektor. In short, whoever receives this torma is dispelled far into the distance. It includes the visualization of the vivid presence of the wrathful deity and emanations of deities in all directions to arrest the evil forces. Then they are being commanded with the use of the dance movements, vajras, mantras, magic substances, burning incense, and the state of samadhi. All that is included within gektor. As all of these aspects are combined in what is called the "auspicious coincidence," every one of them is significant.

The important thing to understand here is that the obstructor (*gek*) is your own thoughts, your own projections; therefore, the moment you simply let be in the composure of samadhi, every single type of obstructor immediately dissolves—they all simply vanish.

Once you have chased a thief out of your house, you then lock the door; similarly, the next two lines describe the protection circle followed by a mantra:

> In the nondual wisdom state of deity, mantra, and dharmakaya,§
> The boundary mandala is naturally self-perfected.§
> Hung hung hung vajra raksha raksha brhrum§

The protection circle is comprised of a vajra scepter in the center, surrounded by a dome built of vajra crosses; the floor also has a huge vajra cross. Any spaces in between are filled with ever-smaller vajras, until the dome and floor become completely impenetrable. The dome is surrounded by flames, water, a roaring wind, lightning, and thunder—in other words, the five elements. In addition, there are male and female wrathful deities. One faces outward and the other one faces inward, as explained in the general method of the development stage. The deities facing inward and outward prevent external obstacles from interfering in the practice and blessings and accomplishments from slipping away. So everything has its purpose.

Karmey Khenpo had a skillful hand and was a very good artist. When he received the empowerment for Mawey Senge, the Lion of Speech, from Chokgyur Lingpa, he took an oath to compose or draw something with divine quality every day. Thereafter, no matter where he went, he always had paper and pen. He lived to an advanced age and made many drawings, designs, and paintings. Over the years, he made drawings and sketches of almost all the mandalas, and so forth, in the *Chokling Tersar*. Karma Khenpo's drawing of a protection circle shows what it should look like. I have managed to secure some of these drawings, but not that many. Apparently, there is a monk at a monastery in Eastern Tibet who has many more. However, I do have a drawing of the protection circle he made.

THE DOWNPOUR OF BLESSINGS AND CONSECRATION OF OFFERINGS

OM AH HUNG

Hosts of Trikaya Guru Deities, manifest from dharmadhatu!

Let resplendence descend on this place and bestow empowerments
and siddhis!

Please bless this great offering mudra of appearance and existence
as manifest ground

To be an ocean-like display of Samantabhadra!

Om ah hung vajra guru dheva dakini gyana abeshaya a ah

Hung hung hung om sarva puja megha ah hung

Samaya.

The first two lines comprise the downpour of blessings. For this, you visu-alize that light rays stream out from your heart center in all directions, espe-cially to the buddhafields, where the chief figure of the mandala resides. In this case, it would be the pure land of Padmasambhava, the Glorious Cop-per-Colored Mountain, where he is seated in the three-kaya palace. Then, from Padmasambhava and his retinue, a shower of blessings descends onto you, your surroundings, the shrine implements, offerings, and so forth. Just like water drops falling on a huge lake, these blessings dissolve into you and become indivisible from you. But the real meaning is that our incor-rect, impure way of seeing things subsides, both externally and internally, so we see purely and correctly. Even though we do not perceive things as being totally pure, they actually are already pure. In the *Trinley Gyepa,* there are some very special lines for invocation, where the wisdom beings, who remain in the basic space of dharmadhatu, are invoked to arise and become indivisible from us, the samaya beings.

Hung Hrih!

From the land called the northwestern Chamara Continent,

The spontaneously present place of wondrous great splendor,

From the celestial palace of lotus light, the Glorious Mountain,

Orgyen Tötreng Tsal, embodiment of all the Three Roots,

Together with all the sugatas and victorious ones throughout the
directions and times,

And your retinues of vidyadharas, dakas, and dakinis,ᵍ
Do not neglect the samaya of your former promise.ᵍ
When I invoke your mindstream with the overwhelming, intense
    power of yearning,ᵍ

With your beautiful forms in free-flowing dance movements,ᵍ
With the tones of your voices roaring as sounds of vajra mantras,ᵍ
And with your compassion as the luminous state of self-existing
    wakefulness,ᵍ
Please come here from the unmanifest dharmadhatu!ᵍ

Shower the great vajra resplendence of body, speech, and mindᵍ
Onto the outer, inner, and innermost mandala and samaya articles.ᵍ
Quickly display wondrous signs and indications!ᵍ
Bestow empowerment and blessings upon all the practitioners of
    this supreme sadhana!ᵍ

So even though there are just two sentences here, you still imagine
that the sky totally fills up with deities, who then dissolve into you, the
shrine offerings, and so forth. In this way, you, your surroundings, and so
forth are all blessed.

In order to awaken to enlightenment, we need to perfect the accumulations and remove any obscurations. To perfect the accumulations,
we make offerings, but offerings need to be sanctified first, so the next
two lines are for the consecration of offerings. *Appearance and existence
as manifest ground* refers to the Dzogchen view. From the very beginning, all that appears and exists, the world and beings, are in fact forms
of the original ground, the primordial state. That is the true form of the
deity indivisible from the primordial nature. To put it simply, whatever
you perceive is an expression of Padmasambhava's mind. Even more
simply, whatever you perceive is a projection of your own mind. Whatever you perceive, all that you experience, is in itself devoid of any solid
existence, apart from your projecting ideas, as if they existed in themselves. But, when you face this reality, then, through the practice, you
will realize that nothing is apart from the state of primordial purity.
As everything is a state of emptiness to begin with, there is great flexi-
bility. If emptiness were not the basic state, then everything, including
ourselves, would be frozen in one state from the beginning. But, in this
state of emptiness, you are free to imagine an infinite number of offer-

ings. There would be no space for you to imagine anything if it weren't empty to begin with.

Here *Samantabhadra* means "immeasurable display." As explained in the commentaries on *The Way of the Bodhisattva*, each pore of Bodhisattva Samantabhadra's body emanates a cloud bank of offerings that fills the sky with exquisite sense pleasures. Each of these emits rays of light, from which another bodhisattva appears. Again, from each pore of this bodhisattva's body, offering clouds fill the universe, and so on, to infinity.

Tulku Urgyen Rinpoche pointed out mind-essence with a simple gesture of his hand. If one recognized it and remained for even a few instants in the state of rigpa, many eons of negative karma would be purified instantly. In the same way, the ocean-like display of Samantabhadra is also an extremely effective purification. If you cannot imagine an infinite display, try to imagine a large one. Even without all the details, it is still very beneficial. Until we attain the state where everything naturally manifests out of emptiness, we need to use our imagination, though we should still make the offering in a state of complete equality. Though development stage, in this case, is the process of mental visualization, according to the ultimate meaning, whatever appears and exists is actually the manifestation of the ground itself.

OM AH HUNG VAJRA GURU DHEVA DAKINI GYANA ABESHAYA A AH is the mantra for the downpour of blessings, and HUNG HUNG HUNG OM SARVA PUJA MEGHA AH HUNG is the one for the consecration of offerings.

In the elaborate sadhana, one separately consecrates each of the outer, inner, innermost, and secret offerings. Outer offerings include the rinsing and drinking water, perfume, lamp, food, music, and so forth. The inner offerings are for the wrathful deities; they include blood, fat, the five sense organs arranged as a flower, and so forth. The secret offerings are the amrita, rakta, and torma. But here, all you do is chant OM SARVA PUJA MEGHA AH HUNG, which actually includes all outer, inner, and innermost offerings, because *sarva* means "all" and *puja* means "offerings." Imagine that everything is included in one consecration. At this point, imagine all seven general offerings—drinking water, rinsing water, food, lamp, perfume, musical instruments being played, and flowers—as well as the inner offerings. However, for wrathful deities, they are human fat, which is used as a lamp, the flesh as fruit, perfume, and music created with thigh bone trumpets, drums made from skulls, and so forth. On the innermost level, amrita is made out of the one-thousand ingredients, of which there are eight primary ones; rakta is comprised of a substance that brings an end to all of samsaric existence; and the torma emanates a cloud bank of desirable objects. Even though you can imagine each of these in great detail, here you should at least bring them to mind to a certain degree. The seven general offering bowls as well as the amrita, rakta, and torma on the shrine are the supports for visualization. Though you should have these supports, you should also do the visualization.

When we make the actual offerings later in the sadhana, we add the ultimate offerings of the union of liberation and the offering of thatness, emptiness, and so forth. However, we do not need to consecrate them at this point.

In these offerings, we are not holding onto concepts of self and other, because we have already exorcised the demons of dualistic concepts during the gektor. In the *Trinley Gyepa,* we say:

> Within the primordially pure mandala of all that appears and
>   exists,
> There are no names, such as dualistic fixation, obstructor, or
>   deceiver.
> Yet, not realizing this, due to the dependency of momentary
>   confusion,
> All you demons who prevent us from attaining enlightenment,
> Take this torma as payment for our debts
> And disperse leisurely to your respective dwellings.

We offer the peaceful deities pure water to drink, which is in complete harmony with normal concepts. The blood we offer the wrathful deities to drink is vaster than the ocean. Even if you killed everyone in the world, their blood would not fill the ocean. The flesh, organs, and so forth, all develop from blood; therefore, when somebody gets a cut, we respond very differently than if someone is spilling water on the ground. People get very upset at the sight of blood, and they usually do not drink it. Therefore, the purpose of making an offering of blood in our visualization has nothing to do with killing people and offering their blood, but rather with dissolving our fixated notions. As for wrathful deities, we turn it completely around. As we must offer them something humans don't drink, we use blood. Also, when hearing that blood is offered as a drink, one thinks, "Is it my blood or someone else's blood? If it is someone else's blood, wouldn't it be sad for them? So, I would rather offer my own." This reflects a perceived duality of self and other, and until you transcend that duality, you should definitely continue to offer blood in your visualization.

It is similar when offering rinsing water. For the peaceful deities, of course, you offer clean water to rinse their feet; but for a wrathful deity, it has to be the opposite of pure, clean water. That is why we offer poison as rinsing water for the wrathful deities' feet. One may then develop dualistic concerns, "Won't it hurt their feet? If you offer poison to the deity, won't their skin fall off, the whole thing going to pieces?" When you hear the word *poison*, you immediately form a strong mental notion, thinking, "It's bad, it's horrible, it's deadly." However, you must overcome value judgements such as these, using the many subtle techniques Vajrayana employs to this end. That is why people who do not know the true meaning and purpose of the symbolism often get a completely wrong impression of Vajrayana.

Finally, the word *samaya* means all seven aspects of preparation are now complete.

The Main Part

The Three Samadhis

Training in the development stage of the main part involves the extraordinary method of visualizing the deity. Beings are born in one of four ways—by egg, womb, heat, or moisture, or instantaneous appearance (a type of ethereal rebirth). These four correspond to each individual's habitual tendencies. The particular methods of visualization found in the development stage purify the tendencies related to the four modes of birth as well as the habitual tendencies related to passing away. Many of the details for visualizing can be found in *Light of Wisdom, Volume II* (*Lamrim Yeshe Nyingpo*), which states:

The *Lamrim Yeshe Nyingpo* root text says:

Manifesting as the resultant from the causal purifies egg birth.[8]
The wisdoms of the fivefold true perfection purify womb birth.[8]

Being instantly present from a mantra purifies birth through
warmth.[¹⁰]

The deity in completeness by mere recollection purifies miraculous
birth.[¹²]

These four types of rebirth have four points: the very extensive development stage, corresponding to egg birth, for the complex beginners with
dull faculties; the development ritual of *true perfection,* corresponding
to womb birth, for the slightly complex people with medium faculties;
development through just a mantra, corresponding to warmth and moisture birth, for noncomplex people of sharp faculties; and development
as instantaneous perfection, corresponding to miraculous birth, for the
extremely noncomplex people of the highest faculties. Thus, there are
four types of rituals for development of the deity.[3]

One can also begin the visualization according to one of the many
styles of Mahayana, Anu Yoga, or Ati Yoga. My explanation is based on
the *Tukdrub* itself and seems to correspond to the visualization for purifying the concept of womb birth. The aspect of knowledge (*prajna*) is of
primordial purity and the aspect of means (*upaya*) is of spontaneous presence. Their indivisible unity manifests in the form of the seed syllable,
out of which everything appears. At the same time, you can also say that
out of dharmakaya the sambhogakaya appears, out of sambhogakaya the
nirmanakaya appears, and so forth.

The words we have here are: *Dharmakaya's basic space of suchness is
the realm of luminous wakefulness. Sambhogakaya's unceasing illumination
is compassionate expression.* Then this emptiness and compassion combine
into *Nirmanakaya's seed samadhi, the white HRIH.* The method of purifying
is called the "three samadhis," (the samadhi of suchness, the samadhi of
the illumination, and the samadhi of the seed syllable). This process purifies conception based on the meeting of the father's sperm and the mother's ovum. You could compare the letter HRIH to the consciousness that
enters the fertilized egg. It is the seed from which the deity will appear.

The seed syllable then develops into the full-fledged form of the deity
and takes birth. A newborn baby is not yet fully grown; it needs to be
nurtured and to mature. Symbolizing this process, the deity still needs to
be consecrated with the three syllables and empowered with the five Buddha families, even though it manifests fully. Having grown up, the child
can now carry out the responsibilities of adulthood, which correspond to

the various recitation intents. Finally, just as everything begins to disintegrate at death, we dissolve everything at the end of the sadhana. Then, to symbolize the nirmanakaya's unceasing activity to benefit beings, we again appear in the form of the deity.

In other words, the development stage purifies an ordinary person's habitual states of delusion and ways of perceiving, from the moment of conception and birth until death, when everything disintegrates. The practice begins with the three samadhis, goes through all the various parts of the sadhana, and ends with dissolving and then re-emerging. Every single feature totally fits together, not only purifying habitual tendencies, but also maturing a practitioner into the completion stage. Moreover, it does not finish there. It extends to the final resultant stage of buddhahood, where endless, boundless benefit will manifest for beings. The *Light of Wisdom, Volume II* also explains this very carefully. So the development stage has many levels of impact and effect.

If you practice Vajrayana, there is no way to avoid understanding the three-kaya principle. The awakened state of the Buddha, which is dharmakaya, expresses itself as sambhogakaya, in order to influence beings. Out of the sambhogakaya, the magical forms of nirmanakaya are conjured forth, to provide sentient beings with a tangible connection and to teach the nine vehicles, in order to bring them to enlightenment. Having turned the wheel of the Dharma in boundless ways, which are called the "Inexhaustible Adornment Wheels of Enlightened Body, Speech, and Mind," and so forth, then the nirmanakaya deities dissolve into the sambhogakaya, and the sambhogakaya dissolves into the dharmakaya. The structure of the development stage reflects this cycle.

The main part begins with unfolding the framework of the three samadhis. Next, you visualize the support, which is the mandala, and the supported, which is the deity. Third, you invoke the wisdom beings to dissolve indivisibly into you, as the samaya being. Then you pay homage; make outer, inner, and innermost offerings; and offer praises. Finally, you train in the vivid presence, which is the visualization of the principal figure of the mandala, followed by the recitation of mantra. All of this comprises the general system of development stage, according to Mahayoga.

> Ah
> Dharmakaya's basic space of suchness is the realm of luminous
>   wakefulness.

Sambhogakaya's unceasing illumination is compassionate
  expression.§
Nirmanakaya's seed samadhi is the white HRIH.§
From it light radiates, purifying the clinging to a real universe with
  beings.§
On gradually piled elements, amidst the vajra protection circle,§
From BHRUM comes the jeweled palace with perfect qualities.§

The first of the three samadhis is the samadhi of suchness. The syllable AH signifies non-arising, non-dwelling, and unceasing. The *Manjushri
Nama Sangirti* describes it as the most eminent among all verbal expressions, while the *Guhyagarbha Tantra* mentions it as being the basis for all
sounds and words. In this particular context, the syllable AH signifies "letting be" in the state of dharmakaya, the awakened mind of all buddhas,
which is the nature of our own mind's emptiness, primordial purity, or
rigpa; these are all synonymous at this point.

The first sentence means that dharmakaya—the state of unconditioned suchness, the primordial purity that pervades all of samsara and
nirvana—is endowed with a spontaneously present, luminous wakefulness.

To apply this personally, the ideal is to mingle your state of mind with
the dharmakaya of all buddhas. To do this, we simply drop our visualization and totally relax into the state of awareness or emptiness, naturally,
without following after any thoughts of the past, present, or future. For
a short while, simply let be in naturalness. If you have already had the
state of rigpa pointed out to you by a master, and you have recognized
it, then this is the occasion to remain in the state of composure, sustaining the continuity of rigpa, which is a wakefulness that defies thoughts,
words, and descriptions. But if you have not had the pointing out instruction, then you should do the following: Focus on your faculty of sight, the
eye consciousness, and simply direct your gaze into the openness of space
before you. Let your tongue remain suspended in your mouth, not touching the upper palate or gums. Remain totally disengaged, uninvolved in
either recollecting the past or planning the future. Just allow the present
moment to be, like a drawing on water. Then, for a short while, you will
experience some openness, a naked state of being open and awake, and
that's it. However, if you are not able to just let be, then, at least think
that all phenomena in samsara and nirvana, whatever appears and exists,

are, by nature, emptiness. This emptiness is not a blank void state; it is endowed with *luminous wakefulness.* This concept, of course, may not be dharmakaya, but if one does not know how to recognize the natural face of dharmakaya, then one must at least use thought to loosen one's dualistic concepts.

The next sentence, *Sambhogakaya's unceasing illumination is compassionate expression,* refers to the samadhi of illumination. This compassion is nonconceptual and undirected, embracing of all those who fail to understand their basic nature of suchness. It is the natural expression of the dharmakaya of all buddhas, which is the sambhogakaya. So to practice this, let the awakened state of the first samadhi manifest as a magical compassion for all sentient beings who fail to recognize this intrinsic wakefulness.

All beings without exception are already the dharmakaya of all buddhas. Their basic nature of suchness is the sugata-essence, but failing to realize that, they continuously stray into the deluded ways of experiencing. That is the reason for compassion. Since only a buddha, the awakened state, is completely free of delusion, and everyone else, you could say, is submerged in a deluded way of experiencing, there is reason for compassion. This delusion causes our present experience of samsara to emerge. As compassion manifests from the state of emptiness, sambhogakaya appears from dharmakaya. The unity of the two, the indivisibility of emptiness and compassion, takes the form of the seed syllable, which is the third samadhi. That syllable, HRIH, corresponds to nirmanakaya. Whether it is in the shape of the Indian or Tibetan syllable, the HRIH we visualize is indivisible from our own minds. The syllable radiates brilliant rays of light, symbolizing that our buddha nature is naturally endowed with inconceivable great qualities.

In the vast space of emptiness, sambhogakaya's illumination takes the form of a white HRIH. In other words, imagine that in the middle of the vastness of space, a brilliant white HRIH emits light in all directions. This is the samadhi of the seed syllable, which corresponds to nirmanakaya.

In short, out of the dharmakaya space of suchness, compassion manifests, fulfilling activity that assures the welfare of all sentient beings. These three samadhis are incredibly profound. In the pure aspect, they correspond to the dharmakaya, sambhogakaya, and nirmanakaya of all buddhas. On the impure level, they purify any habitual tendencies related to birth. All Mahayoga sadhanas include training in these three samadhis. This could all be explained in great detail, but it is important to know how to apply it in a practical way, by means of the pith instructions of a master. According to Mahayoga, unless you are able to apply the teachings, there is no framework for the sadhana. On the other hand, if you do not know all the finer details, but do practice these three basic principles, then at least the framework for sadhana has unfolded. This is an extremely vital point. This is why the *Trinley Gyepa* has a four-line verse for each of the three samadhis. These are chanted with a very special slow tune that allows the practitioner to bring these three samadhis to mind to the fullest and actually apply them as one goes along.

Om!

From the all-pervasive state of the utterly pure dharmadhatu,

A manifold display manifests as occurring in dependent connection.

From the very moment it manifests, it is the primordial nature beyond concepts.

This is the suchness stated by the Lotus King.

Dharmadhatu jnana vajra svabhava atma koh ham

Ah

Though everything is the nature of dharmakaya, the awakened state,

For all beings equal to space, who do not realize this,

The radiance of the nonconceptual self-expressed great compassion

Shines throughout, like the sun in the sky.

Bodhichitta utpadaya mi

Hung

Since all things originate as effects from causes,

In order to free the six kinds of beings, in the manner of compassionate emptiness,

The white letter HRIH, brilliant, with rays of light,

Appears immutable within the expanse of space.

Hrih sapharana phat sangharana hung

Even though there is only one sentence for each of the three samadhis in the *Trinley Nyingpo*, as we chant, we should allow the meaning of each word to bring to mind the natural face of dharmakaya, the mind of all buddhas; to the best of our ability, we should remain in this continuity. Then, within the continuity of dharmakaya, we allow primordial purity to be expressed as compassion. Of course, the best is to have totally spontaneous, genuine, uncontrived compassion; but if that does not happen, then one must contrive it.

From the HRIH *light radiates, purifying the clinging to a real universe with beings.* The light of the seed syllable purifies the tendency to cling to things, such as the world and sentient beings, as if they were solid and real. We must dissolve this tendency in order to train in development stage, just as a cup must be empty in order to be filled. If we still cling to our notions of material existence, we will not be able to imagine a pure land, like Sukhavati, where the scenery is entirely composed of insubstantial gemstones, and the palace itself is immeasurable.

The details of the mandala temple are very complex, but according to the tradition of pith instructions, you can simply imagine that you are in a magnificent house, a wonderful mansion, made of insubstantial jewels. Dilgo Khyentse Rinpoche said this to a few students, when he was in the West. So, we try to think of it as being the best possible, the most exquisite, whatever we can imagine beyond the ordinary.

The words *On the gradually piled elements, amidst the vajra protection circle* mean that various types of seed syllables, like E, YAM, RAM, LAM, BAM, emanate from the HRIH and turn into the mandalas of the elements in different colors, shapes, and so forth. This too is very complicated. At this point, just imagine the syllables emerge, and that is good enough. The vajra protection circle is outside of that, like a huge dome.

From BHRUM, comes the jeweled palace with perfect qualities. The celestial palace is situated at the center of the huge vajra cross, which is on the floor of the vajra protection circle. Its proportions, dimensions, decorations, and so forth are all complete and perfect, just as the *Magical Net* tantras (*Mayajala*) explain. In-depth descriptions can be found in Karmey Khenpo's *Detailed Explanation of Mawey Senge*[4] as well as in the *Guhyagarbha Tantra.* An important point to remember, however, is that the celestial palace is a manifestation of the principle deity. In other words, the building is none other than the deity itself, and from every single little bell, the sound of the Dharma resounds.

Visualizing Padmasambhava and His Retinue

In its center, upon a lion throne with a lotus, sun, and moon,

Is my awareness as Padmasambhava, the embodiment of all
sugatas.

With an expression of peacefully smiling wrath, and a white and
red complexion,

I wear the lotus crown, secret dress, gown, Dharma robes, and a
brocade cloak.

My right hand holds a vajra and my left a skull cup with a vase.

The supreme consort is embraced in the concealed form of a
khatvanga.

With my feet in the playful, royal posture, I am poised in a sphere
of five-colored light.

The floor of the celestial palace is mainly white, but there is a design on
it, and it has various levels. The light in each of the four directions is of a
corresponding hue—red, yellow, green, and white. Water flows in the four
corners of the main floor, and then the inside of that is raised up above the
rest. There are also various designs made of jewels in diverse colors.

In the center of the palace, imagine a deep blue platform with eight
sides, on which there is a lotus, sun, and moon. The fully blossomed lotus
flower is huge, has four petals, and is either lapis blue or multicolored.
In the center of the lotus is a raised throne supported by eight lions, two
on each side. On top of the platform of the throne, there is a lotus flower
with both a sun and a moon disc. The syllable HRIH, which is actually our
own mind in the state of rigpa, now comes to settle on the main throne
and turns into Padmasambhava.

Padmasambhava, the embodiment of all sugatas... Padmasambhava, or
Guru Rinpoche, has white skin, but it glows with a reddish hue. He is
smiling peacefully, but his gaze is a little wrathful, a bit wild. His eyes
look directly at those to be tamed.

The lotus crown is like the ones Tulku Urgyen Rinpoche copied;
Chokling Rinpoche has one. It is unique in that the rear flap does not
hang down. It is described in the *Trinley Gyepa* as being *adorned with vulture's feathers, mirror(s), and jewels, and is endowed with silk streamers.* Even
though it is often depicted as blue, its base color is actually red, symbol-

izing the Lotus family, whose activity is magnetizing. The front flaps are blue and green, and there is a vulture feather at the peak, symbolizing the summit of all views. There is also an eye-of-a-peacock feather to symbolize that the five poisons are automatically transmuted into the five wisdoms. These days it is often made with just a peacock feather and no vulture feather, as if the summit of all views were not needed. Finally, according to the tradition of *Chokling Tersar*, there is a tiara of ribbons hanging down from the crown.

The secret dress is a white undergarment worn next to the body. Over this, Padmasambhava wears a blue spangled gown; and over that, he wears the three Dharma robes. He also has a monk's skirt, which is unique to the *Tukdrub Barchey Künsel*. Over all this, he wears a maroon colored brocade cloak tied with a *tantrika's* belt, which is a special kind of sash.

He raises a vajra in his right hand and supports a skull with a vase of longevity in his left. Most Nyingma traditions show his hand supported on his right knee, which is called the *Nangsi Zilnön* style, whereas in the *Tsokye Dorje* style, he holds the vajra in front of his chest. In the *Chokling Tersar,* his hand is raised and most likely slightly forward. The skull cup is filled with the nectar of immortality, in which the vase of longevity rests.

In the *Nyingtik* tradition, Padmasambhava's consort is visualized, but here she is in the hidden form of a khatvanga. The khatvanga is the trident resting in the crook of his arm, and it has a profound significance. For example, the three prongs symbolize piercing the three poisonous emotions to reveal they too have the nature of basic space, and the three heads symbolize the three kayas. The garland, silk streamers, damaru, bells, and so forth, all embody profound symbols that can be learned elsewhere.

Padmasambhava sits in the "playful, royal pose," which is not full lotus; instead, one leg is slightly extended, as can be seen in *thangkas*. This is probably how the Indian kings of the past sat. He is also *poised in a sphere of five-colored light.* He is not sitting perfectly erect, but leans slightly to the right.

As you visualize all of Padmasambhava's details, as described in the extensive version of the sadhana, imagine that all these details, accessories, and so forth have a divine nature.

There are also four deities to dispel obstacles; they are magical manifestations of the four emblems. Arya Tara appears from the khatvanga;

the Lord of Secrets, Dorje Bechön, springs forth from the vajra; Achala emerges from the skull cup; and Mewa Tsekpa arises from the vase of longevity.

> Above my head is the white lord, Sambhogakaya Avalokiteshvara.ᵹ
> With four arms and palms joined, he holds a crystal rosary and a
>   white lotus.ᵹ
> Above his head is Dharmakaya Amitayus.ᵹ
> Red in color, he holds a nectar-filled life vase in equanimity.ᵹ

Padmasambhava is the embodiment of all the buddhas in a single form. Behind him, another branch of the lotus rises above, where it unfolds a lotus flower. On this lotus, Avalokiteshvara sits upon a lotus disc. He is white and has four arms. The first two are joined in prayer in front of his chest. He holds a white crystal rosary and a white lotus in the other two. He wears a deer skin across his left shoulder.

This same lotus has another branch, which extends up behind Avalokiteshvara. Dharmakaya Buddha Amitayus sits upon this branch, wearing the sambhogakaya attire and appearing like Amitayus Buddha. He is red, has two hands in the gesture of equanimity, and holds the vase of longevity. As sambhogakaya deities, both Avalokiteshvara and Amitayus wear the sambhogakaya attire, consisting of the eight types of jewelry, the silken garments, and so forth. When practicing Amitayus as an independent sadhana according to the *Barchey Künsel*, visualize him embracing his consort; however, here his consort is simply a radiance of light. These are the Trikaya Gurus, the gurus of the three kayas. They are also called the dharmakaya, sambhogakaya, and nirmanakaya deities. They are the three primary deities in the mandala of *Tukdrub Barchey Künsel*.

In addition to these, there are the twelve retinue deities.

> Around, on the anthers of the four-petaled lotus flower,ᵹ
> Are, in the east, the white Gyalwey Dungdzin,ᵹ
> In the south, the radiantly white Mawey Senge,ᵹ
> In the west, the yellow Kyechok Tsülzang,ᵹ
> In the north, the dazzling light-brown Dükyi Shechen.ᵹ

Guru Rinpoche's throne is situated upon an octagon, and he faces east. Directly in front of him, on a petal of the four-petaled lotus beneath his throne, is the white Gyalwey Dungdzin. He holds a flaming sword in his right hand and a mudra shaped like a hook in his left hand. He is semi-wrathful, meaning half peaceful and half wrathful, and he wears a skirt made of tiger skin with bone ornaments. He is also half-seated, which means he is either seated or standing, either of the two. Some people claim it makes a big difference whether he is sitting down or standing up, but actually it does not matter; as Padmasambhava said, "If you visualize me sitting, fine, visualize me sitting. If you visualize me standing, fine, visualize me standing." The *Güjang* states that Gyalwey Dungdzin is one of the eight manifestations called Lotus King, who is the deity of magnetizing activity. In the sadhana specific to Gyalwey Dungdzin, he has a retinue of four dakinis in the four directions, and it is said that its practice brings the three realms under one's control, develops the magnetizing and wrathful activities of yogic discipline, and so forth.[5]

In the south, meaning to Guru Rinpoche's right, on the second lotus petal is the radiantly white Mawey Senge. His two hands are in the gesture of expounding the Dharma. Wearing the attire of a fully ordained monk, he holds the stems of two lotus flowers in his hands. The flowers bloom at the level of his ears and support two volumes of scripture. To his right, is the *Prajnaparamita,* condensing all the Sutra teachings into a single volume. To his left, is a volume of Kilaya scripture, for dispelling all types of hindrances and achieving all kinds of siddhis, which condenses all the Vajrayana teachings. His legs are in the full vajra posture (commonly known as full lotus). He wears the kind of pandita hat that has a peak. The *Güjang* says it should be yellow, which Dilgo Khyentse Rinpoche confirmed, when I asked him if it shouldn't be orange. So though it is commonly said that Tsongkapa created the yellow hat, it is probably not true as there must have been a tradition in India for some panditas to wear yellow pandita hats. Nonetheless, beneath the pandita hat, he is wearing the crown of the five Buddha families with the five jewels, and so forth, as well as the syllables OM AH HUNG TRAM HRIH AH. When Mawey Senge is one of the retinue deities, as in this case, you do not visualize anyone else around him; but when you practice his own sadhana, he has his own retinue of the four families of Manjushri, the four families of Sarasvati, and the Four Guardian Kings. Mawey Senge is the manifestation of intelligence and insight, and his supreme knowledge is indivisible from Manjushri's. Mawey Senge is also indivisible from one of the eight manifestations called Loden Choksey.

Behind Padmasambhava is the yellow Kyechok Tsülzang, who holds a five-pronged vajra in his right hand and a small reliquary box in his left. He wears the three Dharma robes of a monk and the orange lotus crown, inside of which you should also visualize the crown of the five Buddha families. In the *Güjang*, it says that *together with his vajra, he holds a banner of victory*, which spontaneously brings forth all desirable things and fulfills all wishes, like a shower of rain. That is how he is described in the separate sadhana for Kyechok Tsülzang, or Lama Norlha, as he is known. Here it only mentions the vajra, but tertöns often don't divulge everything—some things they mention explicitly, others they keep secret. I am not sure why he is not holding the victory banner here, but that's the way it is. In his own sadhana, Lama Norlha is surrounded by his own retinue, the four families of Jambhala, who are the wealth gods of devas, humans, nagas, yakshas, as well as *kuvera* and many other deities, the four kings of the four directions, and so forth.

In the north, meaning to Padmasambhava's left, is the dazzling light brown, Dükyi Shechen. He looks similar to Padmasambhava, but he is standing and does not have any charnel-ground attire. He has a Kilaya dagger raised in his right hand. In his left hand, he has an action dagger pointing downwards. Usually when people hold a knife, they point it away from themselves, but here it is important that the *phurba* is pointed at oneself. His two eyes are gazing heavenward, and he is chanting the syllable HUNG. He is in a mass of flames, with his two legs in the striding stance. In some old tangkas, he is depicted standing on a corpse, but I have not found any evidence to support this. He is indivisible from the yidam Vajra Kilaya (Dorje Phurba), which symbolizes that Guru Rinpoche has completely perfected activity.

In the independent sadhana, he is surrounded by different deities, including the lion-faced dakinis and the herukas of the eight classes. In the *Tukdrub Barchey Künsel*, the "lower activities" are connected with this deity; there are a lot of rituals for suppression, annihilation, destruction, and so forth. In that sadhana, all you need to do is simply remain in the form of Padmasambhava, while in the sky before you is Dükyi Shechen together with his retinue. There, Padmasambhava's lotus crown is blue instead of red, and it has five skeleton heads on the outside. The mantra for Dükyi Shechen is the same as for Vajra Kilaya.

Now we move on to the eight deities seated in the points of the octagonal platform:

> Outside, surrounding these, are, on the eight-faceted jewel,⁺
> In the east, the blue-colored Dzamling Gyenchok,⁺
> In the south, the radiantly clear blue Pema Jungney,⁺
> In the west, the white Kyepar Pakpey Rigdzin,⁺
> In the north, the dazzling red-maroon Dzutrül Tuchen.⁺

Directly in front is the blue-colored Dzamling Gyenchok. He is dark blue and wrathful, wearing a two-layered dark blue brocade cloak. On top of the cloak he wears the charnel-ground attire, which includes an elephant skin on his torso, a tiger skin wrapped around his waist, human skin wrapped like a scarf around his neck, and a triple bandolier of human heads. He does not wear a crown, but there are skeleton heads in his hair. His braids are turning upward and his eyes are glaring. His fangs are bared, and he holds two Kilaya daggers raised to the right and left. He has another Kilaya dagger tucked into the human skin he wears as a sash around his waist. Like Padmasambhava, he is wearing boots, though he is in a striding stance. With his feet, he holds down the corpse of a demon. He is indivisible from the deity Yangdag or Vishuddha Heruka.

In the individual sadhana, Dzamling Gyenchok is surrounded by a retinue of the eight *gaurima* goddesses. Six doctrines connected to this deity bring awakening through meditation practice, such as *tummo* (inner heat), dream yoga, illusory body, *bardo*, and *phowa*. When we do phowa according to Chokgyur Lingpa's style, we visualize Dzamling Gyenchok.

In the south, the radiantly clear Pema Jungney is clear blue, like the sky. His hands are crossed in front of his chest holding a vajra and bell. His consort is white, and she holds a curved knife and skull cup. He is naked except for jewel and bone ornaments. Sometimes he is depicted wearing a tiger skirt, like the Tötreng Tsal form of Padmasambhava, but that is not necessary here. The five families of Tötreng Tsal surround him. According to the chapter of the teachings discussing this form of Padmasambhava, there are *six wondrous doctrines that bring awakening without meditation*. These doctrines—such as liberation through seeing, hearing, touching, or wearing—bring enlightenment without one having to do anything whatsoever. If you want to train in the Dzogchen instructions according to the *Tukdrub Barchey Künsel,* then you should train in the instructions connected to Pema Jungney. There is also the root tantra of the *Barchey Künsel,* called the *Lotus Essence Tantra,* which gives the accessory instructions connected to him.

In the west, the white Kyepar Pakpey Rigdzin is wearing the normal attire of Padmasambhava, although he is standing. In his right hand, he holds a vajra pointed at the sky, which symbolizes pointing out the right path. He is holding a khatvanga staff in his left hand. In the *Güjang,* it says he is Guru Nyima Özer, who is one of the eight manifestations. In his individual sadhana, his retinue includes the eight drekpa aspects. When making a huge consecration, for events like blessing a piece of land or embarking on a great effort to benefit beings, assume the identity of Kyepar Rigdzin.

To the north, the dazzling red-maroon Dzamtrül Tuchen is none other than Dorje Drollö. He is standing on a tigress' back and is wearing Dharma robes. He holds both a vajra and a Kilaya. In the *Güjang,* it says he has a horse's head sticking up on the crown of his head and that many scorpions emanate from the hand holding the phurba. In the long version of the sadhana, it does not say that he stands on a tigress; it says he has mounted a pregnant tigress and he is eating the hearts of the *damsi* spirits. In his individual sadhana, the ten wrathful deities surround him.

Having completed the deities in the four main directions of the octagon, now come the four in the intermediate directions.

> In the southeast, the red Vidyadhara Dorje Draktsal,
> In the southwest, the flaming dark-blue Kalden Drendzey
> In the northwest, the majestic dark-brown Raksha Tötreng,
> And in the northeast, the radiantly clear-red Dechen Gyalpo;
> All perfectly adorned with the appropriate ornaments and objects.

In the southeast, the red Vidyadhara Dorje Draktsal is none other than the wrathful form of Padmasambhava, known as Guru Drakpo. In his right hand, he holds a vajra and with his left hand he is holding a scorpion by the neck. He wears the eightfold charnel-ground attire. In some termas, he is a solitary figure, but in the *Barchey Künsel,* he is in union with his consort, Varahi (Dorje Palmo), who is dark blue and bears a curved knife and skull cup. In the individual sadhana, Dorje Draktsal has the five aspects of the five armor deities surrounding him.

This yidam's activity is to suppress the samaya violating *gongpo* spirits.

In the southwest, the flaming dark-blue Kalden Drendzey is holding a vajra, wearing the full tenfold wrathful attire, the charnel-ground attire, and jewel rings. His consort is the light-blue Sky-Faced One. He has one face and two arms. This deity is often used in the making of the sacred medicine known as *mendrub*. The activity connected to him is the supreme activity. Kalden Drendzey is Chemchok from among the eight herukas (*kabgye*); in fact, in the individual sadhana, Kalden Drendzey is surrounded by the eight herukas.

In the northwest, the majestic dark-brown Raksha Tötreng wears only the charnel-ground attire. Though he is a wrathful deity, he does not have wings or wear the general wrathful ornaments. He holds a vajra and skull cup and is embraced by his consort, Blazing Light Blue. In his individual sadhana, he has a retinue of ten wrathful deities, just like Vajra Kilaya. The many lower activities connected to this deity include subjugating the thirteen types of sea spirits. In the Sutra teachings, the Buddha taught how to make subjugating *yantras*, but probably only Chokgyur Lingpa has the actual sadhana for applying them. I have not seen such sadhanas in any other tertön's collection, and Jamgön Kongtrül has stated that there aren't any. Karmey Khenpo wrote that the *Güjang* contains many more details, but I have yet to find any copies of this. In the root text for the *Tukdrub*, nothing else is mentioned.

And in the northeast, the radiantly clear-red Dechen Gyalpo is in essence Padma Vajra as well as Chakrasamvara. Like Chakrasamvara, he has a consort. They are naked and wear only bone and jewel ornaments. He has three eyes, bears his fangs, and glares with wide-open eyes. The teachings connected to this deity include the path of means (*upaya*). In the individual sadhana, he is practiced as five families. The completion stage practices connected to Dechen Gyalpo are *chö* and Dzogchen. The Dzogchen guidance manual connected to *Barchey Künsel* is a fusing together of instructions from Pema Jungney and Dechen Gyalpo; it covers both Trekchö and Tögal.

The appropriate ornaments and objects is a phrase that is further explained in the *Trinley Gyepa*, which you should definitely consult.

> At the four gates are the four kinds of dakas and dakinis with their consorts,[8]

And in the spaces between, the Three Roots and dharma protectors
    are gathered like cloud banks.

These magical wisdom forms of united appearance and emptiness

Are spontaneously present as the essence of the three vajras

And perfected with the supreme empowerments of the five
    wisdom families.

Om ah hung

Om hung tram hrih ah abhikhincha hung

The four kinds of dakas and dakinis refers to the dakas of the four families—Buddha, Ratna, Padma, and Vajra—in union with their consorts.
They are in the colors of their respective families and have curved knives,
each with specific ornaments on the handles—a vajra, jewel, lotus, and
vajra cross. The *Trinley Gyepa* describes them this way:

At the four gates, in the center of lotus flowers with sun discs:

To the east is Vajra Daka; his body is white.

With a peaceful expression, he is joined with the consort of his own
    light.

To the south is Ratna Daka, with the color of gold.

In a playful demeanor, he is joined with the consort of his own
    light.

To the west is Padma Daka; his body is red.

With a passionate expression, he is joined with the consort of his
    own light.

To the north is Karma Daka; his body is green.

With fierce majestic splendor, he is joined with the consort of his
    own light.

All are adorned with silks and ornaments of bones and jewels.

They hold skull cup and curved knife fashioned with their
    individual insignia.

While standing in playful striding stances,

They are vividly present as the forms that spontaneously
    accomplish the four activities.

When you do the fire puja according to the *Tukdrub Barchey Künsel*, these are the four deities at the four gates who carry out the activi-

ties. There are also independent sadhanas for each of the four dakas with their dakinis and each sadhana has its own mantra.

At this point, we have visualized the samaya being, and that is the basis for invoking the wisdom being. We have visualized body, speech, and mind, which should be complete, no matter which deity it is. These three aspects should be present, vividly brought to mind. When you turn a consecrated tangka around, you see the three syllables OM AH HUNG written on the back. Now, this needs to be perfected with the supreme empowerments of the five wisdom families. The crown of the five Buddha families symbolizes the three poisonous emotions being naturally purified into basic space. In order to bring this to mind, we say the mantra OM AH HUNG, which is for vajra body, vajra speech, and vajra mind. OM HUNG TRAM HRIH AH is for the five Buddha families. Then *abhikhin-cha* means "empowerment." We imagine we receive the empowerment for that, which is necessary at first. Visualize the samaya being and then invoke the wisdom beings to confer this empowerment. This is very profound actually.

This means we should visualize ourselves as the samaya being, the deity. We should also invoke and invite the wisdom being, definitely, without thinking of one as being superior to the other. Can you think like that? In the lower tantras like Kriya Yoga, for sure one thinks of the deity as being superior to oneself, but in Mahayoga, one doesn't. That's a very significant point, actually. Then, we're finished.

Up to this point covers the general visualization of the principal deity as well as the deities of the retinue.

The Three Principles of Visualization

The vital essence of development stage is summarized in three principles: vivid presence, pure recollection, and stable pride. Vivid presence means that your visualization is as clear and distinct as the reflection of the sky on the surface of a smooth lake. It is simply a vivid, insubstantial presence that is mentally visible and not made of any material substance. Vivid presence also means that the visualization is not vague, blurred, incomplete, or mixed up. It is complete, distinct, and clear.

The Light of Wisdom, Volume II, describes the steps of development stage in great detail, which one can apply in a very expedient, progressive order until one achieves certain meditative experiences. But one practical approach is to use a consecrated tangka or copy of one as a support for your visualization. Study the painting, then close your eyes and visualize as much as you can remember. Then open your eyes and look at the tangka again. After a bit, again close your eyes and visualize the deity to the best of your ability. Growing accustomed like that can be quite helpful in the beginning, and after a while you will not need to use the tangka at all. You will be able to just let all of it appear naturally in your mind's eye. At first, you visualize the deity with his retinue in front of you, but when you have become adept at the visualization, you imagine yourself as the central deity surrounded by your retinue. Over time, your mind will become totally flexible, and then you can emanate, multiply, and so forth. Anything is possible.

Stable pride is the confidence and insight that the deity is none other than buddha nature itself; in other words, the nature of this mind is the deity. You need to realize that there is no other deity apart from that. As we are veiled by ignorance, we do not recognize this at first. The whole purpose of yidam practice is to remove this veil. When the veil has been lifted, we recognize the fact that we ourselves are the deity. According to Mahayoga, one never thinks of the deity as better than oneself. That's a very important point. If you think you and the deity are at all different in status or quality, you will be further nurturing your notions of duality, and you will never accomplish the deity.

The pure recollection of symbolism involves a lot of detail, as every feature of the deity has a specific meaning. The face, arms, attributes, ornaments, seat, palace, and so forth, are all symbolic. However, we can summarize all this into one key point: the deity is the state of awareness-emptiness, and all the aspects of the visualization are the naturally occurring expression of emptiness. Neither the deity nor its mandala has any concrete reality.

If you are a practitioner of the highest capacity, then it is best to visualize the entire retinue distinctly and completely. If, however, you have not fully mastered the development stage, then you likely will not be able to see everything that clearly; therefore, it suffices to focus on the main deity. As the retinue is the expression of the central figure, it will eventually appear, just as a king's retinue automatically follows him wherever he goes. This is how it is taught in the stages of meditation practice for the sadhana entitled, *Assemblage of Sugatas according to the Eight Herukas* (*Kabgye Deshek Düpa*).

At the same time, we should train with the development and completion stages in unity. To do this, we visualize in terms of development stage, while training in the completion stage. This is the meaning of *these magical wisdom forms of united appearance and emptiness.*

EMPOWERING AND SEALING

Then we imagine that all the deities, including the deities of the three kayas and the entire retinues, have the three syllables at their heart, throat, and forehead, signifying the vajra body, speech, and mind of all buddhas. The white OM at the crown of the head is Buddha Vairochana as vajra body; the red AH at the throat is Amitabha as vajra speech, and the blue HUNG at the heart is Akshobhya as vajra mind. In this way, we see that all deities have the nature of vajra body, speech, and mind.

It is also said that one should always combine deity, mantra, and mudra; therefore, together with the OM AH HUNG, one makes the hand gestures of the five, three, and single-pronged vajras at the three places. According to the *Tantra of the Magical Net* (*Mayajala*), you should visualize that the five fingers of your right hand have the nature of the male buddhas and those of your left hand have the nature of the female buddhas. Then you make the mudras corresponding to OM HUNG TRAM HRIH AH at the appropriate places around your head symbolizing the five Buddha families. Then these eight syllables all emanate light in all directions, inviting the wisdom beings (*jñanasattvas*) from their own abodes. They then arrive, confer empowerment, and finally dissolve indivisibly into you.

According to the intent of Mahayoga, all the empowerment deities are in union with their respective consorts and settle in their respective places, according to which Buddha family they belong to. They sport in union, and the bodhichitta of melting bliss reverts upward and overflows, transforming into the deity of that particular family. This transforms the five poisonous emotions into the five aspects of wisdom and purifies the habitual tendencies, so that the five wisdoms perpetually adorn our heads like a crown. One also develops the assurance that from the very beginning, the five sense aggregates have the nature of the five male Buddhas

DISPELLER OF OBSTACLES

and the five elements the nature of the five female Buddhas. The chief figure of the *Tukdrub* mandala is peaceful in nature, but it is interesting to note that when the central figure is wrathful, the five Buddha families dwell inside the five skulls adorning his head. If the main deity has more than one head, such as Chemchok Heruka who has twenty-one, then each head would have the crown of the five Buddhas.

In some systems, there is no need for empowering and sealing. As there are so many deities and symbols and mudras, one can easily become confused; therefore, one just focuses on the meaning or intent.

In short, these two, sealing and empowering, are very profound aspects and are also necessary when consecrating a statue.

INVOCATION

After the empowering and the sealing comes the invocation in seven lines, followed by the Tötreng Tsal mantra:

HUNG HRIH!
From the land whose name is the southwestern continent of
    Chamara,
The supreme nirmanakaya realm Lotus Net,
Trikaya inseparable, Orgyen Tötreng Tsal,
With your ocean-like assembly of infinite Three Root deities,
When I invite you yearningly to this place of devotion,
Please come through the power of your compassionate vow.
Dispel all obstacles and bestow the supreme and common siddhis!
OM AH HUNG VAJRA GURU PADMA TÖTRENG TSAL VAJRA SAMAYA DZAH
    SIDDHI PHALA HUNG AH
DZAH HUNG BAM HOH
SAMAYA TISHTHA LHAN

Here, still imagining that you are Padmasambhava, rays of red light stream forth from the HRIH in your heart center. The very tips bend inwards forming small hooks. They extend into all directions, but primarily to the Trikaya Buddhafield of Padmasambhava at the Glorious Copper-Colored Mountain, where they touch the heart center of Padmasambhava, Avalokiteshvara, Amitayus, and the surrounding deities.

In this way, the deities' samaya is automatically invoked, and they are reminded of the oath they took to always act for the benefit of beings. Padmasambhava said that he would come from the Glorious Copper-Colored Mountain and appear before anyone who chants the *Seven Line Prayer*.

The wisdom being never departs from the basic space of dharmadhatu, yet it appears in the perception of those to be influenced. The wisdom being, since primordial time, is indivisible from the samaya being. In other words, what you have just visualized is already saturated with the wisdom being, yet you need to bring this to mind by means of the invocation. As you sing in a melodious tune full of yearning and devotion, sound the musical instruments and burn incense. Then, due to the power of their past vow of compassion to benefit beings, the wisdom beings will manifest with all their intrinsic qualities.

Moreover, invoking Padmasambhava with deep yearning, devotion, pure samaya, and complete sincerity creates the proper circumstance for the natural manifestation of Padmasambhava's awakened state. The most vital element, however, is a deep yearning, like a child longing for his mother or a mother thinking of her child. If one has that kind of devotion, a complete surrender, seeking no other refuge, then there is no doubt Padmasambhava will manifest.

In principle, as the innumerable wisdom beings arrive, they become indivisible with you, like flames merging into one or snowflakes falling on a lake. But according to Dilgo Khyentse Rinpoche's commentary on *Barchey Künsel*, you should imagine that the wisdom beings remain at a slight distance for a short while.

At this point, you imagine that the goddess *Khakuma* emanates from your heart center. With the syllable DZAH, she invites all the deities to approach the eastern gate of the mandala. Next, with HUNG, the goddess with the shackles, requests all the deities to come close, to be indivisible from the samaya beings. With BAM, the goddess with chains ensures that the wisdom beings and the samaya beings melt one by one indivisibly and firmly. And with the fourth syllable, HOH, the goddess with the bell expresses great delight and joy that the wisdom beings and the samaya beings have dissolved into each other indivisibly. In the *Ngakso* drubchen, it is slightly different. The first goddess, with the hook or the noose, invites them to come closer; the second, the goddess with the shackles, draws them in; the third, with the chains, melts them indivisibly; and the fourth one enjoys this with great delight. In our case, it is the former example. In the more elaborate and the medium lengths of the sadhana, in requesting them to remain firmly, one chants lines of poetry aloud at this point. Here, we just chant the four syllables and then SAMAYA TISHTA LHEN. The whole visualization should be compressed into these mantric syllables. The four goddesses invite the wisdom deities, they come closer, and then they dissolve and remain firmly as indivisible from our visualization.

In order to avoid binding yourself in dualistic concepts, please remember that it is always important to know the actual meaning of any visualization. In this case, the samaya being symbolizes the buddha nature, which is already present in every single sentient being as the nature of mind. This basic nature is and always has been pure; otherwise, it would not be called deity. The realization of this divine nature or purity is represented by the indivisibility of the wisdom and samaya beings. Though we visualize the samaya being and invite the wisdom beings, in fact they are already indivisible. Also, dissolving the wisdom beings into the samaya beings does not mean we are inserting one entity into another, where they remain as one thing inside the other; nor does it mean we are creating something unnatural that was not already that way from the beginning.

The four syllables DZAH HUNG BAM HOH are used in many different contexts, such as summoning, invoking, and so forth. This is called "binding with the four mudras," but the meaning varies according to the context.

HOMAGE

HUNG HRIH!
Without arising, ceasing, or changing, you perfect all activities.
Your self-existing compassion frees all beings.
Like a wish-fulfilling jewel, you shower a rain of siddhis.
Assembly of vidyadharas, I pay homage to you!
ATI PUHO
PRATICCHA HO

Ultimately and actually, the true homage is simply to let be in equanimity, fully aware that the deity is indivisible from the nature of your own mind. According to Mahayoga, simply acknowledging that the samaya and wisdom beings are indivisible is sufficient for paying homage. The ultimate homage is recognizing that whatever appears and exists already has divine nature and acknowledging that sights, sounds, and awareness are deity, mantra, and dharmakaya. While chanting these four lines, it would be ideal to perform the ultimate homage; otherwise, you should visualize the following: Still imagining yourself as Padmasambhva, emanate a replica from your heart center. This figure is known as a karma or action deity. Then imagine that the goddesses at the four gates turn toward the karma deity and pay homage by prostrating, while saying ATI PUHO. The karma deity then prostrates in return and says, PRATICCHA HO. After that, the karma deity dissolves back into your heart center. This exchange acknowledges that the chief figure and the retinue of deities are equal.

THE OFFERINGS

OM AH HUNG⁑

I present you, as outer offerings, an ocean of desirable objects
 amassed like cloud banks;⁑

As inner offerings, an inconceivable feast of amrita, rakta, and
 torma;⁑

And, as secret offerings, the unity of bliss and emptiness, the basic
 space of wakefulness.⁑

Accepting these, please bestow the supreme and common siddhis!⁑

OM VAJRA ARGHAM PADYAM PUSHPE DHUPE ALOKE GHANDHE NAIVIDYA⁑

SHABTA SARVA PANCHA RAKTA BALINGTA MAHA PUDZA AH HUNG⁑

These words are very profound and could be explained in great detail, but here I will just outline the main points.

First, in brief, once more a karma deity emanates out of your heart center and assumes a place in the center of the celestial palace. Then, as you form the various offering mudras, countless gods and especially goddesses appear. These gods and goddesses magically conjure forth the outer, inner, and innermost offerings and present them to the karma deity.

The outer offerings are an inconceivable number of sense pleasures *amassed like cloud banks.* The inner offerings are *amrita, rakta, and torma.* Amrita is connected to the partaking of siddhi, and rakta symbolizes the emptying of samsara. The torma represents the inexhaustible amount of sense pleasures. The secret offering is *the unity of bliss and emptiness.* For this, you offer female figures to the male deities and male figures to the female deities. Finally, as the state of primordial purity is the "thatness" offering, simply remain in the equanimity of primordial purity.

One accompanies each word of the Sanskrit mantra with its respective hand mudra and visualizes that the corresponding offering goddess makes an offering to each of the deities. For example, for ARGHAM, imagine that the goddess holding the rinsing water presents it to each of the deities personally and simultaneously. After making her offering, as a token of blessing and accomplishment, each goddess dissolves into each of the deities as you go along.

Do not get caught up in any ordinary mundane concepts during this; otherwise, all the deities will end up drowning in the ocean of rinsing water. As the drinking water is like the flow of the River Ganges, no deity could drink all of that. If you cling to ordinary concepts, you will become overwhelmed. In fact, the offerings are inconceivable in order to shatter one's ordinary concepts.

There are both material and mental offerings. No matter how generous you might be and how nicely you arrange them, material offerings are still limited. On the other hand, mentally created offerings can be infinite. For example, it would be hard for one to arrange a whole ocean of rinsing water, drinking water that flows like the River Ganges, and butter lamps that shine like the sun and moon on one's shrine. However, mentally, we are free to imagine these things. The materials arranged on the shrine are a support for what we imagine mentally.

If you have concepts of clean and unclean, neat and messy, then you should keep the shrine as neat as possible. If you have transcended any concept of clean and unclean, neat and sloppy, then this does not really matter. Similarly, if you have concepts such as superior and inferior quality, large and small, then you should try your best to offer large amounts of the finest things. And as Jamgön Kongtrül says, it is not enough to just set up musical instruments, you should play them. Even if you only have a bell, you should ring it. Pleasant sounds can be regarded as offerings to the peaceful deities, whereas harsher, abrasive sounds can be considered offerings to the wrathful deities. In short, you should have all the offerings required from rinsing water to music.

ARGHAM is rinsing water, PADYAM drinking water, PUSHPE flowers, DHUPE incense, ALOKE lamps, GHANDHE scents, NAIVIDYA food, and SHABTA sound. SARVA PANCHA is for the amrita, RAKTA is RAKTA, BALINGTA is for the torma, MAHA PUJA means great or inexhaustible offering, and AH HUNG means presented. Whether you practice in a large gathering or alone, you should play the musical instruments for a while. The purpose of this is to provide a sufficient amount of time to do the visualization. You should think of each aspect of the outer and inner offerings and also bring to mind the ultimate offering in completeness. Then, even if your pronunciation is not that great, if you are able to bring all of these aspects to mind, it is still okay.

At the end, all the offering goddesses and gods dissolve back into you, and you remain in the state in which offerer, offering, and offered are indivisible.

THE PRAISES

> HUNG HRIH!
> From your essence, the luminous state of dharmakaya,
> Your nature manifests as sambhogakaya's empty bliss.
> Your capacity, the all-taming nirmanakaya, accomplishes the
>   benefit of beings.
> I prostrate to and praise the whole assembly of mandala deities!

These are extremely profound words; in fact, no ordinary poet or scholar could write anything as impressive.

Praising is based on the same principle as flattering someone, but it's possible to make a more elaborate praise, where you combine three principles of symbol, meaning, and sign. At this point, in the *Trinley Geypa,* the symbolism of each of Padmasambhava's features is included; but here, it is simply the ultimate praise of essence, nature, and capacity.

While chanting these lines of praise, imagine that all the buddhas and bodhisattvas of the ten directions and the three times are strewing flowers that gently rain down upon the entire surrounding area. The gods and the guardian kings of the four directions, Brahma, Indra, the universal monarchs, and so forth, all join in and chant along with you. Then again, all these deities dissolve back into your heart center.

Making offerings and praises is extremely effective in perfecting the accumulation of merit and purifying obscurations. When performing them, always remember there are two aspects of accumulation, with and without concepts. Material offerings and mentally created ones are both examples of perfecting the accumulation with concepts. Acknowledging the nature, in which the offering, the donor, and the recipient are indivisible in nature, is perfecting the accumulation beyond concepts.

RECITATION OF MANTRA

Now comes the recitation phases.

First there is an invocation:

> HUNG HRIH!
> In the essence mandala of bodhichitta,
> Gathering of deities reveling in wisdom magic,
> Without departing, remember your vajra samaya
> And bestow blessings, empowerments, and siddhis!

In the elaborate version of the sadhana, one invokes with verses for each of the deities of the three kayas, the twelve manifestations, and the dakas and dakinis. Here these are compressed into these four lines, which act as a general invocation.

Thus, beseech them. Then, with one-pointed concentration, say:

> Light radiates from the heart of the Crown Buddha Amitayus
>   above,
> Gathering the life essence of samsara and nirvana,
> Which dissolves into the vase in his hands.
> The flow of nectar falling from this vase
> Enters me through the gate of Brahma and fills my body.
> Purifying sickness, harm, misdeeds, and obscurations,

The twofold accomplishment is achieved.^ॐ
OM AMARANI JIVANTIYE SVAHA^ॐ

That was gathering the blessing for the benefit of oneself.^ॐ

This sadhana has three main purposes: accomplishing one's personal aim of gathering the blessings, emptying samsara for the benefit of others, and achieving the nondual intent of self and others. This verse is related to the first of these and deals with fulfilling your personal objective of longevity.

In Amitayus' heart center, upon a lotus and a moon disc, is a red letter HRIH surrounded by the syllables OM AMARANI JIVANTIYE SVAHA. The seed syllable HRIH and the encircling mantra all radiate five-colored light. All the life force and merit throughout samsara—the five elements, the potent essences, and so forth—and nirvana—wisdom; compassion; the capacity of all buddhas and bodhisattvas; the essences of the five elements; the essences of plants, flowers, trees, and so forth—is all gathered back by the light, just like bees gather honey into their hive. It all dissolves into the life vase held by Amitayus, filling it until it overflows with lustrous white nectar. This nectar flows directly into you, as Padmasambhava, through the crown of your head. It fills up your body just like a crystal vase filled with milk, purifying all sickness, evil influences, negative karma, and obscurations, so that the twofold siddhis are achieved. As you visualize, chant Amitayus' mantra of longevity, OM AMARANI JIVANTIYE SVAHA. If you are accumulating recitations in retreat, follow the terma root text, which says, *Chant this mantra 1.2 million times.*

The best sign of accomplishment is to meet the deity in actuality. Hearing the sound of the mantra is a sign of progress in samadhi. Another excellent sign is if the nectar on your shrine boils over or your butter lamp ignites by itself. The next best is to experience these things in a vision. The third best is to dream of the sun and the moon, of ascending the peak of a mountain, of a lake overflowing, of crops ripening, and so forth. All of these are indications of accomplishing immortality.

Light radiates from the heart of the Noble Tamer of Beings^ॐ
And pervades all the realms of the six kinds of beings.^ॐ
It purifies each of their disturbing emotions^ॐ
And turns them into forms of the Great Compassionate One.^ॐ

OM MANI PADME HUNG HRIH༔

That was the all-pervading activity for the benefit of others.༔

To accomplish the second intent, imagine that Avalokiteshvara is just above your head as described previously. In his heart center, is a six-petalled lotus flower with a moon disc resting on it. In the center of this is a white letter HRIH, and on each of the six petals is one of the syllables of OM MANI PADME HUNG. In the *Trinley Gyepa*, one imagines that each of these six syllables has its own distinct color and radiates light to one of the six realms. The beings in each realm are purified of their negative karma, obscurations, and habitual tendencies. Here it is all compressed into just four lines, and you imagine that the letter HRIH and the mantra simultaneously purify the six realms of samsara with rays of light and turn all beings into forms of Avalokiteshvara. You should accumulate one million repetitions of this mantra.

The signs of accomplishment are having spontaneous compassion and being able to benefit others in actuality. Next best is to dream that out of compassion you guide many beings to safety.

Next is:

In the heart center of myself,༔
The guru embodying all families,༔
There is a five-spoked golden vajra on a moon disc.༔
In its center is HRIH, encircled by the mantra.༔
Light radiating from it makes offerings to the noble ones༔
And gathers the blessings and siddhis into me.༔
By radiating again, the universe becomes a pure land༔
And the inner contents, all the beings contained in it, are forms of
    deities.༔
Resounding sounds are the tones of vajra mantras,༔
And thoughts are the luminous state of wakefulness;༔
Everything is the single mandala of nonduality.༔
OM AH HUNG VAJRA GURU PADMA SIDDHI HUNG༔

In that way, and without the duality of self and other,༔
Recite in the unity of development and completion.༔
Samaya.༔

Continue to imagine yourself as Padmasambhava, in the form that unifies appearance and emptiness—as visible yet insubstantial. In your heart center, there is a lotus and moon disc, upon which a golden five-pronged vajra stands upright. In the central sphere of the vajra is the syllable HRIH surrounded by the Vajra Guru mantra, OM AH HUNG BENZA GURU PADMA SIDDHI HUNG. The mantra is spelled anti-clockwise but spins in a clockwise direction. Here, your own bodily form is the samaya being, while the vajra is the wisdom being, and the syllable HRIH is the samadhi being. The HRIH and the mantra radiate light in all directions, thus making offerings and honoring all the buddhas and bodhisattvas of the ten directions and bringing back all the blessings, accomplishments, compassionate capability, and so forth. In other words, there is an exchange between the light radiating out in all directions and light coming back at the same time, which accomplishes the benefit for oneself. But light also radiates throughout the universe, transforming the perception of the world into a pure land, the inner contents of beings into deities, sounds into mantras, and thoughts into the luminous state of wakefulness. In other words, the recitation of one single mantra combines all four recitation intents of approach, full approach, accomplishment, and great accomplishment (the analogies for these are: the moon with a garland of stars, a revolving firebrand, the emissaries of the king, and a beehive breaking open).

There's a very profound instruction that Paltrül Rinpoche clarified, called the *Fourfold Stake of Recitation*. These four are: the stake of the deity, the stake of the mantra, the stake of emanating and absorbing rays of light, and the stake of unchanging samadhi. One can accomplish all of them while reciting this one mantra.

According to the oral tradition of the Old School (*Nyingma Kama*), one performs the recitation of each of the four intents individually with one mala round for each. However, according to the tradition of pith instructions, which is the specialty of Padmasambhava, they can all be combined into one or done alternately. It is quite flexible.

The seed syllable encircled by the Vajra Guru mantra, shining rays of light into all directions, corresponds to the approach, which is like the moon encircled by a garland of stars. When the moon rises in the sky, simultaneously you can see all the stars in all directions, vividly and distinctly.

The recitation intent of the emissaries of the king is when you imagine that the seed syllable and encircling mantra each send out countless rays of light in the ten directions to all buddhas and buddhafields surrounded by an infinite number of bodhisattvas. Then all these rays of light present offerings to their body, speech, and mind, invoking their blessings and compassion. Finally, the siddhis of the body, speech, and mind of all buddhas are drawn to you and dissolve into your forehead, throat, and heart centers.

The great accomplishment is like a beehive breaking open. All the syllables now resound with their own distinct sounds. They don't stand still any longer, but begin to spin and revolve, while sending out even more rays of light to all the buddhas making offerings, praises, and so forth. They extend even further, to any realm with sentient beings, dispelling and annihilating all obscurations, negative karma, habitual tendencies, and suffering—and transforming the six realms into pure lands. All sentient beings become male and female deities, their minds the awakened state, and so forth.

The stake of emanation and re-absorption, which is for all-encompassing activities, means that you are free to imagine whatever you want. When Shabkar Tsokdrug Rangdröl stayed in his retreat in Amdo (Northeastern Tibet), some young women, who had been robbed of all their possessions, including their food, came to him. Shabkar wanted to help them but could not escort them back to civilization, for he would have had to break his retreat vow. So, he tried something else instead. He visualized that rays of light emanated out from his heart center and touched his benefactors' hearts, causing the notion, "I must go and see the guru" to arise in their minds. Over the next couple of days, numerous people showed up at his retreat and safely escorted the women home. It really is true that once you accomplish the development stage, you can adapt your visualization to whatever is necessary. Then there are no restrictions as to what one is or isn't allowed to visualize. There is no limit to deity, mantra, and samadhi.

When you are doing a great accomplishment practice, a drubchen, the recitation is like a revolving firebrand. You visualize another mandala reflected in front of you, so you have self-visualization and front visualization simultaneously. Then, while reciting the mantra, you imagine that each syllable comes from your heart center, goes out of your mouth, travels through space, and enters the mouth of the corresponding deity in the sky before you. It enters their mouth, dissolves into the heart center, and then comes out through their navel. It then enters your navel and goes back up to your heart. The mantra chain continues circling in this way without break. From each of the syllables of this huge chain, rays of light stream out into all directions, transforming the universe into a pure land, sentient beings into male and female deities, and so forth.

If you have been introduced to the state of rigpa by a master and have recognized it, with the ability to remain unwavering from the basic nature of awareness during the sadhana, then it is perfectly fine, while reciting the mantra, to firmly plant the stake of unchanging samadhi, rather than deliberately focusing on conceptual attributes.

To chant the mantra Om ah hung vajra guru padma siddhi hung has immeasurable benefits. Padmasambhava himself said, "If you recite like this, your state of mind will be indivisible from mine." You should accumulate at least 100,000 for each syllable or 1.2 million—but it's best to do 4.5 million.

> *Having thus finished the approach recitation,*
> *Now comes the recitation of accomplishment and of great bliss.*

From forms of myself and the mandala deities,
Bodies are emanated, filling the universe.
Our speech, as songs of recitation, roars with the sound of
    mantras.
Our minds are the changeless state of luminosity.
The victorious ones throughout all directions and times are pleased
    by the offerings,
And the twofold purpose of beings in the three realms is achieved.
Everything is completely perfected
As the inconceivable great mudra mandala.
Om ah hung vajra guru padma totreng tsal vajra samaya jah siddhi
    pala hung ah

Sometimes "mount the horse" of melodious tune,
Sometimes sing the song of hung,
Especially perform the vajra recitation of great bliss,
While joining with the breath.
Samaya.

Here *my form* refers to the samaya being, namely you as Guru Rinpoche, who along with all the deities of the mandala, manifests countless replicas, which stream out in all directions filling the entire universe. Each syllable of the respective mantras resounds simultaneously and continuously. The various seed syllables also emanate light in all directions and resound as well. All the while, nothing and no one parts, or even wavers from, the state of primordial purity, the awakened state of all buddhas. With these rays of light, inexhaustible offerings emanate, pleasing the buddhas and bodhisattvas in all directions and purifying the negative karma, sufferings, obscurations, habitual tendencies, and so forth, of all sentient beings in the three realms of samsara. In this way, the twofold purpose is completely achieved and perfected.

Sometimes chant the Tötreng Tsal mantra with the tune unique to the tradition of Chokgyur Lingpa. It is said that chanting with a melody multiplies the effect of the mantra billions of times. What is more, the special *Chokling* melody for the Tötreng Tsal mantra has great qualities, like bringing one's conceptual mind to a halt just by hearing it. It captivates the attention and interrupts the flow of normal thinking.

The song of HUNG is the fivefold HUNG of five different colors. The visualization for that is explained in the extensive sadhana's *Recitation Manual*.

> Fivefold HUNG syllables from the letter HUNG in the heart centers
> Of myself and all the mandala figures
> Roar their thunderous self-sound,
> Pervading the entire phenomenal world.
> They make offerings to the victorious ones, gather back siddhis,
> And purify all beings' karmas and kleshas,
> Especially their clinging to ordinary experience.
> The main figure and the entire retinue sing the song of HUNG
> And, through this vajra melody,
> The experience of the wisdom of great bliss blazes forth
> And the supreme empowerment of awareness-expression is attained.

Imagining this, chant:

HUNG HUNG HUNG HUNG HUNG

Chant HUNG in sets of five, while combining the visualization with your breathing. While exhaling, imagine that the HUNGs stream out of your heart center, also in sets of five, filling and purifying the entire universe; you then inhale them along with your breath. There is a lot of explanation about how HUNG represents the awakened state of all the victorious ones. Its shape and features have profound meaning; but in short, HUNG purifies our attachment to ordinary concrete experiences.

The most profound way to perform *the vajra recitation of great bliss* is by unifying your breath and mind with the mental recitation of the mantra, while performing the vase breath.

This belongs to the accomplishment intent. Next comes the enactment of the activities.

Now comes the activity application.⸎

> The light radiating from my heart⸎
> Invokes the minds of the four families of dakas⸎
> Whose emanations and re-emanations pervade the universe,⸎
> Spontaneously fulfilling the four activities.⸎
> Harinisa racha hriya chitta hring hring dzah sarva siddhi phala
> hung⸎

At this point, rays of light emanate from Padmasambhava and touch the dakas and dakinis dwelling at the four gates of the mandala in their respective colors. This compels them to carry out the four activities of pacifying, increasing, magnetizing, and subjugating. If one performs this more elaborately, then the four recitations are separated, corresponding to the four times of day, the four directions, the four types of focus and attitude, and so forth.

Here it just says the Harinisa mantra, but in other places, Chokgyur Lingpa says that for specific purposes, like empowerments, and so forth, it should be appended to the end of the Tötreng Tsal mantra, OM AH HUNG VAJRA GURU PADMA TOTRENG TSAL VAJRA SAMAYA JAH SIDDHI PALA HUNG AH. The syllables of the Harinisa mantra are the essence or heart syllables of the dakas and dakinis of the four classes, so it is the mantra that attracts all the blessings and accomplishments.

> *Recite in that way. Apply the change of concentrations*⸎
> *As described in the Sheldam Nyingjang.*⸎
> *Samaya. Seal, seal, seal.*⸎

The *Sheldam Nyingjang* is the root text of *Barchey Künsel*. It explains how to change the mantra with the visualization, corresponding to the twelve manifestations, the dakas and dakinis, and so forth, in order to accomplish a specific need or aspiration. Both Khyentse and Kongtrül said that the *Sheldam Nyingjang* is like the treasury of a universal monarch, because it gives an abundance of instructions and various activity applications. It contains an incredible number of teachings for accomplishing the supreme and common siddhis, casting spells, making medicines, and so forth. Tulku Urgyen Rinpoche said that some of the recipes described at the end of the *Sheldam Nyingjang* for preparing medicine are incredibly effective, much more so than normal medicine.

In his commentary, Jamgön Kongtrül states that if you have been incapable of practicing perfectly, then you need to make some amendments. To make up for what you may have left out of the visualization, chant the Sanskrit Vowel mantra; to make up for any mispronunciations, missed words, and so forth, one chants the Sanskrit Consonant mantra; and to make up for mental distractions and the like, you repeat the Hundred Syllable mantra. You should also repeat the offering and praise verses. It is also a tradition to include the supplication *Barchey Lamsel, Clearing Obstacles from the Path,* and various Dharma protector offerings (*sölkha*), especially for the guardian of the teaching, *Tseringma,* and the guardian of the terma, *Khyung Tsünma.* You can also chant the *Narak Kongshak,* the *Mending Apology for Narak,* or the shorter *Jömey Dönshak,* the *Apology for the Ineffable Meaning.*

THE FEAST OFFERING BETWEEN SESSIONS

Between formal sessions, the most eminent way of perfecting the accumulation of merit is to perform the feast offering. *Feast* in Tibetan is *tsok,* which means "many gathered together." This refers to a gathering of male and female participants, all coming together to perform a feast. It is also a gathering of all kinds of food and drink as offerings. The Sanskrit word is *ganachakra. Gana* is "gathering," in the sense of feast. *Chakra* means "wheel;" the Tibetan word *khorlo* actually means "cutting into pieces," like a wheel of weapons. The *Light of Wisdom* explains that one gathers the accumulations of merit and wisdom and cuts to pieces whatever interrupts or prevents the perfection of the accumulation of merit and wisdom, namely all concepts of duality.

According to the tantras, a feast has many requirements, of which food and drink are indispensable. These are then heaped on top of either a human or animal skin. Terdag Lingpa said that performing a feast has many incredible virtues. These days, feasts are very pleasant, because there is a lot to eat and drink, often including wine and various meats.

In the terma text of the *Rigdzin Düpa* from the *Longchen Nyingtik*, it says liquor and meat are indispensable ingredients for the feast offering. Paltrül Rinpoche, however, said that placing the flesh of sentient beings in front of the wisdom deities is like slaying a child and giving its flesh to its mother. Many people agree with him and will never include meat in the feast offering. Personally, I am happy when there is no meat in the feast offering. At the same time, the teachings do not prohibit it, and often they encourage its inclusion. The exact type of meat to offer, like the five meats and the five nectars, is too complex an issue to go into here.

> RAM YAM KAM᳴
> The seed syllable in the heart center of myself visualized as the
>   deity᳴
> Emanates RAM YAM KAM, purifying the clinging to offering articles
>   as being real.᳴
> The light from the three syllables transforms them into wisdom
>   nectar,᳴
> Which becomes an offering cloud of desirable objects filling the
>   sky.᳴
> OM AH HUNG᳴

Still visualizing yourself as Padmasambhava, emanate RAM YAM KAM from your heart center. RAM is the fire that burns all the material offerings to ash; YAM is the wind, scattering the ashes into all directions; and finally, KAM is the flood of water rinsing away anything that remains. Next, visualize an enormous skull cup the size of the billionfold universe resting on a tripod. Within this skull cup are offerings of the five meats and nectars. Underneath is wisdom fire being fanned by the wisdom wind. As the skull cup heats up, the offerings melt together and boil. Then, from the rising steam, the three syllables OM AH HUNG invoke all the blessings of the body, speech, and mind of all the buddhas. It returns in the form of the nectar of body, speech, and mind. These wisdom qualities become indivisible from the samaya substance, creating an inexhaustible ocean of nectar. In this way, the wisdom and samaya beings are indivisible within this nectar. We should imagine this nectar has such a quality that even a single drop flung into the air can emanate cloud banks of desirable objects.

The vajra master is sitting in the center facing down the row. On his right side are the male tantrikas and on his left are the female tantrikas. Children should sit facing the vajra master, and all the feast articles should be piled up in the center.

First, the vajra server consecrates the feast articles, using vajra urine. If that were done in a normal way, no one would even think of eating any of the feast. However, transcending concepts is one of the most vital aspects of a feast offering. At the beginning of the feast offering, you should totally transcend such concepts as clean and unclean, good and bad, edible and inedible, and so forth. Next, you invite the guests with:

> HUNG HUNG HUNG
> Ocean-like assembly of Trikaya Jinas,
> Please manifest from the unconstructed state of luminosity.
> To enable us to accumulate merit and purify obscurations,
> Please come, reveling in your wisdom magic.
> VAJRA SAMAYA JAH JAH

Rays of light from the heart center of Padmasambhava invite the guests, who are his own gurus and yidams as well as the dakas, dakinis, protectors of the wisdom classes, and so forth. They all arrive, filling the immeasurable palace right up to the ceiling, like cloud banks.

There are three steps to the feast. The first is presenting the feast:

> OM AH HUNG
> The essence of the feast offering is a cloud bank of wisdom nectar
> In the form of goddesses with desirable objects filling the sky.
> May this enjoyment of unconditioned great bliss
> Please you, assembly of mandala deities of the Three Roots.
> SARVA GANA CHAKRA PUJA HOH

Here, countless offering goddesses make offerings to all the assembled guests. This verse is repeated three times. It pleases the gurus, mends samayas with the yidams, and removes grudges of the dharma protectors; it also mends the samayas and purifies the male and female practitioners, and so forth.

The second part of the feast is the apology and mending. In our tradition, we insert the chant known as *Kangwa Yushelma, The Turquoise-Covered Tsogkhang Pema*, written by Jamgön Kongtrül. Its words and meaning are both exquisite. I requested Dilgo Khyentse Rinpoche to write an explanation of it, but he never completed it. In front of all the guests, we apologize as follows:

> Hoᴴ
> For the misdeeds, veils, faults, and failings created since
>   beginningless time
> And especially for the infractions and violations
> Of the root and branch samayas,
> I apologize and mend them by offering this feast of desirable
>   objects!
> Samaya shuddhe aʜ

We purify breaches of samaya mentally; just going through the motions and repeating the words will not purify anything. The best way to mend any breach is with the view that transcends the notion of breaking, and so forth. At the very least, you should have deep-felt regret and remorse for any transgressions.

The last part of the feast is the "deliverance." The *Light of Wisdom* describes the required qualifications of a vajra master for performing a true deliverance. It also details the seven acts of transgression, the tenfold objects that qualify someone to be delivered, the methods of delivering, and so forth. Here, however, the deliverance is summarized in the following verse:

> Hung
> Vajra Gingkara, heart emanation of Palchen Heruka,
> Summon and dissolve the demons and obstructors of dualistic
>   fixation!
> Freeing them into luminous space, their flesh, blood, and bones
> I present to the assembly of the mandala deities of the Three
>   Roots.

SARVA BIGHANAN SHATRUN MARAYA KHA KHA KHAHI KHAHI
HA HA HI HI HUNG HUNG PHAT

These days, deliverance is simply the portion of the feast one puts aside. It is now placed in front of the vajra master, who performs a specific act of summoning. Visualize that the enemies and obstructors, which are the manifestation of ego-clinging, the three poisons, and the five negative emotions, are summoned and dissolved into a symbolic receptacle (*lingam*). The ones who perform the summoning are emanations of the chief figure, who in this case is Palchen Heruka, with his male and female *gings*. The obstructors and demons being summoned and gathered here represent the clinging to perceiver and perceived, ego-clinging, and so forth. Those are the demons. For the deliverance, visualize that the enemies and obstructor demons are being stabbed in the heart of delusion with the Kilaya dagger; their life force and merit dissolve into you. Their consciousness, delivered into the realm of dharmadhatu, dissolves indivisibly with the awakened state of the chief figure, and so forth. There are many necessary aspects of this visualization here. The remnants—the flesh, blood, bones, and so forth that remain after the spirit has left the body upon deliverance—are offered for the enjoyment of all the deities. That is called the final part of the feast, the deliverance.

Generally speaking, the two unique features of Vajrayana practice are union and deliverance, but if they are practiced literally, there is something terribly wrong. A more complete explanation of deliverance would include some very horrifying details.

At the end of the deliverance offering, one enjoys the feast ingredients and articles, as the substance of siddhi. The terma root text says this should be done within the state of bliss and emptiness, maintaining the dignity of the deity. Enjoying the feast as a deity in the state of blissful emptiness is very significant. If the vajra master has a high level of realization, then this can be accompanied by vajra song and dance.

Having enjoyed the feast, you make a residual offering without hoarding or keeping anything for later. The residual offering is first consecrated with the breath, or actually the vapor from the mouth of Palchen Heruka, the central figure of this mandala. In the best case, the vajra master first takes some of the food and then spits it out again over the residual offering. These days, however, the residual is usually consecrated with the space mudra instead, as one chants:

Внуо⸗

Servants of Palchen, host of messengers,⸗

Accept this enjoyment of residuals,⸗

And according to your past vows,⸗

Remove all obstacles and increase favorable conditions.⸗

Мама нкимс нкимс ваlingta кнани⸗

There are many deities and participants who have taken the pledge to remain at the periphery of the mandala and not participate in the central part. They will not partake of the main offerings but only the remnants, so the remnants should be carefully placed seventy-two steps away. If you are staying in retreat, then you save the remnants until the end of your retreat, when you can put them at the appropriate distance.

After this, make offerings and praise, pray for siddhis, and apologize for faults.⸗

By HUNG *dissolve the wisdom mandala into basic space.*⸗

By PHAT *manifest the deity and continue activities.*⸗

At the end of the feast offering, repeat the verses for offering and praise, followed by the chant known as *Nyingpo Jangchub Sem*. If the feast ritual has been conducted over several days, then you should receive the siddhis, but this is not necessary for a short, occasional practice. Next, apologize for any mistakes you may have made by chanting the *Rigdzin Khyilkhor*. If you have a shrine, you should perform the *Tenshuk*[16]

Then, while chanting the triple HUNG, you imagine that the buddha-field dissolves into the celestial palace, the celestial palace into the surrounding deities, and the surrounding deities into the central figure of Padmasambhava. Padmasambhava then slowly dissolves into the seed syllable in his heart center, then the seed syllable itself vanishes, at which point you simply remain in equanimity. As you utter the triple PHAT, just like a fish jumping out of water, you re-emerge in the form of Padmasambhava, marked with OM AH HUNG at your three places. This dissolution and re-emergence purifies the habitual tendencies for passing away and taking rebirth.

---

16 These can all be found in various chants published by Rangjung Yeshe. Translation and Publications.

CONCLUSION

Dedication of Merit and Aspirations

Dedicate the merit and make aspirations:⸎

> Hoн⸎
> By the power of accomplishing the mandala of the Vidyadhara
>   Guru,⸎
> May I and all the infinite sentient beings without exception⸎
> Spontaneously accomplish the four kinds of activities⸎
> And be liberated into the luminous space of dharmakaya!⸎

When chanting the dedication and aspirations, your attitude should be no different from that of Manjushri or the Bodhisattva Samantabhadra. Ideally, if you know how, you should perform the ultimate dedication, which guarantees that any aspirations you make will be accomplished.

For the next four lines, imagine that all the buddhas and bodhisattvas scatter flowers. Gods and goddesses perform songs, dances, and so forth. Then chant the verse of auspiciousness:

> May the blessing of the root and lineage gurus enter my heart!⸎
> May the yidams and dakinis accompany me like a shadow follows
>   the body!⸎
> May the dharma protectors and guardians dispel all obstacles!⸎
> May there be the auspiciousness of attaining the supreme and
>   common siddhis!⸎

> *In between sessions, always increase*⸎
> *The two accumulations of merit and wisdom.*⸎
> *Especially train in devotion to the guru*⸎
> *And in the unity of basic space and awareness.*⸎
> *Samaya.*⸎

Every kind of Dharma practice is included in these last four lines. If you practice according to these four lines, you will fulfill all your dharmic aims. The accumulations of merit and wisdom include all nine vehicles;

among these, the highest vehicle, Ati Yoga, is the most simple to train in and the most convenient. In an instant, one can awaken to complete enlightenment, fulfilling all of one's purposes. In other words, it is a teaching on how to attain immediate buddhahood.

Specifically, devotion to the guru is indispensable on the path of *Tukdrub Barchey Künsel*. Unless you have sincere devotion and confidence that your root guru is indivisible from the mind of Padmasambhava in person, you will not truly enter the stream of blessings. Without devotion, the blessings wither. Expecting to receive blessings without devotion is fruitless. There is no higher practice than devotion to your guru. The proper way to perform any drubchen or feast offering is to combine it with guru devotion, mingling your mind with the guru's as basic space and awareness. Therefore, always keep devotion to the guru, and accomplishment will be guaranteed. To do this, regard your guru as someone very special, obey his or her every command, perceive that whatever he or she does is perfect, and regard him or her as the embodiment of all objects of refuge.

COLOPHON

This quintessence of all the profound teachings:
Is easy to apply and simple to practice, bringing swift blessings.:
It will remove obstacles, increase experience and realization,:
And perfect the activities of taming beings.:
Samaya. Seal, seal, seal.:

I, Chokgyur Dechen Lingpa, revealed this from beneath the foot of Palchen Heruka at *Da-Nying Khala Rong-Go* on the tenth day of the ninth
month in the year of the Earth Monkey (7.11.1848). Having kept the seal
of secrecy for eight years, on the tenth day of the tenth month at the Kar-
tika Constellation in the year of the Wood Hare (19.11.1855), accompanied by perfect conditions of place and timing, I decoded the letters from
the wisdom dakinis' secret script, which were written down by Khyentse
Wangpo, the joyful servant of the Lotus-Born Guru. May there always be
happiness!

Near the Nangchen town of Shonda, in eastern Tibet, there is a cliff
called *Da-Nying Khala Rong-Go*, with the shape of Palchen Heruka, or
Vajra Kilaya, on it. Chokgyur Lingpa revealed the *Tukdrub Barchey Künsel* from below the large, brown boulder forming the foot of that figure.
Chokgyur Lingpa was born in the Ox year, so he would have been about
twenty-five-years old at the time. He kept this terma secret for eight
years; then, in the Wood Hare year, he decoded the dakini script, and
Jamyang Khyentse Wangpo wrote it down. Around this time, Jamyang
Khyentse had a dream, in which he came to a vast plain where hundreds
of thousands of people were building stairs of various heights. He asked,
"What are you doing?" They replied, "We are building a staircase for
Padmasambhava's arrival." Even though they were all extremely indus-
trious, they didn't succeed, and it was said that only Chokgyur Lingpa
together with Jamyang Khyentse and Kongtrül could build a workable
staircase. Jamgön Kongtrül said that this dream had a special significance
and meaning, and I feel that the *Tukdrub Barchey Künsel* can still bring
great benefit.

Concluding Remarks

The disciple's job is to train in the actuality of the samadhi of suchness; but, to be honest, few people are able to remain in samadhi while visualizing. The teacher's job is to explain it, and I feel I have tried my best. I have spelled it out as best as one can, and there's not much beyond that, really. If you are not able to train in actuality in the samadhi of suchness, then train in the second class way, in the resemblance of it. When that is the case, you have no choice but to train conceptually in imagining what it is supposed to be like. And imagining is just thinking, right? Whatever appears and exists, all phenomena, is emptiness. That's a thought, right? So you should do your best to mimic the tradition of the pith instructions and keep your body straight but relaxed, your eyes mingling with space, your mind indivisible from awareness and emptiness, your tongue not touching the palate, and so forth. That is called the tradition of pith instruction, given as a way to approach that. Honestly speaking, the reality of this does not often happen during the visualization practice. But, on the other hand, how much you fool yourself is up to you.

Then, even if you don't understand all the symbolism, at least you are forming a link. As long as you are trying your best, your practice will slowly advance, and you will gain confidence both in yourself and in the teachings. Your devotion to the guru will become ever more profound. In the beginning, just trust that you are already there and proceed from that point. If you have trust and take one step after another, sooner or later you will reach your destination. No matter how feeble you are, if you continue to practice, you will get closer and closer to the goal. You may not reach it this lifetime, but at least you will be moving in the right direction and forging a link.

Other people approach sadhana practice thinking they have to be perfect from the beginning; but as with most things in life, this just isn't possible. You must start where you are and continue to practice, while aiming towards perfection. On the other hand, if you start out with a closed mind, thinking, "Whatever I am unable to do right now is not really necessary. It is useless, and I don't want to deal with it," then you will never progress. Some teachers may say, "Just believe it is all there. It is okay, you don't really need to try too hard." However, that is definitely not the authentic way, as described in the basic scriptures of the *Nyingma* tradition, such as the *Magical Net Tantra (Mayajala)*. *The Guhyagarbha Tantra* explains very precisely and exactly what is necessary and what the measure of perfection is when performing the group assembly sadhana, the elaborate version of the mandala, the mudras, the mantras, and everything else.

Every day we chant the lineage prayer, *Kunsang Dorsem,* which contains the names of the great masters of the lineage, who attained accomplishment by practicing the *Magical Net Tantra*. Great masters, like Longchenpa and Rongdzom Pandita, spent their entire lives practicing the *Magical Net,* and Chokgyur Lingpa's termas are in perfect harmony with these original tantras. At the beginning of the empowerment, the master puts on the crown and explains that this teaching is combined with the intent of the tantras, authenticated by the strength of the nature of things, and so forth.

Of course, there can be many types of Buddhist teachers; some are good, some are bad; they are people. You should not lean exclusively on one teacher's words as being the only thing; there is nothing that special about one person's statement. Even if it's written down, it's just somebody's opinion, which doesn't make it more special. On the other hand, you can consider the tantras themselves, like the *Magical Net,* as being really special. You can verify what is correct or incorrect through the original scriptures, where you authenticate or measure the practice, and through your own intelligence as well. If you pay attention to the exact purpose of each development stage aspect, how it purifies habitual tendencies and prepares for the completion stage and enlightenment, you will see the necessity of each feature. Otherwise, you can place a torma on the shrine, play the damaru and bell, and say the sounds without even thinking about what it means, like some people do, going through the motions meaninglessly.

The most important point is to try one's best. The Buddha himself taught that one should listen to the teachings and instruction, think about what has been taught, clarify it in one's own mind, and then actually apply the teachings in one's life.

Sometimes it appears inevitable that over time traditions will wane and people's practice will become superficial. That is how it goes. Many masters write that drubchens and major ceremonies these days are mere reflections of what they once were. It is said that when Padmasambhava and King Jah performed the ganachakra and drubchen rituals, they could magically conjure the mandala in mid-air. Just by chanting Benza Samadza, all the wisdom beings would appear. But even our feeble versions are still better than nothing, because, really, if the practices disappeared altogether, what would be left? Sadly, time appears to be running out. The great masters are passing away one after the other, and all the great qualities of purity, goodness, and wisdom seem to be vanishing with them. There are also a lot of internal disputes nowadays. In fact, the Buddha said that the Dharma can only be ruined from within—not from the outside, but from disagreements among the sangha.

Personally, I would prefer if the reflection could at least remain for a little while longer. Whether or not the teachings remain depends upon people studying and reflecting, not only on the extensive Sutra teachings, but also on the Vajrayana. Just hanging around Dharma centers and visiting lamas without studying, reflecting, and practicing is not going to amount to much.

I would like to say one last thing: Please do not think you only need to practice thirty minutes or so a day together with the occasional retreat. You should apply yourself 100 percent every minute of every day.

Also don't divide your time, where you have special time for practicing and the rest of the time you're not practicing. The whole time is practice, because then we can bring the fruition to maturity. Otherwise, it's not going to be that fruitful to just practice this month and that month out of the year and totally give up practice the rest of the time. Of course, it gives positive imprints, but on the tenth and twenty-fifth days, we should not break the special practice. It's actually one of the samayas of Padmasambhava to never interrupt the practice of the tenth day of the lunar month and to always keep the vajra and the skull cup. The *Tukdrub Trinley Nyingpo* is very good to practice on the tenth day.

NOTES ON COMPLETING THE RECITATION WITHIN THIRTY-FIVE DAYS

Based on Trinley Nyingpo,
The Yoga of the Essential Activity
The Short Practice Manual of Tukdrub

Jamyang Khyentse Wangpo

OM SVASTI

If you are to perform the recitation of *Tukdrub* in a little more than a month, arrange in front of yourself any suitable image of the Precious Master, either a painted or sculpted one. In front of that, you should place the *Shining Jewel* torma with amrita on its right and rakta on its left. Arrange the seven enjoyments in front of that as well. To the right of the amrita, place the torma for the teaching guardian *Tseringma*, which has upon its central bulb a white torma with four petals, with one morsel on each of the four sides of the bulb. It is surrounded by pills in the intermediate spaces and has a white staff. To the left of the rakta, place the torma of the treasure guardian *Kharak Khyung Tsünma,* a triangular red torma with ornaments. Triangular pellets surround this torma.

Following this, at the beginning of the afternoon session, finish as far as the guru yoga, in accordance with the liturgy for preliminaries, the *Seed of Supreme Enlightenment*. Carry out the refuge, bodhichitta, and expulsion of the obstructors, as contained within the *Extensive Practice Manual*, planting the poles at the time of throwing the gektor outside. Return back inside and proceed with the visualization of the protection circle and the rest of the Seven Preliminary Points.

For the main part, practice up to the praises, following the *Extensive* or *Short Practice Manual,* whichever is suitable. Then open the recitation mansion and recite an appropriate number of mantras. Chant the *Barchey Lamsel* once. If you are following the *Extensive Practice Manual*, make praises and dissolve the recitation mansion according to that text. Or, if you are following the *Daily Practice*, make short offerings and praises; after three repetitions of the Hundred Syllables, dissolve the front visualization into yourself with JA HUNG BAM HO. Carry out the dissolution with the triple HUNG and the emergence with the triple PHAT. Then chant the dedication, aspiration, and utterance of auspiciousness.

For the evening session, carry out the refuge, bodhichitta, and consecration of offerings, according to the *Short Practice Manual*. Follow the root text of the *Short Practice Manual*, as above, and, in the state of dissolving with the triple HUNG, begin the yoga of sleep.

Emerge from that state as the deity the next morning and carry out the preliminaries. Focus on refuge for one day, while concluding each session by reciting some repetitions of the bodhichitta verses and the Seven Branches. Proceed with the meditation and recitation of Vajrasattva, and so forth, for the sake of continuity, ideally doing four sessions a day. Then do one day of the meditation and recitation of Vajrasattva.

Since the guru yoga here serves as the outer means of accomplishment, emphasize it by doing it for three days. On the first day, chiefly perform mandala offerings. On the second day, make the supplications *Düsum Sangye* and *Barchey Lamsel*. On the third day, practice primarily the Vajra Guru recitation and the visualization for receiving empowerments. For the sake of continuity while practicing the preliminaries, conclude each session with the *Medium Practice Manual*, beginning with the deity visualization and ending with dedication, aspiration, and utterance of auspiciousness. Having thus finished five days of preliminaries, begin the main part.

When carrying out the main practice, do the preliminaries once before the refuge at the beginning of the first session. In the other sessions, do the refuge and bodhichitta of the *Short Practice Manual* three times. When expelling the obstructors, change the words *Take this torma* to *Don't remain here*. Continue up to the consecration of offerings in the usual way; then do the deity visualization. At the end of the praises, open up the recitation mansion. To begin with, chiefly recite Amarani mantras for seven days; then chiefly recite Mani mantras for seven days. After that, complete 400,000 Vajra Guru mantras, the principal recitation. This is of utmost importance. This seems to require approximately ten days.

While completing these, it will suffice to do one rosary for each of the other mantra recitations to maintain continuity.

Finally, take three days for the Tötreng Tsal mantra, which signifies accomplisment. For the activity application, recite the appended Harinisa mantra for about one day. At the end of the session, recite the Ali-Kali and Om Yedharma mantras three times, in order to amend the duplications and omissions of the mantra and to increase the blessings. Make offerings and praises and recite the *Barchey Lamsel* once and the Hundred Syllables three times.

Dissolve the recitation mansion with the triple HUNG and then re-emerge with the triple PHAT. Chant the verses for the dedication, aspiration, and utterance of auspiciousness.

In particular, in your afternoon session after *Barchey Lamsel,* follow the *Extensive Practice Manual* from the consecration of the feast articles through the liberation offering. At that point, recite the petition offering of *Tseringma* up to the praise and then the petition offering of *Kharak Khyung Tsünma*. At the end of that, chant any suitable supplications to Orgyen Guru Rinpoche, such as *Barchey Lamsel* and *Sampa Lhündrub*. Then chant the verse for the residuals. However, as tradition holds, you should not take the residual torma outside before the retreat is finished; collect it in a container instead. Following the ritual for the residuals, make offerings and praises, repeat the Hundred Syllables, dissolve the recitation mansion, and so forth, as above.

The *Short Practice Manual* is sufficient for daily use. On the tenth day of the waxing and waning moon in the afternoon session, perform the *Extensive Practice Manual,* and so forth. It is excellent if you can chant the *Tseringma* mending prayer, prayers for the mending of disharmony, and the petition offering to the *Tenma* goddesses.

For the prayer of mending disharmony related to *Tseringma,* put amrita in a skull cup mixed with mendrub and a prime serving of wine. For the petition to the *Tenma*, the *serkyem* alone will suffice.

Finally, on the day before finishing retreat, if you don't do the fire puja, focus on reciting as much as you can—one thousand, for example— of the Hundred Syllables at the end of all four sessions, in order to amend duplications and omissions of the mantra. In the evening on that day, make new offerings and lay out an abundance of whatever feast articles you have. Getting up earlier the next morning, follow the root text of the *Extensive* or *Short Practice Manual*, whichever you find suitable, and complete as much recitation as you can. After that, do the *Barchey Lamsel* and make elaborate offerings, praises, and confessions of faults.

According to the *Extensive Practice Manual,* at the time of receiving the siddhis, instantaneously visualize the torma as the deities, touch it to your three places, and eat a little. Dissolve the recitation mansion and so forth. It is the tradition to receive the siddhis at daybreak.

After that, follow either the *Extensive* or *Short Practice Manual,* as you find suitable, and perform the feast offering in the manner of a thanksgiving as much as you can—for example, one hundred times. If you do carry out the hundredfold feast offering, go through to the residual offering each time, following the *Extensive Practice Manual,* while continuing to save the residuals. At the end, send out the residual, according to the *Extensive Practice Manual,* and also send out all the residual offerings gathered earlier. Finally, perform the invocation, covenant, and so on, through the verses of auspiciousness, according to the *Extensive Practice Manual*.

This much recitation practice is feasible and also sufficient. It seems like you can complete it within approximately one month and five days.

This was composed by Khyentse Wangpo. May it be virtuous.

CONDENSED TEACHINGS ON THE TRINLEY NYINGPO THIRTY-FIVE-DAY RETREAT

Lama Putsi Pema Tashi

Editor's note: This teaching has been condensed, in order to not dupli-cate material. The explanations on the different aspects of the sadhana have been deleted, as they appear very extensively in Orgyen Topgyal Rinpoche's commentary on the *Trinley Nyingpo*. Points that have a differ-ent syle of explanation have been included, as well as all of the pertinent material relating to the thirty-five-day retreat.

PRELUDE

If you do not have time to practice the *Trinley Nyingpo* sadhana in its more elaborate version, known as the *Trinley Gyepa*, you can perform a sadhana found in the *Chokling Tersar,* called the *Thirty-Five-Day Practice*, composed by Jamyang Khyentse Wangpo. Here you can practice the abbreviated *Trinley Nyingpo* in a more extensive way. It is called the *Da-chig zhag-nga*, which means "one month and five days," during which you engage in the ngöndro, the preliminaries, and the main practice, itself, in a complete manner.

These are a few notes on how to practice the short version of the *Tukdrub* sadhana, based on the *Trinley Nyingpo*, in which you do the recitation in a suitable way for one month and five days.

First, place a tangka or statue of Guru Rinpoche on the shrine in front of you. Here, he is called Lobpön Rinpoche, the "Precious Master." In front of and beneath him, as seen from the shrine's point of view, place the torma called *Rinchen Barwa*, or *Shining Jewel,* which is the general torma of the *Tukdrub*. To the right of this torma, place the amrita, and to the left, place the rakta. In the very front, set out the seven general offerings, such as water, rice, and so forth. This is the simple way of arranging the shrine.

You should also have a *Tseringma* torma in the center of the shrine. This torma can either be very simple or elaborate, where it has four lower levels; either style is fine. The sphere of the torma is white. It has four petals and also small pellets in the four directions of the sphere as well as in the intermediate directions. This torma symbolizes the five *Tseringma* sisters. The torma should be placed to the right of the amrita.

The other protector is called *Kharak Khyung Tsünma*. *Tseringma* is called the guardian of the teachings (*kasung*), while *Kharak Khyung Tsünma* is called the guardian of the terma (*tersung*). The torma for *Kharak Khyung Tsünma* should be placed on the other side of the shrine, to the left of the rakta. It is a red crescent-shaped torma encircled by pellets.

It isn't written down here, but there is something else we should remember. Since we are doing this as a retreat, we should draw a white swastika on the floor under our meditation cushion. On the ceiling above our head, we should tie a packet of sacraments, such as mendrub and a bit of hair from our root guru. Doing this will help us avoid interferences, such as illness, and complete the practice.

If we are doing this practice as a thirty-five-day retreat, we should begin during the waning of the moon, meaning between the twentieth and thirtieth of the Tibetan lunar calendar. We should finish the retreat at the beginning of the month, between the first and the fifth. The first fifteen days of the month in the Tibetan calendar are called the waxing period, while the last fifteen days are called the waning period.

Closing the door, you should begin the retreat in the evening. Begin the practice by chanting the supplication to the lineage masters, first the general supplications and then the specific ones for *Barchey Künsel*. After this, it is good if you can offer the white torma (*kartor*) in a general way.

Then, begin with the preliminaries, called the *Seed of Supreme Enlightenment*. Start from the very beginning and go all the way through, including the guru yoga section. It was composed by Jamyang Khyentse Wangpo and later expanded and lengthened slightly by Tersey Tulku, the incarnation of the son of Chokgyur Lingpa. Tersey Tulku was also Tulku Urgyen's uncle. Both versions of this text, Jamyang Khyentse Wangpo's and Tersey Tulku's, are found in the *Chokling Tersar*.

PRELIMINARIES

When starting retreat, you begin by chanting the verses of refuge and bodhichitta up to and including the guru yoga verses found in the *Seed of Supreme Enlightenment*. After that, you start again with refuge and bodhichitta, expelling the obstructors, and so forth, while reading from the extensive sadhana, the *Trinley Gyepa*. If you do not have the long sadhana, it is okay to chant the same sections from the *Trinley Nyingpo*.

There is a little text of appended details that we use in conjunction with the *Trinley Nyingpo*. It's called the *Zurdeb*, the *Appended Details*, written by Jamyang Khyentse Wangpo. This text has extra lines that you should insert, at certain points, into the *Trinley Nyingpo*. As the first insert explains, visualize yourself in front of the refuge assembly, with light rays radiating from the HRIH in your heart center throughout the ten directions, calling upon the samayas of all the buddhas, bodhisattvas, and gurus. By saying VAJRA SAMAYA JAH, you invite them to appear in the sky before you.

At this time, you imagine the white letter HRIH in the center of your heart. Of course, you should always think of yourselves as the deity and keep the pride of being the deity. So, you are Guru Rinpoche, and the light from your heart invokes the vows made in the past by the gurus, buddhas, and bodhisattvas. Therefore, you should imagine that they all respond, by appearing in the sky before you. If we just imagine that all the buddhas and their spiritual sons have arrived and are in our presence, then they are actually there. The Buddha himself said he will be right in front of whoever thinks of him.

In truth, there is nothing the buddhas and bodhisattvas don't know. Therefore, whenever someone supplicates them, they know this immediately. It doesn't matter if you are among a group of one hundred people. When the rays of light emanate from your heart, the refuge will still appear before you. Most of you have already heard the extensive explanation of how to take refuge and so forth, when you received teachings on the preliminaries. Whether we are chanting from the extensive version of the *Trinley Gyepa* or from the *Trinley Nyingpo* together with the Seven Branches, the visualization stays the same.

The main difference between "outsiders" and "insiders," meaning Buddhists and non-Buddhists, is the act of taking refuge. This really marks the difference, because non-Buddhists don't rely on the Three Jewels, while Buddhists do. The very moment a few strands of our hair are clipped, the dividing line is drawn between being Buddhist or not.

After refuge comes bodhichitta. These are both extremely important components of any sadhana practice. They are the foundation and very basis of all practice. We need a firm foundation, just like when we build a house of many stories. Without a very solid foundation, the house will be in danger of collapsing. During the winter in Tibet, it is possible to construct even a very large house on top of the frozen ice, and it will remain firm until spring and summer arrive and the ice melts. Then the whole structure will begin to shake and fall apart. So refuge, especially, is the very basis of all Buddhist practice.

At the conclusion of taking refuge and forming the bodhisattva resolve, where the text says JAH HUNG BAM HOH, imagine the objects of refuge dissolving into you. The *Thirty-Five-Day Practice* text mentions dispelling the obstructors. In order to give the obstructor's torma and erect the poles, there are various lines to chant in the text.

If we are in retreat, this is the time when we erect the poles in the four cardinal directions for the *Four Guardian Kings*. When we set up the poles of the four kings in the four directions, or simply place a single placard at the doorway with them painted on it, we have created a dividing line. No one crosses this line, either going in or out. We imagine the four kings are truly present as guardians who prevent obstacles from entering and blessings from slipping out. It's like having a good watchdog at the front gate. We also take the vow or pledge to not go outside or let other people come inside. These poles are erected at the outset of a drubchen, and we do the same for our retreat.

These days, it is difficult to make a drubchen really strict, due to the time and setting. It will not suit our surrounding environment, but drubchens performed in Tibet were done exactly according to the book. From the time the poles were set up, no one could leave the circumscribed area, and no one from the outside could enter—without exception. Not even food or supplies were allowed in or out. Participants in a drubchen were not permitted to communicate with anyone outside the mandala. A specially appointed "go-between" would pass on any messages from outside and convey any responses from within. If something really had to be brought in, a special *gek-trey* would be pronounced over it to dispel any obstructors, and then it could be brought in.

At this point, if you knew that someone who you had to meet would unavoidably arrive later, you would imagine that this person had been granted entry from the very beginning of the drubchen, permitting them to arrive later. Jamgön Kongtrül said, "If you erect a pole, but don't respect its significance and just talk to whoever comes by or just stroll out whenever you please, there is no point in erecting a pole at all. It is meaningless. If you erect a pole to the four kings, you should not cross it or let others from outside do so."

After erecting the poles, you return inside, sit down, and visualize the protection circle. Then you begin with the seven preliminary points found in the instructions of the extensive *Trinley Gyepa*. If you are only doing the *Trinley Nyingpo* sadhana, you just continue by blessing the offering articles and bringing down the resplendence according to the text.

Cast off the obstructors and create the protection circle to dispel disharmonious circumstances. Consecrating the articles and bringing down the resplendence improve or increase positive conditions.

All sadhanas have three sections—the preparation, the main part, and the conclusion. In this case, we have now finished the preparation.

Main Part

According to the commentary, after having completed the seven points of the preliminaries, you proceed with the main part of the sadhana text up to the praises, whether it is extensive or condensed. Since this is a teaching on the condensed version, the main part begins with AH and the visualization of the deities. The letter AH represents great emptiness, the state of nonarising of all phenomena. Since the very beginning, all phenomena are totally free from mental constructs. By uttering the syllable AH, we just remain in the state in which things are as they are.

There are a few major points for the main part of development stage: the three samadhis, the visualization of the celestial palace, the visualization of the deities, and the empowerment and consecration.

The Three Samadhis

In development stage, the three samadhis are actually the most important aspect. They are the samadhi of suchness, the samadhi of illumination, and the samadhi of the seed syllable.

In the *Trinley Nyingpo*, the first line refers to the samadhi of suchness:

> Dharmakaya's basic space of suchness is the realm of luminous wakefulness.

The next line refers to the samadhi of illumination:

> Sambhogakaya's unceasing illumination is compassionate expression.

The third line refers to the samadhi of the seed syllable:

> Nirmanakaya's seed samadhi is the white HRIH.

It is said that one should erect the framework of the three samadhis in the same way one pitches a tent. The three samadhis are explained in

Tibetan in terms of what is to be purified, that which purifies, and the outcome of purification.

The first, the samadhi of suchness, purifies the experience of dying. At some point or another, we are going to die. The experiences that occur while we pass away can be purified by means of training in the samadhi of suchness. There are different bardo states, which include the bardos of death, dharmata, and becoming. These states occur from the moment of leaving the body up until and including the moment of taking rebirth within one of the six realms. Some beings remain in the bardo of becoming for a very short period and some remain for a long time, but generally speaking it lasts about forty-nine days. Training in the samadhi of illumination purifies the bardo state. At some point, we reconnect with a new life in a womb, egg, or such, and this birth process is purified by the samadhi of the seed syllable.

The outcome of the three samadhis is attaining the three kayas: the samadhi of suchness leads to realizing the dharmakaya, the samadhi of illumination leads to realizing the sambhogakaya, and the samadhi of the seed syllable leads to realizing the nirmanakaya.

The samadhi of suchness is necessary as long as we have something to purify when our physical body, composed of the four elements, passes away. During the death process, the power of these four elements begins to dissipate: earth dissolves into water, water into fire, fire into wind, wind into space, and space into consciousness. At that point, there is a moment called the "dharmakaya of death," which is luminous cognizance. Ordinary people fall unconscious, if they do not recognize this moment as the basic state of all things, which is empty and free of constructs. But this is the moment when good practitioners remain in *tukdam*, samadhi after the body dies.

This failure to recognize is exactly what needs to be purified. You clear it up by training in something that corresponds to that moment, something that has a mode similar to the dharmakaya of death. You train in the pride or self-assurance that this state of cognizant emptiness, totally free of constructs, is the emptiness of all phenomena—both outside and inside, whatever appears and exists, all of samsara and nirvana. The samadhi of suchness is simply resting your mind free of concepts for a while, until you start to think again. Understand this to be the basic framework of the entire sadhana practice. The samadhi of suchness also purifies clinging to the view of permanence—taking the world as solid, real, and permanent—which is one of the two extreme views. It purifies this view and the habitual tendency for taking rebirth in the formless realms.

In short, by training in the state of emptiness free from all constructs, we purify three things: the death state, the view of permanence, and the habitual tendency for taking rebirth in the formless realms. Moreover, we plant the seed for realizing the state of dharmakaya.

The Secret Mantra path of Vajrayana has two aspects: means and knowledge. *Means* is the development stage, while *knowledge* is the completion stage. In the development stage, we visualize the deity and attend to all the other details, such as training in keeping these things in mind. The completion stage involves seeing that even the deity is devoid of any concrete identity whatsoever; it too is emptiness, free of constructs. In this context, the samadhi of suchness is the completion stage. It is the most vital point. There is nothing more crucial than this.

The general Buddhist teachings describe *suchness* as the three gates of emancipation—emptiness, signlessness, and wishlessness—corresponding to ground, path, and fruition. We need to train in these to purify the moment of death. However, most people fall unconscious shortly after dying, when the three experiences of whiteness, redness, and blackness occur. This unconscious, oblivious state usually lasts for three days, although the length of time is not certain. The body is still present, but the mind is in a blank, unconscious state. After several days, one awakens with the thought, "Where am I? What's happening?" Thinking is reactivated, and the bardo of becoming begins. This bardo experience is purified by the samadhi of illumination, which in the tantras is also called the state of magical compassion that illuminates everything.

The second of the three samadhis also acts as a purifier. After dying, when the bardo of dharmata begins, there is a spectacle of light rays and colors. Practitioners who have trained in Tögal experience these as deities. Unless you have some training in Tögal, the whole event flickers past, with nothing more than a shimmering of lights and colors, which are intensely bright and overwhelming. For more details, you can read Padmasambhava's *Liberation through Hearing in the Bardo*.

At this time, the soft, cozy lights of the six realms also appear, more readily attracting one's attention. These soft-colored lights seduce you back into the realms of the six classes of beings. To purify this experience, train in the samadhi of illumination. How do you do this? Within the state of great emptiness devoid of constructs, direct your attention toward all sentient beings, who do not realize their own basic nature of emptiness. Filled with compassion and loving-kindness, think, "How sad that sentient beings have not realized this!" Let your compassion be like the sun emitting rays of light in all directions. It is said, "The moment of realizing emptiness is the same moment as manifesting compassion." This compassion is the second of the three samadhis.

The samadhi of illumination purifies the bardo state, and it has two aspects: the main part and the subsequent part. The main part is simply to remain without any concepts in emptiness, filled with the light rays of compassion. When we begin to think again, the first thought that should arise is the assurance that the purity of the bardo state is the sambhogakaya. Besides purifying the bardo state, this samadhi also purifies the habitual tendency to hold the view of nihilism, as well as the habitual tendency for taking rebirth among the gods in the form realms. Finally, this training plants the seed for realizing the sambhogakaya, the form of the deity adorned with the major and minor marks of excellence. This second samadhi, which relates to sambhogakaya, is also called magical compassion.

The third is the samadhi of the seed syllable. Here the object to be purified is the moment before taking rebirth, when one is just about to enter one of the six classes of sentient beings. The seed syllable grows into or gives rise to the deity. The deity could be an unelaborate form of a single figure or an elaborate form with many faces, numerous arms, and so forth. The seed syllable produces all of these. We should first visualize the seed syllable, as the natural manifestation of nondual compassionate emptiness, in the middle of space, like a radiant moon.

The seed syllable is the source of the entire mandala of deities. At the very outset of the development stage, visualize the seed syllable again and again until it becomes clear. Whenever the seed syllable is not clear, return to imagining it until it becomes so. This purifies the mind-energy principle, which takes rebirth. Visualizing the mind-energy principle in the form of a seed syllable purifies this tendency for taking rebirth. It also establishes the basis for realizing the nirmanakaya. This explains the samadhi of the seed syllable.

No matter what yidam you practice, you should perfect an additional set of three aspects: distinct appearance, stable pride, and recollection of the pure symbolism.

Distinct appearance means imagining the complete form of Padmasambhava, or any other yidam, including the attributes, garments, and complexion's hue, everything down to the black and white of the eyeballs. Everything should appear very distinct, not blurry or mixed together. If some detail does not appear clearly in your mind, simply train in visualizing this repeatedly until it becomes distinct. Your visualization should not be flat and two dimensional, like a painting, but three dimensional, like a statue. In the beginning, visualize the appearance as clear and distinct, yet empty, like the reflection in a mirror or the moon in water. It is visible but devoid of self-nature, like a rainbow, transparent and insubstantial.

Next is stable pride. Mundane pride is to think, "I'm great, greater than others. I'm rich. I know this and that. I'm special." This is the normal type of conceit or pride, but that is not what is meant here. Here we are dealing with the pride of self-assurance, the confidence that one's sugata-essence is identical with that of all the buddhas. Our buddha nature, too, is endowed with the qualities of the fourfold fearlessness, ten strengths, and so forth. Yet we ourselves are at the stage of the ground. In the case of the Buddha or Padmasambhava, they are at full-fledged realization, the state of fruition. Nonetheless, we should have the assurance and pride that our own buddha nature is, in fact, identical with that of Padmasambhava himself in the state of complete buddhahood. That is the kind of confidence we need to have.

Lastly, recollecting the pure symbolism is a matter of utmost importance. Recollecting the purity can be applied to any deity, regardless of whether it is peaceful or wrathful, two-armed or six-armed. In short, every single detail means something, and you should learn this meaning.

Returning to the text, the next line reads:

> From it light radiates, purifying the clinging to a real universe with beings.[8]

We have the tendency to think things really exist—the vessel and its contents, the world and its beings, appearance and existence. So, at this point, imagine that the syllable HRIH sends out a tremendous amount of five-colored light in all directions, totally purifying the habitual tendency of clinging to the world and beings as real and solid. Having removed that tendency, remain again in the state of equanimity, emptiness free of constructs.

The whole principle of the development stage is to purify our different types of habitual tendencies. The various aspects of the development stage then become a real remedy to counteract our obscurations and tendencies. Therefore, these steps of training should somehow correspond to the different ideas and tendencies we presently have.

[For teachings on the palace and the deities, see OTR's commentary.]

An extremely important line of the text reads: *Is my awareness as Padmasambhava, the embodiment of all sugatas...* Stating that one's mind is the embodiment of all the sugatas, Padmasambhava, this line appears at the beginning of the visualization of Guru Rinpoche. Thus, in order to actualize this basic state, we should visualize our mind, endowed with the qualities of complete enlightenment, like the twofold knowledge and so forth, in the form of the deity, Padmasambhava. This deity is not someone else to whom we pray for long life, good health, and business success. It's not like that. Here, you are the deity; the deity is none other than you. In this way, the deity is spontaneously present.

The word *rigpa* here refers to the buddha nature; one's awareness or rigpa is the basic element or constituent of the buddha nature. This is present in all sentient beings, without any exception. The awakened state of buddhahood, endowed with the twofold knowledge and all the enlightened qualities, and our own buddha nature, are not different in any way whatsoever. There's not even an atom of difference. We should understand this. This buddha nature, or *sugatagarbha*, is present in everyone. When we recognize, trained in, and perfect the twofold knowledge, it fully unfolds, endowing us with the capacity to act for the welfare of beings.

But in our case, we have not recognized the sugata-essence, so the buddha nature remains clouded or enveloped within the two obscurations. Just like the example of holding a medicine bottle within one's hand, the qualities of enlightenment are not manifest. Hence, in our present state, we are unable to act for the welfare of beings. It is like the cloud-covered sky, in which the sun is unable to shine forth and give warmth, even though it is present. When the clouds disperse, the sunlight shines forth. In the same way, when our obscurations are removed, we need not invent a new buddha nature as though it were not already present. The sun does not need to be created anew each time.

It's very important to understand that the buddha nature we already have is exactly the same as the state of complete enlightenment. The only difference is that it is now obscured. However, these obscurations are not intrinsic to the buddha nature, and they don't adhere to it. For example, when I open my fist and release the eraser, the hand doesn't stick to the eraser. This is what is meant here. We have not abandoned the obscurations yet, but they are not intrinsic either.

Complete enlightenment is endowed with the twofold purity, the purity of the primordial essence and the purity of having removed the temporary defilements. We possess the first of these two; therefore, we are the buddhas of the primordially pure essence. But the real buddhas also possess the second purity, the purity of having removed the emotional and cognitive obscurations. Our nature is exactly the same as that of all fully enlightened buddhas, but our buddha nature does not function as a fully enlightened buddha, because it is still enveloped by obscurations. Here, *temporary* means "not innate." They can be removed. This principle is very important to understand.

In order to remove these obscurations, according to the general path of Mahayana, we train in the five paramitas of means: generosity, discipline, diligence, patience, and meditation—remaining in meditative equanimity. We also cultivate discriminating knowledge. According to Vajrayana, we train in the path of unifying means and knowledge. The development stage is the skillful means aspect, and the completion stage is the knowledge aspect. As we train in these practices, we gradually remove the covers, realizing our in-born nature. This is not a new achievement; rather, it's a realization of what was present to begin with.

How can we know we have buddha nature? Evidence proves the buddha nature is definitely present within our stream-of-being. We are able to feel loving-kindness and compassion for others; we can feel devotion, renunciation, and disenchantment with samsara; and we can take delight in virtuous actions and regret misdeeds. These are only possible because we possess the sugata-essence. Otherwise, these feelings would not arise. The scriptures say that if this potential were not present, we would never feel weary of samsara, nor would we have the desire to become liberated and fully enlightened.

Among the synonyms for buddha nature are *potential* and *element*. A poisonous snake has the potential to be poisonous; when it bites, it can instantly inject the poison. In the same way, we possess the potential for, or basic element of, enlightenment, and that is why we can awaken to it.

Right now, we have the basic element of disturbing emotions, because we have not abandoned the emotional obscurations. Since we have this potential, we can become angry, attached, or proud when we encounter difficult circumstances. Nevertheless, we also have the potential for enlightenment. If we remove the obscurations, we can immediately realize the awakened state. This is like extracting gold from gold ore. The ore possesses the basic element of gold, so if we smelt it, the gold will appear. Similarly, milk has the basic component of butter, and if we churn it, the butter will appear. Water, however, does not have the potential to yield butter. We can churn water for as long as we want, but it will never produce any butter.

Buddha nature is unformed, which means it is not created due to causes and conditions. It is like space—changeless. If you praise space, it doesn't feel delighted; if you blame space, it doesn't feel sad. Our basic nature does not improve when we become enlightened, nor does it worsen when we are deluded in samsara. It is unchanging, because it is unformed.

Some of the scholars from the New Schools object to the idea that buddhahood is spontaneously present and unformed in all sentient beings. They ask, "What about an old dog? Why doesn't it have the thirty-two major and eighty minor marks of excellence, and why doesn't it turn the wheel of Dharma if it has the complete potential?" The response is that the buddha nature, although fully perfect and already present in all beings, is not yet effective. It does not fulfill its own potential, because it is covered by the two obscurations. However, once sentient beings eliminate the two obscurations, they realize their own true, inherent nature, which was already there to begin with.

Why are there varying viewpoints concerning our buddha nature? Viewpoints vary because the intent taught in the sutras differs. The Buddha taught in different ways, adapting the teachings in accordance with different people's capacities. Therefore, we hear about the three turnings of the wheel of Dharma and the three sets of teachings. The second set of teachings is the Turning of the Dharma Wheel on the Absence of Attributes. In other words, it emphasizes that all things are empty of an entity or an identity—the empty essence. By nature, all phenomena are devoid of a self-nature. That is what is chiefly taught in the second turning.

People who stress the second turning of the wheel of Dharma consider this the definitive meaning. They view the teachings on buddha nature as the temporary, expedient meaning, which eventually leads to the definitive, ultimate teachings.

Other people consider the third turning of the wheel of Dharma, called the Turning of the Dharma Wheel on the Complete Uncovering, to be the definitive meaning. This emphasizes the cognizant, luminous buddha nature, endowed with the twofold wisdom present within all sentient beings. From that point of view, exclusively teaching that things are empty is the expedient meaning, not the final one. They consider the teachings on buddha nature to be the definitive meaning.

Both of these approaches are fine, and both are ways of understanding the Buddha's intent. They are just meant for different types of people. The different schools of philosophy seem to differ on several points, because they emphasize different sets of teachings. Some emphasize the second turning of the wheel of Dharma, whereas others emphasize the third turning, the final set of teachings. However, they are not making up anything on their own. They are all following the Buddhist teachings.

Kagyü and Nyingma lineages primarily follow the view that the sugata-essence, present in all sentient beings, is already endowed with the perfectly enlightened qualities in a potential way. Using the practices of the path as circumstances for removing the obscurations allows the indwelling enlightened qualities to manifest.

The *Uttaratantra Shastra* describes the way in which the sugata-essence is veiled or obscured. It uses nine analogies to show how the sugata-essence is obscured in an ordinary person; in someone on the path, such as the shravakas, pratyekabuddhas, and so forth; in candidate bodhisattvas; in bodhisattvas on the first seven impure stages, or bhumis; and in bodhisattvas on the three pure, final bhumis. Even on the eighth, ninth, and tenth bhumis, there is some degree of obscuration. Although the bodhisattvas at the end of the stream of the ten bhumis are still slightly obscured, from our point of view they appear no different from the fully enlightened buddhas, such as Manjushri and so forth. The other eight sons of the Buddha seem no different, but still there is some very, very subtle cognizant obscuration, which must be removed by means of the vajra-like samadhi, in order to realize the Eleventh Bhumi of Universal Illumination. There is still this slight difference.

How do we remove these obscurations, which cover the buddha nature? We remove them by means of gathering the accumulations, purifying obscurations, and so forth—using all the different trainings along the path. It's like hacking away at a thick wall until it becomes thinner and thinner. Finally, there is nothing left, and we realize the originally pure essence of enlightenment.

In the *Mahaparinirvana Sutra,* the Buddha said, "Now, it is time to teach the definitive meaning, the irreversible, ultimate set of teachings. Anyone here whose mind cannot accommodate these teachings, please depart and don't come back." He then sent Kashyapa to sort out who should remain and who should leave. They checked three times to see if the people who remained could actually accept and grasp the ultimate set of teachings. For example, even if it were said that the father is only ten years old, while the son is one hundred years old, they would grasp and accept that and whatever else the Buddha said. This occurred when the Buddha started to give the definitive meaning, the ultimate teachings.

What did the Buddha teach at this time? In essence, he taught that all sentient beings, from the very beginning, possess the qualities of the awakened state, such as the twofold supreme knowledge, the fourfold fearlessness, the ten strengths, the eighteen unique qualities, and so forth. In their stream-of-being, they already possess these qualities. For some people, this kind of statement is impossible to grasp. It is incomprehensible.

So, what does it really mean? For example, what does the first aspect of the twofold knowledge, the wisdom that sees all that exists, refer to? A scientist, who believes only in the existence of the physical world we see around us, at least accepts that there is a physical world called planet Earth. Even though the Earth's particles are as tiny as the dust motes we see drifting in the sunlight, a Buddha can see how many particles make up this planet. Without having to think about it, in a single instant, he knows exactly how many particles exist in the entire world. In the same way, he knows how many particles exist in the whole universe of worlds. Moreover, aside from the beings in other realms which we, ourselves, cannot perceive, a Buddha knows exactly how many human beings, animals, and sea creatures there are in our world, as well as their exact location, not only in this present moment, but even from the original time of confusion up until now. He knows the personal biography of each living being, one lifetime after another throughout all time, from beginningless lifetimes until now.

For example, a Buddha knows which parents each sentient being had, where he took birth, what he did, where and to whom he was reborn after death, and so forth. A Buddha knows not just the history of a single being, but the individual history of all sentient beings. He knows the histories not just consecutively, one after another, but all simultaneously—in the snap of a finger. This kind of omniscience is, in fact, present in the mindstream of all sentient beings. The question is, can we grasp this? This is how the omniscient knowledge of a Buddha is.

The wisdom knowledge of the shravakas, pratyekabuddhas, and bodhisattvas is deep, but not as deep and vast as the Buddha's knowledge. It is still limited, reaching just so far. The Buddha's wisdom knowledge is limitless. For example, a shravaka might possess knowledge of everything from here to France, while a bodhisattva possesses knowledge of everything between here and America. Nevertheless, this kind of knowledge is still limited.

Right now, we don't know where we were or what we did in our past life. We only know the present life. Yet, at the same time, we have to accept that the omniscient knowledge of the buddhas is present in our being. Right? If it seems impossible to accept this, we would say it is "incomprehensible." However, there is no benefit in merely possessing this quality, because it is, at present, completely clouded over by the two obscurations.

The Buddha gave the following example: Once there was a very destitute person who possessed absolutely no wealth whatsoever. He was forced to roam around begging for his livelihood. Nevertheless, under the fireplace in his own hut, a treasure lay buried underground, but he was ignorant of this fact. The treasure of precious substances did not call out to him and say, "I'm here under your house! Dig me up!" So, he continued to live in dire poverty, not knowing that if he just dug into the earth under his own hut, he would be a very rich person.

One day, someone with clairvoyant "divine sight" came along and saw the treasure buried under the fireplace. He told the poor fellow, "You don't have to live like a poor person, begging for your food. Just dig in the ground under your fireplace, and you'll discover a very precious treasure." The beggar started to dig and first found a cache of silver. This was valuable, of course, but not extremely precious. Nevertheless, he was satisfied and thought, "This is what has been there all along." He brought it up and showed it to the clairvoyant person, asking, "Is this what you meant?" The clairvoyant person said, "Yes, that's part of the treasure, but not the entire treasure. You must dig deeper." The fellow dug for a while longer and brought up gold. He showed it to his friend and said, "Look what I found! Is this the treasure?" The friend said, "Yes, that's again part of the treasure, but not the whole thing. Go back and dig further." The fellow did as he was told and finally uncovered the entire buried treasure.

In the same way, the Buddha's first teachings showed us how to arrive at the level of an *arhat*, by means of the shravaka and pratyekabuddha paths, but this is not the final result. His next teachings showed how to reach the bodhisattva levels of enlightenment, but even these are not the final result. Ultimately, the Buddha taught that one must purify all the obscurations, in order to arrive at the state of complete and perfect enlightenment, called the Eleventh Bhumi of Universal Illumination. This is an analogy taught by the Buddha himself.

Failing to recognize our own buddha nature, we remain covered by the two obscurations and roam throughout the different states of samsara, undergoing great misery and difficulties. For example, we experience the heat and cold of the hell realms, the hunger and thirst of the hungry ghost realms, and so forth—not knowing a precious treasure has been present within us all the while.

Sometimes we use another example the Buddha gave, that of the wishfulfilling jewel lying in the filth of a latrine. No one knows it is lying there, even though it has the capacity to fulfill wishes. Covered with dirt, it is merely waiting for someone to pick it up and clean it again. First, we clean it with water and then with a rough cloth. Later, we use a finer grade of cloth. Later still, we polish it with a very soft cloth, until absolutely no dirt or impurity remains on the surface of the wishfulfilling jewel. Finally, we can mount it on top of a victory banner and make offerings to it. We can then make wishes with it, and they will all be fulfilled. The wishfulfilling jewel had this same capacity all along, but we had to remove the impurities in order to actualize its full potential. In the same way, with great perseverance and fortitude, we should undertake the removal of obscurations and defilements that cover our buddha nature.

To reiterate, we should really understand and acknowledge that all of us possess this basic awareness, the sugata-essence. We visualize this basic awareness in the form of the deity. We shouldn't always think of the buddhas as being up there in the enlightened state, while we sentient beings are down here far, far below, with a difference as vast as heaven between us. In nature, we are identical with the buddhas. In our case, this nature is presently veiled by obscurations. Nonetheless, these obscurations can be removed, and that is exactly what we do when we practice a sadhana.

We visualize ourselves as Padmasambhava in the center of the celestial palace. In the middle of the base within the palace, a square platform is raised above the ground. The octagonal jewel is within that. In the middle of the jewel is a four-petalled lotus. In the middle of the four-petalled lotus is the lion throne, which is a platform of jeweled material supported by eight lions. On top of the lion throne is another lotus, a sun disc, and a moon disc. Padmasambhava sits upon these. Behind our back, a lotus tree is growing. At the level of the second story of the palace, the tree branches out with another lotus appearing at the center of the middle chamber above his head, where Avalokiteshvara sits. At the level of the third story of the palace, another lotus appears above Avalokiteshvara's head, where Amitayus sits. This is how we should imagine it.

[For specific teachings on the twelve manifestations, the dakas and dakinis, empowerment and consecration, invitation, homage, offerings, and praises, see OTR's commentary.]

As we can see in Jamyang Khyentse's explanation, known as the *Thirty-Five-Day Practice*, he suggests that on the first evening of a retreat, we should go through the preliminaries and then the sadhana, all the way down to the praises. He says we can open up the recitation mansion at this point and then chant the *Barchey Lamsel* once. The *Zurdeb*, the *Side Ornament*, mentions this:

At the point of the recitation practice, if you wish to open the recitation mansion after the praises, say:

BHRUNG VISHVA VISHUDDHE HRIH HUNG PHAT JAH

From the root mandala of myself,
Opens up a second wisdom mandala,
Remaining in the sky before me.
Around the seed syllables in both our hearts,

Spin the resounding mantra garlands,⁑
Sending out countless rays of light.⁑

From oneself, the root mandala visualized as Guru Rinpoche and the other two kayas, a second wisdom mandala separates and appears in the sky. It is like a reflection in front, which remains in the sky. In the heart centers of both your own mandala and the second mandala in front, the seed-syllable HRIH is surrounded by a mantra garland. Each syllable resounds with its own sound. They are written counter-clockwise but spin clockwise. They are:

OM AH HUNG VAJRA GURU PADMA SIDDHI HUNG

From the visualization in front, infinite rays of light stream out from the mantra syllables in a variety of colors: white, yellow, red, and green. When we arrive at the recitation section, we will discuss how the mantras are arranged. Now, returning back to the *Trinley Nyingpo*, you should begin with invoking their samaya for the recitation.

Hung Hrih!⁑
In the essence mandala of bodhichitta,⁑
Gathering of deities reveling in wisdom magic,⁑
Without departing, remember your vajra samaya⁑
And bestow blessings, empowerments, and siddhis!⁑

The essence mandala of bodhichitta is the wisdom mandala of the awakened state, rigpa, the buddha nature itself. Its natural expression is to take the form of all the different deities, which are here described as the *deities reveling in wisdom magic.* All of them possess the samaya vow, which cannot be transgressed or abandoned. In the past, when they were on the path, they took this vow to work endlessly for the benefit of all sentient beings. We remind them of this fact, saying, *remember your vajra samaya,* or keep that in mind, and *bestow blessings, empowerments, and siddhis* upon me. This is the invocation.

[For the recitation, see OTR's commentary.]

Recitation — Conclusion

At the end of the recitation, repeat the Vowels and Consonants mantra, the Ali Kali, and the Essence of Causation mantra three times each.

> OM A AH I IH U UH RI RIH LI LIH E EH O OH ANG AH
> KA KHA GA GHA NGA, TSA TSHA DZA DZAH NYA
> TA THA DA DHA NA, TA THA DA DHA NA
> PA PHA BA BHA MA, YA RA LA WA
> SHA KA SA HAKSHA

> OM YE DHARMA HETU PRABHAVA HETUN TEKEN TATHAGATO HAYA
> WADET TEKEN TSAYO NIRODHA EWAM VADI MAHA SHRAMANA SVAHA

Then say the four lines for the offering:

> OM AH HUNG
> I present you as an outer offering, an ocean of desirable objects amassed like cloud banks,
> As an inner offering, an inconceivable feast of amrita, rakta, and torma,
> And as a secret offering, the unity of bliss and emptiness, the basic space of wakefulness.
> Accepting these, please bestow the supreme and common siddhis!

> OM VAJRA ARGHAM PADYAM PUSHPE DHUPE ALOKE GHANDHE NAIVIDYA
> SHABDA SARVA PANCA RAKTA BALINGTA MAHA PUJA AH HUNG

Then say the four lines for the praises:

> HUNG HRIH!
> From your essence, the luminous state of dharmakaya,
> Your nature manifests as sambhogakaya's empty bliss.
> Your capacity, the all-taming nirmanakaya, accomplishes the benefit of beings.
> I prostrate to and praise the whole assembly of mandala deities!

After repeating the praises, add in the *Barchey Lamsel* or *Düsum Sangye*, which is a special supplication to the three kayas, Guru Rinpoche, and the twelve manifestations. Finally, say the Hundred Syllable mantra three times.

DISSOLVING AND EMERGING

When doing the *Trinley Nyingpo* according to the thirty-five-day retreat, at this point, just after the mantras, offerings, and praises, dissolve the front visualization by saying JAH HUNG BAM HO. Imagine that the mandala of the world and beings dissolves back into you. Uttering HUNG HUNG HUNG, dissolve the entire mandala immediately into light. First, the surrounding figures dissolve into you. Then your own body dissolves into the HRIH in the heart center. The HRIH slowly dissolves as well. Do not keep it in mind any longer. You then rest in the state of luminosity for a while. That is the completion stage of dissolution.

By uttering PHAT three times, you again emerge in the form of the deity, with one face and two arms. Imagine that the three syllables OM AH HUNG are in your three places. Then, say the words of dedication and aspiration.

SESSIONS AND BREAKS DURING THE THIRTY-FIVE-DAY RETREAT

We are still on the first day of retreat and have completed one session. Now, we eat dinner and begin the second session, the evening session called the *sö-tün,* which means evening or after dark. Usually in retreat, we do four daily sessions: early morning, morning, afternoon, and evening.

After dinner, during the second session of the first day, the evening session, we again start out with refuge and bodhichitta, blessing the offerings, and so forth, according to the short *Trinley Nyingpo* sadhana. We follow this, as described above, up until reciting the mantras. Then we recite as many mantras as we are comfortable with—it's up to you.

When we dissolve the visualization at the end with the triple HUNG, we go to sleep at exactly that point. Here, this is called practicing the yoga of sleeping. In this way, we fall asleep in the state of luminosity, while practicing the yoga of luminosity.

When waking up in the morning, we immediately awaken with the pride of being the deity. In the *Barchey Künsel* ngöndro, at the very moment of awakening, we recite a special chant to Guru Rinpoche, who appears in the sky overhead, surrounded by dakas and dakinis. They are sounding bells and damarus, while chanting mantras of the self-liberated luminosity of one's mind and so forth. We immediately sit up with the assurance that Guru Rinpoche and all the dakas and dakinis have arrived. We then start the ngöndro practices.[3]

In the *Sheldam Nyingjang,* there is a mantra that blesses our speech to be the nature of the dharani mantras of all the buddhas. It is a short mantra we can say between sessions, yet it is very important.[3]

If we arrange our practice to complete an entire ngöndro plus the sadhana itself within a month, we should spend one whole day on taking refuge in four sessions. We use most of each session for taking refuge; then we engage in the bodhichitta or bodhisattva vow with its Seven Branches and four immeasurables. After that, we do the entire *Trinley Nyingpo* at the end of each session. Thus, in each session, we do the whole ngöndro and also the whole *Trinley Nyingpo*. In the first day, however, we actually spend the major part of the session just on refuge. You can decide how many of each practice to complete daily. Here, we engage in the prostrations with the Seven Branches in the early morning session, starting around 4:00 am, or whenever it's convenient.

The early morning session is before breakfast, from whatever time we rise until we eat breakfast. This is called the early morning session. The practice is the same in all four sessions, and that accounts for the first day of retreat. We go to sleep in the way described above. On the second morning, we wake up and repeat the practices done on the first day.

When we start the ngöndro, we only chant refuge three times and the bodhisattva vows and Seven Branches just a few times. The major part of the session is spent on the Hundred Syllable mantra. At the end of the session, we go through the rest of the ngöndro plus the *Trinley Nyingpo,* while spending the major portion of the session on the Vajrasattva mantra. The next three sessions follow the same pattern.

Now we have spent the first day mainly on refuge and bodhichitta and the second day concentrating on the recitation of the Vajrasattva mantra. We spend the third, fourth, and fifth days focusing on the ngöndro's guru yoga practice.

On the third day, we concentrate on the mandala offering. On the fourth day, we focus on supplicating Guru Rinpoche, with *Düsum Sangye* and *Barchey Lamsel*. On the fifth day, we chant the Vajra Guru mantra as part of the ngöndro. Moreover, we imagine receiving the empowerments, using the major portion of the session on that.

This makes five days altogether. On the sixth day, the ngöndro is more or less finished, so we just do a very short ngöndro in the early morning session. During the other three sessions of the day, we don't need to do the ngöndro; we can just focus on the main practice, which is the guru sadhana itself. Nevertheless, just as before, we should do four sessions, starting in the early morning and concluding in the evening.

It is only necessary to offer an actual gektor in the early morning session, not in the other daily sessions. If we want to simplify things, and we don't want to spend time making actual *gek* tormas, we can just put some rice on a plate and add a little water. Imagining this to be the torma, we offer it up. This is acceptable.

During the next week, we focus on Amitayus' Amarani mantra. Of course, we say a few of the other mantras, but not very many. Then, we spend the following week accumulating Avalokiteshvara's Mani mantra. At this time, we do just one rosary (108) of the Amitayus mantra. When we reach the Vajra Guru mantra, we again say just one rosary (108) of each of the first and second previous mantras.

Over the next ten days, it is very important to do 400,000 of the Vajra Guru mantra, accomplishing this within the ten days. This, of course, depends upon your capacity. During this time, we do just a few of the other mantras, such as a single rosary of each. We should not stop doing them daily.

The above describes the approach. Now we will talk about the accomplishment. We should spend three days on the Tötreng Tsal mantra and one day on the Tötreng Tsal mantra plus the extra Harinisa mantra for the four families of dakas and dakinis.

During each and every session, at the conclusion of the mantras, in order to amend or make up for anything we left out or added and also to consecrate, bless, and increase the mantra's benefits, we say the Ali Kali, Om Yedharma, and Hundred Syllable mantras three times each. Also say the offerings, praises, and either the *Düsum Sangye* or *Barchey Lamsel* prayer once each.

By uttering HUNG three times, we then dissolve the recitation mansion and the entire visualization. By uttering PHAT three times, we re-emerge as the deity. We then dedicate the merit, make aspirations, and say the verse of auspiciousness. This is the same procedure for each session. However, during the afternoon session, which begins at 1:00 or 2:00 PM and lasts until the late afternoon, after the *Düsum Sangye* or *Barchey Lamsel* prayer, we should consecrate the feast offering, according to the long version of this sadhana, the *Trinley Gyepa*, and then continue to the *drelwa,* the deliverance offering.

During the retreat, when we reach the residual offering (*lhagma*), we do not throw it outside. We have a place where we put it and just let it collect there. Don't throw it outside.

On special days, such as the tenth or twenty-fifth, it is preferable to do the *Trinley Gyepa* sadhana. On a daily basis, it is perfectly all right to use the *Trinley Nyingpo*.

We do the offerings, the praises, the *Düsum Sangye* or *Barchey Lamsel*, and the Hundred Syllable mantra three times, and so forth. Afterward, there is the sölkha for the dharma protectors. There is a very abbreviated sölkha, just three four-line verses, to *Tseringma*, which can be inserted here.

If you have received many empowerments for dharma protectors, it is enough just to say the *Lama Yidam* sölkha; however, *Tseringma* is a special protector for this *Barchey Künsel* teaching. The terma protector is called *Kharak Khyung Tsünma*.

In terms of the four sessions of the day, having finished the early morning session and breakfast, do the mid-morning session, from 8:00 to 11:00 AM, for example. The afternoon session runs from 1:00 or 2:00 PM until 5:00 PM, and during this session we add in the *tsok* and the sölkha to the dharma protectors. The sölkha is quite short, and it is fine to keep it brief during rereat. During the evening session, after dark, we do not make any feast offerings or sölkha at all during our retreat. The gektor is offered during the mid-morning session, not in the very early morning session.

Although the *Trinley Nyingpo* text says the feast offering is done between sessions, noble beings never make any distinction between med- itation (*nyamzhag*) and post-meditation (*jetob*). *Nyamzhag* means a "com- posed mental state," and noble beings never stray from that state of mind. Therefore, there is no post-meditation state for such beings. However, normal people, like ourselves, first engage in meditation where we con- centrate one-pointedly on the practice, as in the case of the four intents of recitation explained earlier. When we stand up from our meditation cushion and start moving around, we enter the post-meditation phase. During the breaks, which refer to these post-meditation periods, we engage in different activities. This is the time to make the feast offerings.

FEAST OFFERING

Actually, here the word *feast* (*tsok*) literally means "gathering or many things coming together." There are four types of gathering. The first is the gathering of fortunate male and female practitioners. From the point of view of the shrine, the male practitioners should sit in the right row, while the females sit in the left row. Everyone gathers together, in this way, each with their male or female partners or whatever. This is the gathering of the fortunate ones.

The second is the gathering of deities, or all the guests of buddhas and bodhisattvas, who are invited. These are the ones whom we call upon to receive the feast articles.

The third is the gathering of the articles, which also corresponds to the gathering or accumulation of merit. This refers chiefly to meat and wine. Of, course, there are many other ingredients we can include, but we primarily offer meat and wine. We don't use normal words for these things in the context of a feast offering. Each has its specific term. If we offer dog meat, we don't call it "dog meat," and so forth. It has its particular name, and we can find these terms in the *Great Explanation of Feast Offerings* by Jamgön Kongtrül.

The last of the four gatherings is the great gathering, which is the accumulation of wisdom. Here we train ourselves to relinquish the threefold concept of there being offering articles, the one offering them, and the ones receiving them.

There is something to say about the wine and meat of the feast offering. The sacred medicine (*mendrub*) already contains the five meats and five nectars, but not in a normal way. The mahasiddhas of the past, in particular Padmasambhava himself, specially consecrated the five meats and five nectars. Therefore, if we have a feast offering and we have no meat or wine, we need not worry or feel it is incomplete. If we just sprinkle our oranges and biscuits with the mendrub water, then the feast is complete with the five meats and five nectars. It is not absolutely essential to have meat and wine actually present.

Usually, the five meats refer to the flesh of humans, dogs, elephants, cows, and horses. They depend upon the cultural context in which one is living. In India, in the past, these five animals were never killed for food. Therefore, they were not contaminated by having been put to death for the sake of feeding human beings.

Buddhism is a religion that advocates not harming other living beings. Since the buddhas regard all sentient beings as their own children, we cannot use the flesh of a sentient being that has been slaughtered for food as an offering to the buddhas. Offering the flesh of a slaughtered child to its own mother during a banquet will not please her, and she will not want to eat it. Hence, the animal or human flesh we offer must come from beings who have had natural deaths and have not been violently butchered. In this way, the meat is considered clean. Yet, if we live in a place where people normally eat elephants or horses, then we cannot use this meat. On the other hand, if we live in a country where people do not eat goats or sheep, we can then use this kind of meat, as long as the animal has not been killed. If we do not have such meat, it will suffice if we just sprinkle the food with mendrub.

The articles we offer during a feast depend upon our individual level of realization and meditative powers. We should enjoy the feast articles in a way that does not give rise to thoughts of pure and impure, clean and unclean. For example, if we have a strong feeling that dog meat is very foul, impure, and terrible to eat, yet put it on the shrine and try to enjoy it, it will spoil our state of mind. We will think everything has become contaminated and dirty. If we feel this way, we shouldn't offer such articles.

Furthermore, whatever we arrange as feast articles should be pure in the sense that we don't defile them with attitudes of pride or miserliness. For example, if we arrange a big, spectacular variety of offerings and then regard ourselves as very rich and important, it is the same as putting poison in all the food. On the other hand, we poison the offerings with stinginess if we just offer a few things while thinking, "There's no one here to eat many offerings, so why should I bother to arrange so much. I'm just throwing my money away!" It's best to offer a moderate amount in harmony with our personal level of wealth. Thus, the offerings don't need to be lavish if we haven't much money, and they don't need to be meager if we happen to be affluent. Whatever we arrange is just a tangible support for our visualized offerings, when we mentally increase the articles infinitely. To spend one hundred rupees with impure motivation is not as good as spending one rupee with pure motivation.

We can refer to the *Trinley Nyingpo* for the feast offering. First there's RAM YAM KAM, which represent fire, wind, and water. Then the text says:

> The seed syllable in the heart center of myself visualized as the deity
> Emanates RAM YAM KAM, purifying the clinging to offering articles as being real.
> The light from the three syllables transforms them into wisdom nectar,
> Which becomes an offering cloud of desirable objects filling the sky.
> OM AH HUNG

Visualized in the form of the deity, I am filled with the vajra pride of being the deity, Guru Rinpoche. From the seed syllable in my heart center, the white HRIH, the three syllables RAM YAM KAM shine forth, purifying clinging to the offering of feast articles, such as oranges or biscuits, as being real. The articles are purified through being burned by fire, scattered by wind, and flushed away by the water. In this way, we totally purify any attachment to the articles being real and materially substantial.

When we say RAM YAM KAM, we should actually imagine what the three syllables mean. To simulate the fire aspect, the person standing beside the shrine can first wave an incense stick or a lit match in front of the offerings. To simulate wind, lift the peacock-feather fan out of the vase and wave it over the offerings a few times. To simulate water, use the same wand to sprinkle a few drops of water on the offerings.

Through the light of the three syllables, OM AH HUNG, the feast offerings are transformed into an ocean of wisdom nectar, which then becomes a huge cloud bank of sense-pleasure offerings, such as beautiful sounds, sights, textures, tastes, and smells, as well as the eight auspicious articles and substances, the seven royal possessions, and so forth. Together, these offerings fill the entire sky. Imagining this, we say OM AH HUNG three times.

Afterward, we invoke the guests. If we have already projected a second reflected recitation mansion, we need not think the guests are arriving from elsewhere. If not, then the invocation is important. First, we utter the triple HUNG, and then we say:

> Ocean-like assembly of Trikaya Jinas,⁝
> Please manifest from the unconstructed state of luminosity.⁝
> To enable us to accumulate merit and purify obscurations,⁝
> Please come, reveling in your wisdom magic!⁝
> VAJRA SAMAYA JAH JAH⁝

The Trikaya Jinas, victorious ones of the three kayas—dharmakaya, sambhogakaya, and nirmanakaya—are the buddhas and bodhisattvas, the Three Roots, and so forth, who manifest as an ocean-like gathering. You can invoke them, for example, saying, "In essence, you are the state of luminosity, which is totally beyond any constructs. However, in order for us to gather the accumulations and purify the obscurations, we request you to please appear as wisdom magic. Please approach this place." The two accumulations we gather are the accumulation of merit with form and the accumulation of wisdom without form.

> *We then imagine that the various deities and beings arrive in the sky before us. Then we say, VAJRA SAMAYA JAH JAH, which means "indestructible sacred bond, come come!" The indestructible samaya or bond is the vow deities took in former aeons, pledging to help guide all sentient beings. We call upon the buddhas and bodhisattvas, root deities, and so forth to remember their promise and please come.*

There is a special offering called a hundredfold feast, whereby one hundred feast tormas are offered. Usually, a feast offering has four parts: the pure portion (*phü*), the mending apology (*kangshag*), the liberation offering (*drelwa*), and the residual offering (*lhagma*).

If ten people gather to make a hundredfold feast, and we offer each of these four aspects once, that is the same as offering ten complete feasts, because each person counts as one. Going through this procedure ten times, we will have offered the hundredfold feast. During the execution of each sequence, we offer the pure part first, then the mending apology, and then the liberation offering. We put each one on the shrine as we offer it, chanting the appropriate verse. We gather together the residual offering and put it aside with the previous offerings not given yet. It is called the pure residual.

If you are alone and you want to do the hundredfold feast, you must chant the whole thing slowly one hundred times. It takes some time to complete. Traditionally, if ten people offer a very elaborate version of the hundredfold feast, each time they offer it, the practitioners start at the very beginning of the *Leyjang* (*Trinely Nyingpo*) and go through the tsok. Again and again, they'd start from the beginning of the *Leyjang* and offer ten tsoks during each round. Since we want to get through the puja quickly and don't have much time, we just chant the *Leyjang* once and offer the feast. But, actually, in accordance with the genuine tradition, each time of offering ten, we would start all over again from the beginning of the sadhana practice.

Now, we come to the actual offering of the feast, which is the next four lines, beginning with:

> Om ah hung
> The essence of the feast offering is a cloud bank of wisdom nectar
> In the form of goddesses with desirable objects filling the sky.
> May this enjoyment of unconditioned great bliss
> Please you, assembly of mandala deities of the Three Roots.
> Sarva gana chakra puja hoh

Here, the very essence of the feast articles is a cloud of wisdom nectar that takes on the appearance of offering goddesses of the five families, who fill the sky and present the offerings of sense pleasures. We say, "May this enjoyment of undefiled, unconditioned great bliss please you, mandala deities of the Three Roots." At that moment, we lift up the plate, while contemplating the meaning of the words and presenting the offering to all the deities. SARVA means "all," GANA means "gathering or feast," CHAKRA means "wheel or circle," PUJA means "offering," and HO means "please have." So together this means, "I offer you this entire circle of feast (ganachakra)." This is the first part of the feast, called the pure offering (*phü*), which we mount on the largest plate and place on the shrine, right in front of the mandala deities.

Now, we come to the second part of the feast, called the *tsok barpa* or *kang-shag*, which is the middle feast section, consisting of the fulfillment or mending confession. These four lines include both the mending and the confession. Of course, there is more to recite if we engage in the longer, more extensive version. For example, we can include Jamgön Kongtrül's *kangwa* called the *Turquoise Chamber Mending Chant, Tsok-Khang Pema Drawa*.

Next, contemplate strong regret for all the evil accumulated since beginningless samsara. There are two types of evil: spontaneous wrongdoing and the wrongdoing of having violated a vow to be good. *Digpa* and *dribpa* are spontaneous wrongdoing, negative actions, the obscurations, and so forth. *Nyepa* and *tungwa*—offenses and infractions—are the breaking of vows. First, this refers to breaches and violations of the precepts of individual liberation as well as the refuge and bodhisattva vows. In particular, it refers to the infractions, violations, and transgressions of the pledges connected with taking the four empowerments of Vajrayana, with their implicit twenty-eight samayas, fourteen root downfalls, eight severe downfalls, and so forth. We pray that we can amend all these with this feast offering of sense pleasures. With strong regret, we confess our faults, saying, SAMAYA, meaning "sacred bond," SHUDDHE meaning "utterly pure," and AH, meaning "may it be so."

The portion of the feast torma we give as the deliverance offering should be cut from the torma before consecrating it with RAM YAM KAM at the outset of the feast. But if you have already consecrated everything, there is a way around this. Imagine that the offering goddesses, whom you have visualized, dissolve back into your heart center; then cut a portion of the feast torma.

For the third or last part of the feast offering, called the deliverance (*drelwa*), we first imagine that instantaneously we turn into the Supreme Steed manifestation, Hayagriva, the Great Glorious One. From our heart center, we emanate countless special beings called *gings*, who track down the evil spirits, arrest them, and thrust them into the vajra master's pit. There are different types of gings: some summon, some kill, some chop, and some offer up the demons. All of these emerge from Hayagriva's heart center.

These demons and evil spirits, who are tracked down, apprehended, and brought back, are the natural manifestation of clinging to duality, holding onto subject and object. As long as we have attachment to duality, the manifestation of this attachment takes the form of enmity, hostile forces, and so forth. At the time of capture, the demons dissolve into their effigy, who looks like a little man lying on his back, inside the pit before the vajra master. The vajra master takes his phurba, called the *phurba sec-hog*, meaning the "supreme son." The upper handle of the dagger is Vajra Kilaya, while the lower part of his body becomes the three-sided Kilaya, or dagger, itself. Grasping the dagger in his hand, the vajra master dances the dagger over the effigy, slicing it apart—first the right leg, then the left leg, then the arms, head, and torso. At this point, the vajra master lifts the dagger and touches its point to his own heart center, imagining that the life force, merit, fame, splendor, and so forth of the enemy of the Dharma dissolves into himself.

Again, the vajra master touches the phurba to the effigy and imagines that the consciousness of the evil spirit takes the form of the seed-syllable AH, white in color. Pointing the phurba into the sky, he imagines that the consciousness is projected directly to a pure land, like a shooting star soaring upward. For your benefit, you have absorbed all the merit and glory of the enemy, and for the benefit of the enemy, his consciousness is purified of all obscurations and delivered to a pure buddhafield. The remnants of his body, including the flesh, blood, bones, and so forth, are liberated into the space of luminosity and transformed into wisdom nectar. Although the form is still flesh and blood, the essence is wisdom nectar, which is then offered to the mouths of all the mandala deities of the Three Roots. We should imagine this and say: SARVA meaning "all," BIGHANAN meaning "obstructors" (gek), SHATRUN meaning the "enemies," MARAYA meaning "delivered or terminated," KHA KHA KHAI KHAI meaning "offered up," and HA HA HI HI HUNG HUNG meaning the "response of the mandala deities, who are enjoying this with great delight."

At this point, we should say something important. The enemies that are mentioned here are the projections of our own deluded minds. As long as we mistakenly perpetuate the belief in subject and object—the objects being whatever we perceive and the subject being our dualistic mind, which perceives something as being "other" than itself—then there will always be someone or something appearing "out there," which we perceive as "harming" us. This is nothing other than a projection produced by clinging to duality. This projection of duality is the real enemy, and this is what we summon and terminate. Unless we understand this, practicing this kind of drelwa can create a lot of demerit. Without the proper view, we will be training in the accumulation of bad karma.

It is often said there is a fault in performing the drelwa, if one is unable to perform it correctly. You will create tremendous negative karma if you cultivate the idea that there really is an enemy "out there," whom you should kill to avert his harming you. It doesn't matter whether or not we are really able to kill an enemy; the attitude alone creates a lot of bad karma. Killing the enemy is only half of it—one can feel confident that it's easily possible to destroy one's enemy. However, to guide that consciousness to the pure lands is, for sure, much more difficult. It's better to understand that we are killing our own projections. Otherwise, this can be an exercise in creating bad karma.

Before chanting the four lines for the deliverance offering, say:

NRI TRI BENZA ANGKU SHA JAH JAH HUNG BAM HOH

At this point, sprinkle the torma with a little bit of rakta. There are four lines, in two parts. The first two lines apply to the deliverance of the demons, while the next two lines apply to actually offering it up.

The mantra also has two parts; the first is the deliverance:

SARVA BIGHANAN SHATRUN MARAYA

The second is the offering, or presentation:

KHA KHA KHAI KHAI

Then the deities reply with this expression of delight and enjoyment:

HA HA HI HI HUNG HUNG PHAT

If we are doing an expulsion ritual, we put only half of the deliverance offering on the torma plate and also put a piece of it on top of the residual offering, before giving that. Otherwise, we just place the deliverance offering on the shrine next to the first part, the phü, and the second part, the kang-shag.

Having completed the three parts of the feast—the first pure part, the middle mending-confession part, and the last deliverance part—we then start to enjoy the feast. The male and female participants begin to eat and drink feast articles.

First, offer the articles to the vajra master. If he is male, first offer the nectar, which is the nature of knowledge *(prajna)*. Then offer the food, which is the nature of skillful means *(upaya)*. If the vajra master is female, the procedure is reversed: first offer the food and then the nectar.

The person presenting the feast offerings to the tsok participants should hold the food in the right hand and the nectar in the left hand. When handing the first portion of the offerings to the vajra master, the dorje lobpön, you should give the glass of nectar and the plate of edibles immediately. Since the nectar represents knowledge and the food represents skillful means, the person offering it must cross his or her arms, so that when the vajra master receives the offerings, they should fit into the appropriate hands. As mentioned above, depending upon whether the dorje lobpön is male or female, he or she takes one or the other of the nectar or edibles first. He or she receives the offerings by first making the lotus mudra. Receiving the articles, the dorje lobpön replies, A LA LA HOH.

When serving the others, give everyone an equal share. One person shouldn't have a lot and another person a little. But if someone gets short-changed, no one should mention even a single word of complaint, such as, "I got only a little and you got a lot!" or "Last month we got really nice offerings, but this month the offerings are not very good." There should be no bickering or horseplay. If someone steps on your toes, you needn't scold them with a nasty or silly remark. Totally avoid that kind of arguing and, of course, fighting, which is out of the question. Avoid silly jokes as well. Simply enjoy the feast articles.

After eating, there is an opportunity for special vajra songs and vajra dances to occur. We don't have to do this, but we should know this is the time for engaging in such activities. At the end of this section, in the *Trinley Gyepa,* there is the vajra song:

EMA KIRI KIIRII...

At this point, it is mentioned that we can read the tantras aloud and establish their meaning, thus explaining them. When doing the *Barchey Künsel* drubchen, add the short *Lotus Essence Tantra* here. You can also add it to the *Ngakso* drubchen, but there doesn't seem to be any time to insert it. No matter what puja you are doing, this is always the point at which such tantras can be inserted and expounded upon.

Now, we have come to the residual offering *(lhagma)*. Whatever is left on a person's plate should be gathered back—one shouldn't hold onto things at this point. The residual offering is carried to the shrine for consecrating.

There are two aspects of the residual: the pure and the impure residual. The clean, or pure, residual was put aside some time ago, at the beginning of the feast. The unclean residual is whatever has been gathered from the participants' plates, which is now carried to the altar.

Earlier, the clean residual was placed on a tripod at the foot of the shrine. Now put the gathered impure residual on a plate on the ground in front of the tripod. With the special one-pointed vajra mudra, place a piece of the clean residual on top of the unclean one. Next, put part of the unclean residual on top of the clean one. Then, take all the clean residual offerings and pour them on top of the unclean ones. At this point, we put a piece of the drelwa on top of that. Finally, take a small piece from the *paltor* torma on the shrine. This torma is called the *Legacy of the Glorious Ones;* add it on top of the residuals.

The residuals are blessed in this particular way. If you only place the pure on top of the impure, it is very auspicious, but the activities will not be swiftly accomplished. If you take the impure and place it on top of the pure, the activities will be accomplished quickly, but not in an auspicious way. That's why we first place the pure on top of the impure and then the impure on top of the pure, finally adding it all together. This creates both auspiciousness and swiftly accomplished activities.

The residual offering is carried to the vajra master for consecration. When given the nectar, a highly realized dorje lobpön will eat some it, visualize himself as the Glorious Heruka with consort, and then spit the nectar out onto the residual offering, as the nectar of union. However, if he or she doesn't have this kind of realization, it is better not to do this. The vajra master then makes the pure space mudra, and the shrine master, the *chöpön,* pours the nectar through this, striking the residuals. The residual offering is consecrated by the mantra OM AH HUNG HA HOH HRIH and then returned to the tripod in front of the shrine.

If we look at the four lines found here for the residual offering, it seems very condensed, but the long version has many more details.

When addressing the attendants and emissaries of the Glorious One, meaning the Glorious Heruka, say:

> Servants of Palchen, host of messengers,
> Accept this enjoyment of residuals,

And in accordance with your past vows,⚬

Remove all obstacles and increase favorable conditions.⚬

Your past vows refers to the time when the Heruka liberated Rudra. We then say:

MA MA HRING HRING BALINGTA KHAHI⚬

MA MA HRING HRING refers to the "seed syllables of the ones who receive the residual," while BALINGTA means the "torma," and KHAHI means "please have." The residual offering is carefully carried outside, with a particular manner of walking seventy-two steps toward the southeast. If at all possible, you should do this. When making this offering, you should not tip the plate away from yourself and dump the contents. Rather, tip the plate toward youself, so the contents slip out. Tipping the plate toward oneself, at this point, creates the coincidence for increasing the practitioners' merit and prosperity.

The contents should never be merely thrown away, because this creates the coincidence for increasing the practitioners' fighting among themselves. Also, dogs and beggars should not eat the residuals, because this spreads various plagues and contagious diseases. To make sure this doesn't happen, it is better to place the residuals nicely on a roof top or high ledge, where only the birds in the sky can eat them.

SPEECH BLESSINGS

Now, I will give the special pith instruction on how to bless the voice and increase the potency of the mantra. This very short instruction is from *Khyungpo Naljor*, which Jamgön Kongtrül has adapted. It should be used at the beginning of any recitation.

First, we visualize ourselves vividly present in the form of the deity, whichever deity we happen to be practicing, such as Vajra Kilaya or Padmasambhava. We imagine that on the middle of our tongue is the letter AH, which shines with radiant white light. In an instant, it transforms into a moon disc, with another letter AH standing on it, surrounded by three (concentric) mantra garlands.

The innermost mantra garland consists of the Sanskrit vowels, A AH I IH U UH, and so forth. This white garland is arranged counter-clockwise.

Outside this, a red garland of consonants is arranged clockwise. The outermost mantra is the Om Yedharma mantra, which means "essence of causation." This blue garland is arranged counter-clockwise.

These three mantra garlands symbolize body, speech, and mind. They send out light rays in different colors, which invoke all the blessings of the Three Roots, the Three Precious Ones, and so forth. The blessings return in the form of the deities, the seed syllables of their mantras, and their attributes, such as vajras, lotuses, and so forth. All of these dissolve into your tongue.

Again, the three mantra garlands and the letter AH radiate rays of light, invoking all the mahasiddhas, the vidyadharas of India and Tibet, and the rishis who have accomplished the power of truthful speech. All of their blessings of power gather back and dissolve into the syllable AH, which then melts into your tongue. Imagine this and then repeat the vowel mantra, the consonant mantra, and the Om Yedharma mantra seven times each.

Beginning with the outermost garland, each mantra chain gradually dissolves into the moon disc. The moon disc dissolves into the letter AH, which then becomes a drop of white nectar that melts into your tongue. In this way, we imagine that our tongue is consecrated, so we possess the faculty, or power, of speech of the courageous eloquence of all sugatas. Whatever we say, even a single word, may then have majestic splendor and benefit all sentient beings.

This special instruction, found in a text by Jamgön Kongtrül, called *Dharma Practice for the Breaks* (*Tüntsam Chöchö*), is meant to be practiced in-between sessions, not during them. This small book includes instructions on how to do various things, such as the burnt food offering (*zur*), the smoke offering (*sang*), and tormas.

Key Points for Visualization

In the very beginning, it is probably quite difficult to have a clear visualization of all the details of every aspect simultaneously. If this is the case, here is some advice. The *Yangtig Yeshe Sangtal, Quintessence of Wisdom Openness,* says we can alternate different practices in each session, according to our preferences. For example:

In each session, plant the great stake of the essence mantra.⋮

In each session, rest in the same taste of the deity and your mind,⋮

Whereby the deity and your own mind are of equal taste.⋮

In each session, bring clear appearance of the deity to the limit,⋮

Meaning we imagine how Guru Rinpoche and the other deities appear in minute detail.

In each session, plant the great stake of the essence mantra.⋮

First plant the seed syllable in the center, then the surrounding mantra garland, and so forth.

Regarding the recitation, we should engage in the four intents of recitation: first, like the moon with a garland of stars; next, like a firebrand; then, like the emissaries of a king; and finally, like a beehive breaking open—similes corresponding to approach, full approach, accomplishment, and great accomplishment.

In some sessions, we can simply remain in the unperturbed state, where we feel certain that the nature of our mind and the deity's mind is of one taste.

In some sessions, we can imagine that rays of light shine out in all directions, making offerings to the buddhas, bodhisattvas, and deities of the Three Roots, and returning with the blessings of all their qualities. The light then shines out to all sentient beings, removing their obscurations, negative karma, and habitual tendencies, and transforming each and every one of them into deities, dakas, and dakinis. Thus, everything we see, hear, and think becomes the display of primordial wakefulness.

In every session, always keep the pride of being indivisible from the deity.

Receiving the Siddhis

Now, we have come to the thirty-fourth day of the retreat. Usually, at the end of each recitation session, we say the Hundred Syllable mantra three times. But on the thirty-fourth day, the day before completing the retreat (it doesn't matter if we are doing this as a group practice with many people or alone), we chant many extra Hundred Syllable mantras at the conclusion of each recitation period, as a way to clear up faults. We also recite the *Barchey Lamsel*, and so forth.

If we have time the next morning, the thirty-fifth day, we can use the longer version of the sadhana practice. If not, we can use some parts of it. For example, the *Trinley Gyepa* has a special section for receiving the accomplishments (*ngödrub len*). We can also simply use these four lines from the *Trinley Nyingpo*:

> Hung Hrih!⁸
> In the essence mandala of bodhichitta,⁸
> Gathering of deities reveling in wisdom magic,⁸
> Without departing, remember your vajra samaya⁸
> And bestow blessings, empowerments, and siddhis!⁸

We take blessings from the torma on the shrine, which should be regarded as the Trikaya Deity with the twelve manifestations, the four dakas and dakinis, and so forth. Prior to the start of the retreat, this torma should have been consecrated, just like a statue, with the mantras of all these deities inside.

We take a small piece from the front section and eat that. We also take a little nectar, touch the torma to our three places, and receive the accomplishments. We should do this exactly when the sun rises over the horizon, when the first rays create a spectacular display in the morning sky, with circles and so forth. This is the exact time we should receive the accomplishments.

After this, we can do either the long or short version of the sadhana, whichever is suitable, following it down to the feast section. Here, it says it is good if one can do a hundredfold feast, as described earlier, or the feast according to the long sadhana, the *Trinley Gyepa*, all the way down to the lhagma.

STUDENT: Should we receive the siddhis (*ngödrub len*) before we even start the sadhana itself?

LAMA: It is actually up to you, however you prefer. But there is a tradition of doing the sadhana an extra time after the receiving the siddhis in the form of a thanksgiving, including an elaborate feast offering, and so forth. This is done after having received the accomplishments.

STUDENT: What if we prefer to receive the accomplishments during the practice itself?

LAMA: The *ngödrub len* is done at the end of the recitations. It could be done right before the feast section. After having repeated the mantras, the vowels and consonants, the offerings and praises, the *Barchey Lamsel,* and the Hundred Syllables, we can recite the sadhana verses for receiving the accomplishments. At this point, we could just continue with the feast, if we are doing the short version. According to the *Trinley Gyepa,* if we are doing an extensive practice, including the hundredfold feast, we should go back and start from the beginning of the sadhana after receiving the accomplishments.

FINISHING RETREAT

The stored-up residual offering, which has been kept throughout the whole retreat, is now given away outside for the first time.

STUDENT: The residual is accumulated for thirty-five days?

LAMA: The receivers of the residual feast offering do not have the power to remain within the mandala. They must remain at the periphery. The reason can be traced back to when the Heruka subjugated Rudra. At that time, some attendants remained on the outskirts, not within the main mandala. As a future promise, they would always receive the leftovers, even though they would not be able to participate in the main feast.

It is like inviting an important minister to a banquet. He arrives with many attendants, who do not all sit at the main table. Some sit outside until the minister finishes his feast. Afterward, they may eat. In the same way, we keep the leftovers until the end of the accomplishments and then distribute them.

At this point, if we are not doing a feast in a normal session, we go straight to the dissolution stage. This is the moment of dissolving the mandala. If we have a mandala made of colored sand or powder, we should chant four lines that are called the "request to take leave." If we have a statue or a painted canvas mandala, we chant a different four-line verse, called the "request to remain permanently." We should always chant these verses first.

For example, at the end of a long period of practice, colored sand is scooped together into a pile and taken somewhere else. Prior to this, the deities must be allowed to depart with the four-line verse. If they are represented by a statue or tangka, we ask them to remain.

Afterward, just as at the end of each session, we dissolve the visualization of the mandala by uttering HUNG HUNG HUNG. First, the details of the mandala melt into light, which the deities absorb. The outer deities, above, below, and all around, then dissolve into light and melt into you. The inner deities consist of three sattvas—the samaya being, which is the form of Guru Rinpoche; the wisdom being, which is the five-pronged vajra in the heart center; and the samadhi being, which is the seed-syllable HRIH in the center of the vajra. They dissolve consecutively into one another.

First, the samaya being, the form of Guru Rinpoche, dissolves into the wisdom being, which dissolves into the vajra with the seed syllable and mantra. Then the vajra and the surrounding seed syllables dissolve into the samadhi being, the HRIH itself. The HRIH then slowly dissolves until nothing is held in mind anymore. At this point, there is nothing to be meditated upon, no meditator, and no act of meditation—just emptiness totally free of constructs. We remain like this for a while, in order to eliminate the extreme view of eternalism or permanence.

As you know, non-Buddhist philosophy adheres to either nihilism or eternalism. We dissolve the entire mandala for the sake of destroying one of the two wrong views. This is essential.

Repeating HUNG three times, imagine that the manifest circle of deities dissolves into the space of luminosity. Repeating PHAT three times, as the *Trinley Gyepa* describes, we again imagine ourselves in the form of Guru Rinpoche. Like a fish jumping out of water, this occurs in an instant. We are actually quite accustomed to this procedure already; it is not something new. When we talk about people we know, their appearances immediately come to mind, as soon as we mention their names. It is not a gradual process. Similarly, when a fish leaps out of water, it does not manifest as something that slowly takes the form of a fish. It doesn't happen that way at all. You see the fish in its entirety immediately. In the same way, here we instantly regard ourselves as Guru Rinpoche with one face, two arms, and so forth. At this point, even if it were a different deity with eighteen arms and nine heads, we would still just visualize the deity in a simple form, having just one face and two arms. Then, we should sustain the pride of being the deity in all situations throughout the day. The text says:

> Once more, all appearances, including my own, are the nature of the wisdom endowed with all aspects of the body, speech, and mind of the mandala circle.⁸

All aspects means "everything"—manifest form, sound, smell, taste, and texture. These are all included within the wisdom mandala of all the aspects of body, speech, mind, qualities, and activities; there is nothing impure. In this way, you should emerge, while maintaining the pride of being the deity.

The purpose of this is to destroy the other of the two wrong views, the view of nihilism. In order to destroy this view, you manifest again. There is another reason for this phase as well: it forms the coincidence for our manifesting out of the state of dharmakaya in a form-body, for the welfare of all beings.

At this time, we can also go out and take down the poles that were a support for the *Four Guardian Kings*. Just as we did a short chant at the outset, requesting them to remain, we now do a short chant asking them to depart. If we are in a retreat setting, we need not keep the four kings there. But if we are in a monastery setting, we can keep the four kings as represented by a statue, a painting, or such. At this point, we make a short offering and praise in four lines. With BENZA MU, we ask them to depart. Once the poles have been taken down, people can come in and we can go out.

THE THREE EXCELLENCES

Now, we have reached the dedication of merit and the formation of aspirations. This is the third aspect in the context of the three excellences: the excellent preparation of bodhichitta, the excellent main part of no concepts, and the excellent conclusion of dedication.

It is extremely important that these three excellences imbue any practice you do, even the recitation of one hundred OM MANI PADMA HUNG mantras. In this case, the first excellence is the intention to benefit not just yourself, but also all other sentient beings, by means of the recitation of one hundred Mani mantras. The second excellence is the nonconceptual meditation on Avalokiteshvara, with the seed syllable and surrounding mantra garland, radiating rays of light to benefit all beings. The third excellence is the wish to share the benefit generated by this with all others. This is the excellent conclusion.

There was a great master who lived during the time of the Buddha. At first, he was a non-Buddhist, but later Buddha Shakyamuni converted him. This master wrote some praises, and in one praise, he said, "It is only in your teachings that one dedicates the roots of virtue for the benefit of others. Non-Buddhist teachings never advocate this. This is your superior quality."

Here, the words are very profound:

> Hoh
> By the power of accomplishing the mandala of the Vidyadhara Guru,
> May I and all the infinite sentient beings without exception
> Spontaneously accomplish the four kinds of activities
> And be liberated into the luminous space of dharmakaya!

After the dedication and aspiration verses, we conclude with four lines for auspiciousness. At this point, imagine that all the buddhas and bodhisattvas, deities, and so forth have gathered in the sky in front of you. They utter the words of truthful speech and scatter a shower of Mandarava flowers. While these blossoms are raining down, we utter the four-line verse:

> May the blessings of the root and lineage gurus enter my heart!
> May the yidams and dakinis accompany me like a shadow follows the body!
> May the dharma protectors and guardians dispel all obstacles!
> May there be the auspiciousness of attaining the supreme and common siddhis!

This marks the conclusion of practice.

More Questions on the Thirty-Five-Day Retreat

STUDENT: I have a husband and a child and I have to work, so to do a thirty-five-day retreat would be difficult. What can I do?

LAMA: That's all right. It need not be only thirty-five days in length. This is just how it is prescribed, if you are doing the practice as a retreat. Nevertheless, you should still use the same proportions, stretching it out over a longer period of time, such as three or four months. You should still divide the practice up in the same proportions, using such-and-such number of days on the preliminaries and such-and-such number of days on each of the different mantras. You just stretch it out over a longer period of time.

STUDENT: If I were to try to do this practice as a retreat in my home, I would have to complete a certain number of sessions. However, in the evenings, I would have to interact with my child and my husband, because they need me. Is this possible, or not?

LAMA: Yes, that is all right. You should engage in each session with the best possible qualities; normal conversation should not interrupt it. Compared to repeating one thousand mantras interrupted by conversation, it is far better to say only one hundred mantras, where we begin with bodhichitta, refrain from ordinary speech, and conclude with the vowel-consonant mantra, because this is really pure, like a diamond. Even if the session is very short, at least you will have accrued one diamond for that piece of time. When you practice another first-rate session, you collect another diamond. You end up with a great accumulation of diamonds. That's much better than doing a lot of practice that is not really top quality. You end up with a whole handful of something other than diamonds. The most important aspect is the quality of one's practice.

STUDENT: Does one then still start the retreat by staking up the protector kings of the four directions and so forth?

LAMA: That's not necessary. Mind is the most important. The mind is the one in retreat for that duration of practice, so that's what is essential. It's not just a matter of closing the door, setting up the boundary, and so forth. Concentrating on your practice is more valuable than setting up elaborate boundaries, while sitting and thinking about America and other places. That won't help very much. The physical retreat is mainly for beginners, because a beginner's mind is easily carried away by what it sees and hears. Therefore, it is important to go somewhere where you will not encounter others, will not hear conversations, and will not see or smell things that cause you to create a lot of thoughts. But advanced practitioners can remain in the middle of town and still be in retreat, because the environment doesn't affect them. The sense impressions do not harm them in any way, and this is what is meant by retreat.

CONCLUSION

We receive a reading transmission *(lung)* by simply hearing the sounds, even if we don't understand the words or their meaning. However, receiving guidance in a text entails step-by-step instructions in the meaning of each word and sentence. This need not be passed on quickly.

Regarding the instruction text called the *Thirty-Five-Day Practice* arranged by Jamyang Khyentse, it is very good, of course, if we Dharma practitioners can do a thirty-five-day retreat. On the other hand, we should not think a retreat setting is the only approach to doing this practice. If we think this way, we may never get around to doing it. We can do this practice right now, even if we have no time to do a retreat.

We have a method for doing this practice on a daily basis. Beginners can follow a very short style, whereby just doing the approach aspect suffices. *The Concise Daily Practice Manual, Naljor Gyüngyi Köljang*, is a very short text, only two pages long. It has a brief refuge and bodhichitta, the visualization beginning with the three samadhis, and just a single mantra, the Vajra Guru mantra. After saying this mantra just one hundred times, very nicely, you then say the Vowels and Consonants, the Essence of Causation, and the Hundred Syllable mantras three times each. Conclude with dedication and aspiration. If you can just endeavor in this, it's fine, because it actually includes the entire meaning of both the long and short sadhanas of the *Trinley Nyingpo* in a very concise way. It's perfectly all right, because these teachings are meant to be applied right now, not just kept in mind as a plan to be carried out some day in the future. We all make the mistake of thinking we will have time later to do our practice.

THE BINDU OF TRUE MEANING

The Visualization Stages for
The Concise Practice Manual of Tukdrub

Karmey Khenpo Rinchen Dargye

NAMO GURU MAHA NIDHIYE

For the application of the daily practice of *Lamey Tukdrub Barchey Kün-sel, The Guru's Heart Practice, Dispeller of All Obstacles,* first perform the refuge and bodhichitta from *Trinley Nyingpo, The Yoga of Essential Activity,* while remembering the qualities of the Three Jewels.

Then, by uttering HUNG, rest your mind in the state of suchness, which is empty of both "perceiver" and "perceived."

Space of emptiness refers to the suchness samadhi of great emptiness, which downwardly purifies the death state, upwardly perfects the qualities of dharmakaya, and in between ripens one for meditating on the path of emptiness.

All-illuminating wisdom refers to the illuminating samadhi of magic-like compassion, which downwardly purifies the bardo state, upwardly perfects the qualities of sambhogakaya, and in between ripens one for the path of such magic-like compassion.

The seed-samadhi HRIH emanates light refers to the subtle seed syllable of the seed samadhi, which downwardly purifies the birth state, upwardly perfects the qualities of the nirmanakaya of buddhahood, and in between ripens one for the path of development stage. These then are the three samadhis of the main part.

All appearance and existence is the realm of Padmajala means that in the midst of the perfectly decorated Akanishtha Realm of Padmajala, the Lotus Net, there is an eight-sided jewel, upon a white crystal square. Upon the center of this is a four-petaled lotus, resting upon a jewel throne, sun, and moon. Upon this, the syllable HRIH of the seed samadhi is instantaneously transformed.

In the word *Mahaguru, maha* means "great" and *guru* means "master." In the name *Orgyen Tötreng Tsal, Orgyen* refers to a sacred place, and *Tötreng Tsal* is Guru Rinpoche's secret name.

The majestic splendor of his physical form gloriously subjugates appearance and existence. His body color is white and red, and he has a half-peaceful, half-wrathful expression.

His right hand raises or points a five-pronged vajra into the sky, directly at the level of his heart center. His left hand, in the mudra of equanimity, holds a skull cup *(kapala),* a bliss-sustainer adorned with the life vase of immortality.

At his left side, he embraces his supreme, secret consort in the concealed form of a three-pointed khatvanga, endowed with three stacked heads, a vase, a vajra cross, silk streamers, and bangles of drums and bells.

Upon his head, he wears the lotus crown, which liberates through seeing. He is dressed in the secret white dress, a dark blue gown, red and yellow Dharma robes, and a reddish-brown brocade cloak.

His right leg is bent and his left extended, but even if they are reversed, there is no conflict. So, in the right or left playful royal posture, he is majestically poised, seated within a sphere of five-colored rainbow lights.

On the branch growing from the stem of the lotus behind the bodily form of Orgyen Rinpoche, two flowers blossom above his head. On the lower one, is the mighty sambhogakaya lord, Avalokiteshvara, brilliant white with one face and four arms, holding a jewel, crystal rosary, and a white lotus. On the upper flower, sits the lord of the family, Protector Amitayus, Boundless Life, brilliant red, holding a life vase. Both of them wear the sambhogakaya attire and are seated with their legs in vajra posture.

The masters of the six lineages are above; the yidams, the divinities of the tantric sections, are in between; and an ocean of pledge-holding guardians of the Dharma is below. The twelve manifestations are in the four main and eight subsidiary directions. In all directions, the Three Roots and dharma protectors gather as an ocean-like cloud bank, without any intermediate space.

It is most important to visualize the three main kayas, and it will suffice to merely imagine the retinue as being present. Nonetheless, here is a brief description of their body colors and attributes.

To the east, white Gyalwey Dungdzin wears a crown of dry skulls, bone ornaments, and a tiger skirt. His right hand holds a sword and his left a hook. Smiling semi-wrathfully, he is in half-vajra posture.

To the south, white Mawey Senge, wears a monk's dress and a red[17] pandita hat. His two hands are in the mudra of expounding the Dharma. The upper and lower lotuses support books, and his legs are in crossed position.

To the west, yellow Kyechok Tsülzang wears a monk's dress and a red pandita hat. His right hand holds a vajra and his left a casket; his legs are in crossed position.

To the north, light-brown Dükyi Shechen wears a dark blue and orange lotus crown and cloak. His right hand supports his recitation dagger on the hip, while his left hand stabs the action dagger at the obstructors. He is in a striding stance, with the right leg bent and the left leg extended.

Outside of them, on the eight-sided jewel to the east, dark-blue Dzamling Gyenchok wears the eight charnel ground ornaments, such as the skull crown, and a two-layered cloak. His belt supports the recitation dagger, which he rolls between his right and left hands. Wrathful and awe-inspiring, he is in the striding stance, with his right leg bent and his left leg extended.

To the south, blue Pema Jungney holds vajra and bell in his crossed arms. His consort, the white princess, holds a knife and skull. They have ornaments of silks, jewels, and bones and are seated with their legs in vajra and lotus postures.

To the west, brilliant-white Kyepar Phakpey Rigdzin wears a blue lotus crown and cloak and red Dharma robes. He holds a vajra in his right hand, in the manner of showing the paths and stages; in his left, he is using a khatvanga as a staff. He wears boots on his feet and stands in a walking posture.

To the north, reddish-maroon Dzutrül Tuchen wears a monk's dress, a head garland, and bone ornaments. His right hand holds a vajra and his left a dagger. Ferociously clenching his teeth, he stands upon a lotus, sun, and tiger seat, crushing a male and female rudra.

To the southeast, dark-red Vidyadhara Dorje Drakpo Tsal wears charnel ground attire. His right hand holds a vajra and his left an iron

---

17 Chokgyur Lingpa says yellow pandita hat.

scorpion. He is in union with the dark-blue Varahi, holding knife and skull. With legs in a striding stance, he tramples the male *gyalpo* and female *sinmo*.

To the southwest, dark-blue Kalden Drendzey wears the eightfold charnel ground attire and the ten glorious ornaments. He holds a vajra and a skull cup with blood, one above the other. He is united with his light-blue consort, Namshelma, Sky Faced One, who holds a knife and skull cup. With his right leg bent and his left leg extended, he tramples down a male and female *drekpa*.

To the northwest, dark-maroon Raksha Tötreng wears the charnel ground attire. He holds a vajra and a skull cup with blood and embraces Ting-Ö Barma, Blazing Blue Light, who holds a knife and skull cup. With his right leg bent and his left leg extended, he tramples a male and female samaya corrupter (*damsi*).

To the northeast, brilliant-red Dechen Gyalpo wears jewel and bone ornaments. He holds a vajra and bell in his crossed arms and is in union with his red consort, who holds a damaru and skull cup. His legs are in the striding stance.

At the four gates, the four classes of dakas—white, yellow, red, and green—wear tiger skirts, bone ornaments, skull crowns, and silk streamers. They hold skull cups and knives with vajra, jewel, lotus, and vajra-cross handles. Standing with their legs bent and extended, they are in dancing postures.

All of them are primordially and spontaneously present as the nature in which samaya beings and wisdom beings are indivisible.

The visualization for the recitations follows this. In the heart center of Amitayus, the lord of the family, the syllable HRIH and the mantra garland rest upon a moon disc, emanating rays of five-colored light that is primarily red.

Gathering all the life nectar of samsara and nirvana, the light rays dissolve into me. Uttering this gathers back all your vitality and life energy, which had been cut, degenerated, or dissipated. Outwardly, this life nectar is the essence of the four elements of the world; inwardly, it is the life energy, merit, strength, and wealth of the beings of the three realms; and secretly, it encompasses the wisdom, knowledge, compassion, and power of the victorious ones and their sons. It summons all outer, inner, and secret essences in the form of five-colored nectar. In the context of the *Concise Daily Practice Manual, Gyüngyi Köljang*, you simply let it dissolve into you like falling rain. You do not need to make it flow down from the vase and so forth, as in the medium and detailed versions.

Concerning the Great Compassionate One, in the heart center of the noble and supreme Great Compassionate Tamer of Beings, the letter HRIH stands in the middle of a six-petaled lotus, upon which the Six Syllables are arranged. They face inward and circle clockwise, starting from the front. By the magic of the nadis and elements, the individual lights, white and so forth, emanating from these six letters, purify the sufferings of the six kinds of sentient being, as well as their causes, as follows:

Blue light rays from the mirror-like wisdom of HUNG purify the beings in hell. Yellow light rays from the equalizing wisdom of ME purify the hungry ghosts. White light rays from the dharmadhatu wisdom of PAD purify the animals. Red light rays from the discriminating wisdom of NI purify the human beings. Green light rays from the all-accomplishing wisdom of MA purify the demigods. White light rays from the great luminosity wisdom of OM purify the gods. The five-colored rays of light from the HRIH, emanating to fill the sky, purify the sufferings of beings equal to the sky in number.

This visualization, and so forth, is the detailed version for emptying the realms of the six classes of beings; however, for this daily practice, the condensed way is sufficient.

The actual visualization for the root recitation follows this. In my heart center as Padmakara, the guru in the form that embodies all families, a five-pronged golden vajra stands upon a full-moon disc. On the moon disc, in the hollow of its center, is the spiritual life force, the white syllable HRIH, surrounded by the mantra garland. White and radiant, the outward-facing garland is arranged counter-clockwise, but it circles clockwise. It emanates rays of light, which make offerings to all the noble ones and accomplishes the benefit of beings.

The outer vessel, the world, is the Akanishtha Realm of All-Encompassing Purity. The inner contents, the beings, are the great mudra of the body of *deities of appearance and existence as manifest ground*. In this way, all perceptions are deities. All resounding sounds are the melodious tones of the speech of mantras. All thoughts are spontaneously purified into the mind of nondual luminosity. This naturally fulfills the four common karmas of pacifying, increasing, magnetizing, and subjugating, as well as the all-encompassing activity.

By spontaneously accomplishing the body, speech, and mind of the supremely unchanging great bliss, the level of the Immortal Vidyadhara, we will attain the indivisibility of the three kayas within this very lifetime.

Having uttered this, rest evenly in the continuity of undivided space and awareness. Recite the root recitation of OM AH HUNG VAJRA GURU PADMA SIDDHI HUNG as many times as possible.

Concerning the meaning of the mantra, the *Concise Manual* says, *The three syllables are the inseparable three kayas.* Externally, OM is body, AH is speech, and HUNG is mind. Internally, OM is nadi, AH is prana, and HUNG is bindu. Secretly, HUNG is dharmakaya, AH is sambhogakaya, and OM is nirmanakaya. According to the innermost secret of thatness, HUNG is the empty essence, AH is the luminous nature, and OM is the natural expression of manifold compassion.

VAJRA GURU refers to the Lord of the Family. Externally, this is Guru Dorje Tötreng Tsal; internally, it is Guru Vajrasattva; secretly, it is the unexcelled basic wakefulness; and most secretly, it is the unchanging primordial purity.

PADMA refers to being manifest as the mandala circle. Externally, this is the vidyadhara teacher and retinue in the realm of Padmajala; internally, it is the bindu mandala of bodhichitta; secretly, it is the upaya, teacher, and retinue of great bliss in the space of the consort; and, according to the innermost secret of thatness, it is the unified mandala of undivided space and awareness.

SIDDHI HUNG invokes the siddhis, which are the outer accomplishment of the four karmas, the inner accomplishment of the eight siddhis, and the secret accomplishment of the supreme siddhi. Externally, they are the accomplishment of mastery in the development stage; internally, they are the accomplishment of pliability of the nadis and pranas; and secretly, they are the accomplishment of giving rise to the special realization of one's mind. According to the innermost secret of thatness, they are the absence of both a siddhi to be attained and somebody who attains it.

This vajra mantra condensing approach, accomplishment, and activities into one, fulfills all the activities. These twelve vajra syllables, condensing approach, accomplishment, and activities into one, fulfill all the activities that have not been fulfilled. Without wasting the fulfilled ones, they bring all activities to perfection.

At the end of the session, supplicate the guru, who embodies all the families, and mingle your mind with his. Then seal, by dedicating the gathering of virtue and making aspirations. When you rely exclusively on what is taught here, supplicate with *Düsum Sangye* and so forth and maintain your essence. At the end, in order to clear away the extreme of eternalism, dissolve the presence as deity with HUNG. In order to clear away the extreme of nihilism, emerge in the united form with PHAT. Dedicate the gathering of virtue, as in the case of *Trinley Nyingpo,* and seal with making pure aspirations.

Lobsang Nyima, the diligent practitioner at Yardrok Ganden, the seat of Künkhyen Padma Garwang of the incarnation lineage of Rechen Paljor Sangpo, the chief disciple holding the oral transmission of Künkhyen Bodongpa, made a request expressing the need for the visualization stages of the *Concise Daily Practice of Tukdrub Barchey Künsel.* In accordance with this request, this was committed to writing by Khenpo Karma Ratna Wangchuk, a disciple of the great treasure revealer, on the tenth day of the Monkey month in the year of the Fire Ox, at a time when he was mostly distracting himself with the amusing dramas of high and low people at Rasa Trülnang in Lhasa. May it be a cause for the two stages to flourish.

Tseringma and her Five Sisters

SOURCE MATERIAL

Chokling Tersar

Volume KA:

This volume introduces the texts revealed by Chokgyur Lingpa on the cycle known as *Lamey Tukdrub Barchey Künsel, Dispeller of Obstacles, The Heart Practice of Padmasambhava* as well as the related sadhanas, lineage prayers, and so forth. It also contains commentaries and explanations by other masters of the lineage.

KA 3. *The Essence Manual of Oral Instructions (zhal gdams snying byang)*. The basic terma text of *Lamey Tukdrub Barchey Künsel,* with chapters for historical background, sadhanas for the gurus of the three kayas and for each of the twelve manifestations, and so forth, as well as prophesies for the future. This includes a chapter called *The Quintessence of Wisdom Openness.*

Volume GA:

GA 2. *Bestowing the Splendor of Accomplishment (dngos grub dpal ster)*. The lineage supplication for *Lamey Tukdrub Barchey Künsel.* P.1–4.*[18]

GA 9. *The Recitation Manual for Approach and Accomplishment (bsnyen sgrub dza pra kyi bkol byang)*. Terma text for the recitation part of the *Extensive Practice (phrin las rgyas pa)*. P. 77–96.*

GA 17. *Trinley Nyingpo, The Yoga of Essential Activity (phrin las snying po'i rnal 'byor)*. The short guru sadhana, according to *Lamey Tukdrub Barchey Künsel.* P. 169–178.*

GA 18. *The Concise Manual for Daily Practice (rgyun gyi rnal 'byor bkol byang)*. The concise daily guru sadhana, according to *Lamey Tukdrub Barchey Künsel.* P. 179–182.*

GA 28. *The Seed of the Great Sal Tree (sa la chen po'i sa bon)*. Short notes on the recitation practice of *Trinley Nyingpo,* by Jamgön Kongtrül. P. 395–408.

---

18 Single asterik notes: Available as a booklet from Rangjung Yeshe Translations; www.rangjung.com

GA 29. *Short Notes on Trinley Nyingpo (bsnyen sgrub las gsum bya ba'i yig chung).* Explanation of the *Trinley Nyingpo* sadhana, by Chokgyur Lingpa. P. 409–420.

GA 30. *The Thirty-Five-Day Practice (zla gcig zhag lnga tsam mdzad pa'i zin tho).* Explanation on how to practice *Trinley Nyingpo* in a thirty-five-day retreat, by Jamyang Khyentse Wangpo. P. 421–430.*

Sphere of Refined Gold (bla ma'i thugs sgrub bar chad kun sel las, rig 'dzin padma 'byung gnas kyi rdzogs rim 'od gsal rdzogs pa chen po'i khrid yig thig le gser zhun ces bya ba bzhugs so). The Guidance Text in the Luminous Great Perfection of Rigdzin Pema Jungney according to Lamey Tukdrub Barchey Künsel, by Jamgön Kongtrül.

ADDITIONAL TIBETAN TEXTS

Chokling Tersar

Volume GA:

GA 3. *The Fivefold Consecration (byin rlabs rnam lnga)*. Consecration of the puja articles prior to beginning the sadhana*

GA 5. *The Seven Preliminary Points, the Seven Points of the Main Part, and the Seven Concluding Points. The Extensive Practice (phrin las rgyas pa)*. The extensive version of the guru sadhana, according to *Lamey Tukdrub Barchey Künsel*.*

GA 10. *Opening of the Mansion of Recitation (dza pra khang dbye ba)*. Also called *Gzhi Bstod*. Arrangement liturgy for the recitation part of the *Extensive Practice (phrin las rgyas pa)*.*

GA 12. *The Turquoise Room (g.yu zhal ma)*. The brief fulfillment for *Lamey Tukdrub Barchey Künsel*.*

GA 15. *The Medium Practice of Lamey Tukdrub Barchey Künsel (phrin las 'bring po)*. The medium guru sadhana, according to *Lamey Tukdrub Barchey Künsel*.*

GA 16. *Appendix for the Essence Practice (phrin snying zur 'debs)*. Appendix to GA 17.*

GA 19. *The Secret Mantra That Liberates through Hearing of the Family Lord Vajrasattva (rigs bdag rdo rje sems dpa"i gsang sngags thos pas grol ba)*, plus the *Lotus Essence Tantra* together with the *Reading Method (pad ma snying po'i rgyud bklags thabs dang bcas pa)*.*

GA 20. *The Teaching Protector Sadhana for the Five Sisters of Long Life (bka' srung tshe ring mched lnga'i sgrub thabs)*. The sadhana for *Tseringma* and her four sisters, the dharma protectors of *Lamey Tukdrub Barchey Künsel*.*

Volume NGA:

NGA 6. *The Lamentation of Rudra (smre bshags)*. Confession liturgy.

NGA 7. *The Cloud Banks of Nectar (bdud rtsi'i sprin phung)*. Offering to the dharma protectors, by Chokgyur Lingpa.

NGA 9. *The Cloud Bank of Blessings (byin rlabs sprin phung)*. Supplication to the ocean-like hosts of the Three Roots and the dharma protectors, by Jamyang Khyentse Wangpo.

NGA 15. *Clearing the Obstacles of the Path Supplication (gsol 'debs bar chad lam sel).* The root supplication for *Lamey Tukdrub Barchey Künsel.* *

NGA 16. *The Seed of Supreme Enlightenment (byang chub mchog gi sa bon).* The original liturgy for the preliminary practices, by Jamyang Khyentse Wangpo.

NGA 17. *The Seed of Supreme Enlightenment (byang chub mchog gi sa bon).* The expanded liturgy for the preliminary practices of *Lamey Tukdrub Barchey Künsel.**

NGA 19. *The Essential Meaning (don gyi snying po).* The short commentary on the *Lotus Essence Tantra.*

NGA 21. *The Way to Perform the Extensive Preliminary Practices (sngon 'gro rgyas pa btang tshul).* *

NGA 22. *The Great Gate for Accomplishing Unexcelled Enlightenment (bla med byang chub sgrub pa'i sgo chen).* The extensive commentary on how to perform the preliminary practices of *Lamey Tukdrub Barchey Künsel,* by the second Chokgyur Lingpa.****[19]

Volume CA:

CA 6. *The Blooming of Intelligence (blo gros kha 'byed).* The sadhana, empowerment ritual, and activity applications of Mawey Senge, by Jamgön Kongtrül.

The Oral Teachings That Gladden the Lake-Born Master—A Concise and Clear Guidance Manual Covering the Complete Two Stages of Lamey Tukdrub Barchey Künsel, The Guru's Heart Practice of Dispelling All Obstacles, by Kyabje Dilgo Khyentse Rinpoche.

---

19 **Available from Rangjung Yeshe Publications; www.rangjung.com

ADDITIONAL ENGLISH TEXTS

Dzogchen Essentials, The Path That Clarifies Confusion, Rangjung Yeshe Publications, Hong Kong, 2004.
A Practice of Padmasambhava, Snow Lion Publications, Ithaca, New York, 2011.
The Light of Wisdom, Volume II, Rangjung Yeshe Publications, Hong Kong, 1998.
Vajra Wisdom Deity Practice in Tibetan Buddhism, Snow Lion Publications, Ithaca, New York, 2011.
Trinley Nyingpo Commentaries, Tulku Urgyen Rinpoche, 1984, 1989, 1995. Chokyi Nyima Rinpoche, 1990.
Extensive Commentary on the Thirty-Five-Day Practice, Lama Putsi Pema Tashi.
*The Ocean of Amrita, A Vajrayana Mending and Purification Practice.***
Precious Songs of Awakening, Chants for Daily Practice, Feast & Drubchen.
*Tukdrub Barchey Künsel Drubchen Texts.***
The Lotus Essence Tantra, Fundamental Principles of Buddhist Tantra. Forthcoming, Rangjung Yeshe Publications.
Quintessential Dzogchen, Confusion Arising as Wisdom, Rangjung Yeshe Publications, Hong Kong, 2006.

MP3-4 FILES, VIDEOS, AND PHOTOS

Melodies of Pure Gold.
Trinley Nyingpo, The Yoga of Essential Activity, Audio and Video.
The Best of the Four Dharmas of Gampopa, by Tulku Urgyen Rinpoche. Video. Teachings on the entire path of Vajrayana.
Tangkas and tangka details for the *Tukdrub* cycle.

All practice booklets and photos as well as audio and video files are available from links on the Rangjung Yeshe Publications website; www.rangjung.com

For melodious versions of some of these chants that can be set to music, contact, Erik via email, rangjung@gmail.com or marcia@rangjung.com

Kharak Khyung Tsünma

APPENDIX I

The Supplication to the Lineage of Tukdrub Barchey Künsel,
Entitled Bestower of the Splendor of Accomplishments

Jamgön Kongtrül

Protector of the Blissful Realm, all-pervasive dharmakaya lord,
Shining with thousands of effulgent marks, deathless god of gods,
I supplicate you; dispel the outer and inner obstacles!
Bless me; bestow the supreme and common siddhis!

Lord of Potala, Sambhogakaya Vairochana,
Mighty Compassionate One, Protector of Beings, White Lotus
  Holder,
I supplicate you; dispel the outer and inner obstacles!
Bless me; bestow the supreme and common siddhis!

Glorious Nirmanakaya, Lotus Born,
Splendid Subjugator of All that Appears and Exists, Tötreng Tsal,
  King of Victorious Ones,
I supplicate you; dispel the outer and inner obstacles!
Bless me; bestow the supreme and common siddhis!

Queen of Wisdom, Dakini Gatherings,
Mistress of Secrets, Dhatvishvari Tsogyalma,
I supplicate you; dispel the outer and inner obstacles!
Bless me; bestow the supreme and common siddhis!

Regent Vairotsana, Single Eye of the World,
Manjushrivajra Trisong, father and sons,
I supplicate you; dispel the outer and inner obstacles!
Bless me; bestow the supreme and common siddhis!

Incarnation of Damdzin, Lord of One Hundred Treasures and
   Places,
Tamer of the Beings of the Dark-Age, Chokgyur Dechen Lingpa,
I supplicate you; dispel the outer and inner obstacles!
Bless me; bestow the supreme and common siddhis!

All-Pervasive Lord Jamyang Khyentse Wangpo
And Sovereign of the Mandala, Lodrö Thaye,
I supplicate you; dispel the outer and inner obstacles!
Bless me; bestow the supreme and common siddhis!

Heirs to the profound secret teachings, with fortunate karmic
   aspirations,
Predicted Dharma-holders, and masters of the lineage,
I supplicate you; dispel the outer and inner obstacles!
Bless me; bestow the supreme and common siddhis!

Yidams, dakinis, vow-holders, and guardians of the treasures and
   places,
Magical circle that revels in nondual wisdom,
I supplicate you; dispel the outer and inner obstacles!
Bless me; bestow the supreme and common siddhis!

Supreme Divinities of the Three Roots, accept me until
   enlightenment,
Pacify the eight fears, four maras, and five poisons,
And the outer, inner, and secret obstacles.
Let me swiftly attain the state of the Trikaya Guru.

*This was composed by Padma Garwang Trinley Drodül Tsal, a joyful ser-
vant of Padma, at Devikoti Tsari-Like Jewel Rock (Tsandra Rinchen Drak),
the upper retreat of Palpung, on an auspicious day in the waxing part of the
second month. The scribe was Karma Gyurmey, who is endowed with the fortune of karmic aspirations. May virtuous goodness increase.*

APPENDIX II

The Concise Manual for Daily Practice According to Lamey Tukdrub Barchey Künsel

Padmasambhava

The yogin of true simplicity,
When practicing this essential daily yoga,
Should in solitude gather all the articles necessary
To be a suitable vessel for meditation.
He should then with one-pointed concentration
Enter the meaning of deity, mantra, and wisdom.

Namo

I and all beings equal to the sky
Take refuge in the ones who are the supreme refuge.
Developing the bodhichitta of aspiration and application,
I will accomplish the level of the Trikaya Guru.

Hung

From the space of emptiness, all-illuminating wisdom,
The seed-samadhi HRIH emanates light,
And all appearance and existence is the Realm of Padmajala.
Amidst this wonderfully decorated inconceivable mandala,

Upon a jewel throne, lotus, sun, and moon,
The syllable HRIH transforms, and in an instant I become
Mahaguru Orgyen Tötreng Tsal,
The glorious subjugator of appearance and existence, white-red
    with a peaceful-wrathful expression.
My right hand raises a five-spoked vajra into the sky,

And my left holds in equanimity the skull cup with life vase.

In the crook of my left arm, I embrace the secret consort concealed
in the form of a khatvanga.

I wear the lotus crown, secret dress, gown, Dharma robes, and
brocade cloak.

With two feet in the playful, royal posture, I am majestically poised
in a sphere of rainbow light.

Above my head sits the mighty Sambhogakaya Avalokiteshvara

And the Lord of the Family Amitayus.

The twelve manifestations are above, below, and in all directions,

And an ocean of the Three Roots and dharma protectors gathers
like cloud banks.

This is the spontaneously present primordial indivisibility of
samaya being and wisdom being.

Light rays emanate from the HRIH in the heart center of the Lord of
the Family.

Gathering all the life nectar of samsara and nirvana, the light rays
dissolve into me.

The Noble Tamer of Beings, through his compassionate,
miraculous manifestation,

Purifies suffering and its causes for the six kinds of beings.

In my heart center, as the Guru Embodying All Families,

Is a golden vajra, with the letter HRIH in its center,

Encircled by the mantra chain, wherefrom rays of light emanate.

They make offerings to the noble ones and accomplish the benefit
of beings.

The outer vessel is the Akanishtha Realm of All-Encompassing
Purity.

The inner contents are the mudra deities of appearance and
existence as manifest ground.

Resounding sounds are mantras, and thoughts are the space of
luminosity.

The activities of the four common karmas are naturally fulfilled,

And in the vajra continuity of unchanging great bliss,

The supreme level of the Immortal Trikaya is attained.

OM AH HUNG VAJRA GURU PADMA SIDDHI HUNG

The three syllables are the inseparable three kayas.
VAJRA GURU is the family lord.
PADMA is manifest as the mandala circle.
SIDDHI HUNG invokes the siddhis.

*This vajra mantra condenses approach, accomplishment, and
activities into one,*
Fulfilling all the activities.
At the end of the session, supplicate the guru,
Who embodies all the families, and mingle your mind with his.
*Then seal, by dedicating the gathering of virtue and making
aspirations.*

Ho

By the power of accomplishing the mandala of the Vidyadhara
Guru,
May I and all the infinite sentient beings without exception
Spontaneously accomplish the four kinds of activities
And be liberated into the luminous space of dharmakaya.

May the blessings of the root and lineage gurus enter my heart.
May the yidams and dakinis accompany me like a shadow follows
the body.
May the dharma protectors and guardians clear away all obstacles.
May there be the auspiciousness of attaining the supreme and
common siddhis.

By supplicating constantly with devotion to the root guru,
Inseparable from the Great Master Padma,
All obstacles will be cleared and the accomplishments attained.
Samaya, seal, seal, seal.

*This is the perfect essence of the profound Dharma treasures of the incarnated
great treasure revealer Chokgyur Dechen Lingpa.*

APPENDIX III

Sphere of Refined Gold

The Guidance Text in the Luminous Great Perfection
of Rigdzin Pema Jungney
According to Lamey Tukdrub Barchey Künsel

Jamgön Kongtrül

Namo guru padmakaraya

I bow down at the feet of the Ever-Excellent Padma,
Who proclaims in the spontaneous tones of dharmata
This effortless great vehicle of certainty,
The vajra tantra endowed with the six liberations.

Here, I shall explain the basic intent
Of the essence of the ocean of guiding instructions
That leads to the state of primordial liberation
Within a single life, through the path of direct experience.

When giving the guiding instructions for the Luminous Great Perfection, the pinnacle of the nine vehicles, the single eminent path traversed by all the awakened ones, the master who gives them should possess the empowerments and pure samayas, as well as realization of Trekchö and Tögal. The disciple to whom the explanation is given should have faith, be diligent and intelligent, and cut the ties to this life, thus fulfilling the master's words. The place should have a virtuous quality and be secluded, free from obstacles to meditation. The time is simply when the auspicious link between master and disciple is formed, or when heat and cold are in balance and the wisdom easily manifests. The companion is someone who has pure samaya, pure perception, and an affectionate frame of mind. *The Tantra of the Great Self-Arising Awareness* instructs on how to engage in teaching, listening, and training, when these favorable conditions and elements are assembled.

The actual explanation of the profound guidance, the instruction that is to be given, has three parts: stating the realization in which to train, explaining the practical guidance in how to train, and describing the liberation of having trained in such a way.

STATING THE REALIZATION IN WHICH TO TRAIN

The Root Text of Vajra Speech declares:

> *For the ultimate, supreme completion stage,*⁝
> *The ground space is unconditioned primordial purity;*⁝
> *The ground manifestations of spontaneous presence arise as the*
>   *path;*⁝
> *And realizing their indivisibility matures into the fruition.*⁝
> *This is the intent of the Luminous Great Perfection.*⁝

Out of the universal ground, the essence of which is unconditioned primordial purity, all of samsara and nirvana arises as the self-display of awareness, the nature that is the ground's manifestation, in the form of the eight gates of spontaneous presence. Thus, as the expressions of the capacity stir, the appearances of the paths of samsara and nirvana arise in innumerable ways.

Liberation and confusion arise separately, due to the difference between realizing and not realizing that this is one's own natural expression. However, when realizing the indivisibility of the primordially pure ground and the spontaneously present ground manifestation—due to the circumstance of the guru's blessings and the profound instructions—confusion reverses, the space-display is exhausted into dharmata, and awareness matures into the fruition endowed with the twofold purity at the original state of liberation. This is the intent of the 6.4 million tantras of the Luminous Great Perfection condensed into a single point.

Explaining the Actual Guidance in How to Train

This has two parts: the preliminaries of purifying your stream-of-being and the main part of applying the practice.

The Preliminaries of Purifying Your Stream-of-Being

The preliminaries are of two types: the general and the specific.

The General Preliminaries

The Testament states:

> *Train in impermanence, compassion, and bodhichitta.*[30]

To explain this, the root of the Mahayana path is the precious twofold bodhichitta. In order to let it arise within your being, you must first train your mind in understanding the impermanence of the external world, the living beings within it, and your own body, which will all soon perish. Reflect upon the fact that your support, the human body endowed with the freedoms and riches, is difficult to obtain. Contemplate the fact that cause and effect never fail and that after passing away, you will undergo the intense, extended misery of samsara and the evil states of existence. With a strong and wholehearted attitude of revulsion for superficial, futile pleasures and with renunciation of the whole grandeur of samsaric existence, take refuge from today and until attaining enlightenment, by completely surrendering your plans and aims to the Three Jewels and Three Roots.

Generate the conventional bodhichitta, which has the nature of aspiration and application as the cause, and train your mind in the ultimate bodhichitta as the effect.

To purify misdeeds and obscurations, which are the adverse conditions for experience and realization to arise, exert yourself in the visualization and recitation of Vajrasattva, while completely possessing the four powers.

To increase the two accumulations in combination, creating the favorable conditions, offer the outer, inner, and secret mandalas.

To directly receive the blessings, place special emphasis on the virtuous practice of guru yoga, including the essential supplications, by means of the intense fervor of sincere devotion.

If you wish to begin with the development stage in harmony with the general tradition of Anuttara, you won't need to distract yourself with elaborate details. While possessing the "personal yoga," use the background support of the *Six Wondrous Teachings* or read their essence, the *Lotus Essence Tantra*. The writings of the omniscient master Dorje Ziji Tsal clarify how to practice this.[6]

At the very outset, or at this point, you must receive the unique ripening empowerment for the two stages of development and completion. This bestows the blessings for body, speech, and mind, as well as the twentyfold manifest perfection, which are conferred in the elaborate, unelaborate, very unelaborate, and extremely unelaborate manners, in accordance with the realization of unifying the pith instructions and the oral transmission. Observe the general and special samayas, as if they were your own life.

The Daily Practice

Equalize buddhahood at the four times.[a]

A practitioner of the Great Perfection should exert himself in practicing the continuous river of unceasing dharmata, by means of the vital points of possessing the oral instructions on equalizing buddhahood at the four times.

To seal appearances in the daytime, by not losing the natural stability of awareness throughout the meditation and post-meditation periods, resolve whatever arises in your experience to be the great, unimpeded state of realization, which is nondual and primordially free. When unable to do so, train in seeing all phenomena as illusory. Without letting your mind run wild, lead your perceptions to the space of primordial purity.

To gather the senses naturally at dusk, assume the nirmanakaya posture. Focus your attention on a four-petaled red lotus flower in the navel center within your body's central channel, which is light red, radiant, and straight. At the level of your navel is the ATUNG,, the nature of heat; at the crown of your head is the white HANG, the nature of bliss. Expel the stale breath and hold the vase breath; if you cannot, hold the medium breath. Thus focus your attention on the wisdom of blissful heat generated by the blazing and dripping.

To allow your consciousness to enter the vase at midnight, keep the posture as before. Focus your attention on a radiant white A amidst a four-petaled red lotus in the heart center of the central channel, visualized as before. After that, visualize another white A on the top of your head. Then, between the two, visualize twenty-one very fine white A letters, like a string. Hold either the vase-shaped breath or the soft-breath. On the verge of falling asleep, visualize that all the A letters gradually dissolve into the A in the heart center. Imagine this within the closed lotus bud, radiant like the flame of a butter lamp inside a vase. Thus train in falling asleep, while intending to recognize your dreams.

To naturally clarify awareness at dawn, as soon as you awake from sleep, assume the dharmakaya posture, direct your eyes into midair, and exhale with the HA sound three times. Hence, the lotus in the heart center opens, and the white A shoots out through the aperture of Brahma and remains vividly in the air about a bow's length above you. Focus your attention on it and keep your breath slightly exhaled. If your mind gets agitated, let it descend back to remain within your heart center and focus your attention on it, while lowering your gaze. If you feel dull, practice as above, as it suits your constitution.

DESCRIBING THE LIBERATION OF HAVING TRAINED IN SUCH A WAY

APPENDIX IV

THE CONCISE QUINTESSENCE

The Abbreviated Essential Empowerment for Lamey
Tukdrub Barchey Künsel
Embellished with Additional Notes

Tersey Tulku
Adapted by Tulku Urgyen Rinpoche

NAMO GURU PADMAKARAYE

Padmasambhava, single embodiment of the activity of all the
victorious ones,
Remain forever as the essence of self-existing awareness.
In order to consecrate and accept fortunate followers,
I shall here disclose the essential empowerment, condensed to its
vital substance.

This has three parts: Preparation, main part, and conclusion.

PREPARATION

If you are performing the general offerings and feast, based on either the
medium length or condensed version of the sadhana, and, in particular,
if you are performing the *Grand Guru Torma* or the vase empowerment,
and so forth, then place a *manji* stand upon the mandala made of painted
canvas or heaps of grains. Hereupon, place the vase of victory filled with
nectar, an image of Guru Rinpoche, and the required articles for the four
empowerments of body, speech, mind, and the consolidating empowerment of longevity.

Begin with the supplications and continue the sadhana up to the recitation, for whichever version you are using. Then open up the recitation mansion of the front visualization in the location of the sadhana articles and complete the recitations.

When consecrating the vase, focus on the vase of victory, and say:

> From the syllable BHRUM within the vase, the celestial palace
>   appears, ༔
> Fully complete with all characteristics. ༔
> In its center, the divine assemblage of vidyadhara masters is vividly
>   present, ༔
> Visible and yet empty, like the moon in water. ༔
>
> From the seed syllable and mantra garland in my heart center, ༔
> Light rays shine out in the form of offerings. ༔
> Hereby, the bodhichitta nectar of union ༔
> Completely fills up the vase. ༔

Uttering this, contemplate the meaning and take hold of the dharani cord.
Repeat the above recitation as much as you can. Then say:

> Within the vase of activity, the wrathful, red Hayagriva appears in an instant, holding a lotus club in the right hand and a lasso of flames in the left. From his body, nectar particles flow forth, filling up the vase.

OM HAYAGRIVA HUNG PHAT ༔

After repeating this, say the Vowels and Consonants mantra as well as the Essence of Causation mantra three times each.

If you combine this with the empowerment of longevity, visualize in this way:

> In the five places of the entire divine assemblage, both as self-visualization and front-visualization, the five families of Amitayus are vividly present in a single instant. From their bodies, hosts of *gyokma* goddesses stream forth, like dust motes in a beam of sun light, bringing back all the essences and vir-

tuous attributes of samsara, nirvana, and the path in the form of the nectar of immortal life. This nectar dissolves into you and the sadhana articles, conferring the accomplishment of immortal life and endowing you with its power.

Imagining this, wave the arrow of longevity and sing:

HUNG HRIH!

Vairochana and consort, I invoke your heart-samaya from the dharmadhatu!

Bring forth the power of the hosts of *gyokma* emissaries!

Collect the vitality, merit, and splendor of the buddhas, bodhisattvas, rishis, and vidyadharas

And of mundane beings endowed with merit!

Collect the vitality plundered by the evil spirits above, below, and in all directions!

Collect the essence of space and all the supreme vitality of the Buddha family!

Let it flow together into the auspicious vase of longevity!

Perform the activity of stabilizing our vitality and life force!

Bestow the accomplishment of the unchanging longevity of the Sugata family!

OM AMARANI JIVANTIYE SVAHA

OM BUDDHA AYUR GYANA TSHE BHRUM OM

HUNG HRIH!

Amitabha and consort, I invoke your heart-samaya from the dharmadhatu!

Bring forth the power of the hosts of *gyokma* emissaries!

Collect the vitality, merit, and splendor of the buddhas, bodhisattvas, rishis, and vidyadharas

And of mundane beings endowed with merit!

Bring back the vitality and life force plundered by the naga kings in the western direction!

Collect the essence of fire and all the supreme vitality of the Lotus family!

Let it flow together into the auspicious vase of longevity!

Perform the activity of stabilizing our vitality and life force!

Bestow the accomplishment of the unceasing longevity of the Lotus
    family!
Om amarani jivantiye svaha
Om padma ayur gyana tshe bhrum hrih

Hung Hrih!
Akshobhya and consort, I invoke your heart-samaya from the
    dharmadhatu!
Bring forth the power of the hosts of *gyokma* emissaries!
Collect the vitality, merit, and splendor of the buddhas,
    bodhisattvas, rishis, and vidyadharas
And of mundane beings endowed with merit!
Bring back the vitality and life force plundered by the gandharvas
    in the eastern direction!
Collect the essence of water and all the supreme vitality of the
    Vajra family!
Let it flow together into the auspicious vase of longevity!
Perform the activity of stabilizing our vitality and life force!
Bestow the accomplishment of the nontransferring longevity of the
    Vajra family!
Om amarani jivantiye svaha
Om vajra ayur gyana tshe bhrum hung

Hung Hrih!
Ratnasambhava and consort, I invoke your heart-samaya from the
    dharmadhatu!
Bring forth the power of the hosts of *gyokma* emissaries!
Collect the vitality, merit, and splendor of the buddhas,
    bodhisattvas, rishis, and vidyadharas
And of mundane beings endowed with merit!
Bring back the vitality and life force plundered by the yamas in the
    southern direction!
Collect the essence of earth and all the supreme vitality of the Ratna
    family!
Let it flow together into the auspicious vase of longevity!
Perform the activity of stabilizing our vitality and life force!
Bestow the accomplishment of the effortless longevity of the Ratna
    family!
Om amarani jivantiye svaha

O̱m ratna ayur gyana tshe bhrum tram

Hung Hrih!

Amoghasiddhi and consort, I invoke your heart-samaya from the
    dharmadhatu!

Bring forth the power of the hosts of *gyokma* emissaries!

Collect the vitality, merit, and splendor of the buddhas,
    bodhisattvas, rishis, and vidyadharas

And of mundane beings endowed with merit!

Bring back the vitality and life force plundered by the yakshas in
    the northern direction!

Collect the essence of wind and all the supreme vitality of the
    Karma family!

Let it flow together into the auspicious vase of longevity!

Perform the activity of stabilizing our vitality and life force!

Bestow the accomplishment of the unimpeded longevity of the
    Karma family!

O̱m amarani jivantiye svaha

O̱m karma ayur gyana tshe bhrum ah

Having performed this summoning of longevity, repeat the offerings
and praises, the supplication, and the confession of faults. At the end, say:

O̱m ah hung

Due to the incidence of making desirable offerings, the deities
in the vase dissolve into the essence of great bliss and emptiness, becoming indivisible from the water of the vase.

Imagine that. Initiate yourself by throwing the flower of awareness.
Let the samaya beings and wisdom beings become indivisible and thus
obtain permission.

Following that, offer tormas to the general and specific protectors and
continue the feast offering to the deliverance.

Main Part

Cleanse the disciples while repeating the verse beginning with *Jitar Tampa*.

Sanctify and purify the torma for the obstructors and continue with summoning, allocating, and expelling. Then visualize the protection circle, according to the sadhana text. After that, say:

> By uttering this, imagine the protection circle endowed with vajra foundation, fence, network, and dome blazes with wisdom flames. It is immense, vast, solid, and stable.

Communicate the symbolism. Give out and gather back the flowers, and then say:

> Listen now! Develop the bodhichitta motivation aimed at supreme enlightenment, thinking, "I will attain the precious state of unexcelled, truly perfected buddhahood for the sake of my mothers, all sentient beings equal to space. In order to do that, I will receive the profound ripening empowerments and put their meaning correctly into practice!" Listen, while carefully keeping in mind the correct behavior when receiving Dharma teachings!

This is regarding the teaching you are about to receive:

> The truly and perfectly Enlightened One, the Victorious One endowed with ingenuity in means and boundless compassion, taught an inconceivable number of profound and extensive nectar-like Dharma teachings in accordance with the inclinations of those to be tamed. These teachings can be condensed into the causal and resultant vehicles, as *Kunje Gyalpo Tantra* states:
>
> *There are two kinds of vehicles:*
> *The causal vehicles of philosophy,*
> *And the vajra vehicles of fruition.*

This present teaching belongs to the resultant vajra vehicle of Secret Mantra, which in many ways is more exalted than the causal teachings.

There were no such words as Old or New Schools known in the noble land of India. However, here in the Land of Snowy Ranges, the vajra vehicles are well known as the Old School of the Early Translations and the New School of the Later Translations, reflecting the different periods of translation.

Between these two schools, the Old Vajrayana School of the Early Translations is comprised of the three transmissions of Kama, Terma, and Pure Vision. This present teaching belongs to the short lineage of Terma.

A countless number of terma traditions have appeared, such as the earlier and later ones, but the present one is as follows:

King Trisong Deütsen, who was Manjushri in person, had three sons, of which the middle prince was Murub Tsepo Yeshe Rölpa Tsal, a master of the tenth bhumi. His incarnation, authenticated by the triple means of valid knowledge and extolled unanimously by all sublime beings, was the completely indisputable great treasure revealer and Dharma king, Orgyen Chokgyur Dechen Lingpa, who discovered an ocean-like number of profound termas. His termas were linked with the tantric scriptures, established by factual reasoning, adorned with the experience of the pith instructions, and endowed with the eminent warmth of wondrous blessings.

Chokgyur Lingpa discovered this treasure on the tenth day of the waxing moon of the ninth month in the year of the male Earth Monkey, when he was twenty years of age. He revealed it unhindered from underneath the vajra feet of the Great Glorious One at *Da-Nying Khala Rong-Go*, the sacred place of the qualities of enlightened body.

Keeping it utterly secret for eight years, he applied it in his own practice. Later, in connection with a perfect coincidence of time and place, the wisdom body of the glorious Dharma King of Uddiyana and consort bestowed upon him the empowerments, oral instructions, and special predictions and assurance. From then on, he gradually let the terma of *Lamey Tukdrub Barchey Künsel* flourish.

This terma cycle is the extract of the heart of Padmakara, the knower of the three times. It is the single unique treasure concealed under the earth in Tibet. It is like the great treasury of the universal monarch, filled completely and unmistakenly with all the means for accomplishing the supreme and common siddhis.

In terms of the sections of tantra, this profound path is based on the Great King of Tantras, *The Peaceful and Wrathful Manifestations of the Magical Net of the Vidyadhara Gurus,* which is the root of blessings belonging to the category of the *Eight Sections of the Magical Net.* Due to the certainty of oral instructions, there is no conflict in that it also belongs to the category of *Lotus Speech* among the *Eight Teachings of Sadhana Sections.*[20]

In short, it is like the extracted essential meaning of all stages of development and completion as well as the activity applications of the *Tantra and Sadhana Sections.*

Its root is like a vase filled with nectar; its detailed exposition is like the beautiful lid ornament; its additional sadhanas and background teachings are like the jewel studded decorations; and its special features are like a magnificent latticework. Thus, it is comprised of four grand cycles of teaching.

Among these cycles, this is from the root, which is like a vase filled with nectar, beginning with the performance of the profound steps of the ripening empowerments. Among them, there

---

20 *sgrub sde bka' brgyad.*

are the elaborate, medium, and concise versions. For this step-by-step performance of the *Abbreviated Essential Empowerment,* with the four empowerments conferred as one, based on the torma, together with the consolidating empowerment of auspicious longevity, the duties of the master have been completed.

For your share, first imagine the master as being the indivisibility of the three kayas, Padmasambhava, the glorious subjugator of all that appears and exists. While possessing such devotion, present a mandala offering as the gift for receiving the profound procedures of the blessed empowerments.

Having presented the mandala offering in this way, join your palms while holding a flower and repeat the following supplication three times with the deepest unshakable devotion:

EMAHO!

Dharmakaya Amitabha, I supplicate you.
Sambhogakaya Great Compassionate One, I supplicate you,
Nirmanakaya Padmakara, I supplicate you.
Grant your blessings of bestowing the empowerments upon me!

When you make this supplication, listen to the master as the Precious Master of Uddiyana, who opens the gate of wisdom and compassion and grants his permission in these words:

My Guru, Wonderful Nirmanakaya,
You were born in the land of India, where you studied and
    contemplated.
Journeying in person to Tibet, you tamed the demonic forces.
Residing in the land of Uddiyana, you acted for the welfare of
    beings.

I shall now give you the sublime empowerments
Of Padma Tötreng, the indivisible three kayas.

Next, in order to gather the accumulations, imagine, in the sky before you, the master inseparable from the Immortal Padma Tötreng, emanating an ocean-like cloud bank of the three kayas. An infinite number of the Three Roots and guardians of the Dharma, resplendent and vividly present, surround him. In his presence, form this thought, "I take refuge and generate bodhichitta. By means of the Seven Branches, I will gather the two accumulations!" Then repeat the following three times:

NAMO
I and all beings equal to the sky
Take refuge in the ones who are the supreme refuge.
Developing the bodhichitta of aspiration and application,
I will accomplish the level of the Trikaya Guru.

Thus, repeat the refuge and bodhichitta three times.

OM AH HUNG HRIH
I prostrate to Vidyadhara Padmakara
And to all the objects of refuge in the ten directions.
I present you with a Samantabhadra offering cloud, filling the sky
With materially and mentally created offerings.
I confess transgressing and violating the three vows of individual
    liberation,
The bodhisattva trainings, and the tantric samayas of the
    vidyadharas.
I rejoice in all the noble and ordinary beings
Who engage in the conduct of the sons of the victorious ones.
Please turn the appropriate wheels of Dharma
To relieve the misery of the infinite sentient beings.
Without passing away, remain for the sake of beings
Throughout the countless millions of aeons.
I dedicate all the virtues gathered in the three times
So that all beings may attain the supreme enlightenment.

Thus, chant the Seven Branches.

Having in this way imbued your stream-of-being with the precepts, place your body in the cross-legged posture and sit with a straight back to let the wisdom being descend, laying the foundation for the empowerments. As the key point of speech, bind the movement of the winds with the joining. As the key point of mind, do not let your attention wander elsewhere, but keep the following visualization:

OM HAYAGRIVA HUNG PHAT

OM SVABHAVA SHUDDHA SARVA DHARMA SVABHAVA SHUDDHOH HAM

Out of the empty state, with no ordinary awareness,

You are the great and mighty Hayagriva, red in color,

Holding knife and skull, moving in dance.

In your heart center, a swastika turns anti-clockwise

With Varahi dancing upon it.

Imagine this and give rise to devotion,

Thinking that the master is TötrengTsal in person.

By the power of such deep longing,

Red rays of light shine forth from the HUNG in your heart center

To the realms of buddhas in the ten directions.

In particular, they touch the heart of the Master of Uddiyana

On the Glorious Mountain in Chamara.

Invoking the heart samaya of them all,

The mudras of body, speech, and mind

Shower down, like rain, into you and other disciples.

Entering through the pores, they fill your bodies.

Dissolving completely into Varahi in the heart center,

They activate wisdom, and overwhelming bliss blazes forth.

Uttering this, imagine it and then chant in a melodious tone of voice, accompanied by incense and music:

HUNG HRIH

From the Chamara Continent to the southwest,

The supreme nirmanakaya realm, Lotus Net,

Trikaya Guru, Orgyen Tötreng Tsal,

With your ocean-like assembly of infinite Three Root deities,

Please come when I invite you yearningly to this place of devotion.

Through the power of your compassionate vow,

Dispel all obstacles and bestow the supreme and common siddhis!

Om ah hung vajra guru padma totreng tsal vajra samaya jah
  siddhi phala hung ah
Gyana ahbheshaya ah ah

Chant this repeatedly to shower down the resplendence. Then gather the blessings by saying:

Hung hung hung

Dissolve indivisibly by saying:

Jah hung bam hoh

Place the vajra at the crown of the head or scatter flowers, while saying:

Tishtha vajra

By uttering this, trust that it is stabilized!

After the descent and stabilization of the wisdom beings, the main part of conferring the torma empowerment of blessings begins.

In general, we recognize the torma as being a mandala at the time of approach and accomplishment, desirable objects at the time of offering, the deity at the time of empowerment, and accomplishment at the time of concluding. Here, you should recognize the torma as being the deity during this time of empowerment. Apply the following visualization:

When seen from the outside, this torma, *Radiant Jewel*, is a vast, radiant celestial palace, with utterly perfect proportions and characteristics. When seen from within, the torma has the three kayas dwelling in its center, one above the other, with the deities of the Three Roots gathered like cloud banks and the dharma protectors and guardians carrying out the activities. Thus, it is manifest as the utterly perfect mandala of palace and deities of the immense Magical Net of the Vidyadharas.

Invite them to remain at the crown of your head and bestow their blessings upon you.

From the four places of the chief figure and his entire retinue, marked with the syllables OM AH HUNG and HOH, boundless rays of white, red, blue, and multi-colored light stream forth. As the light dissolves into your four places, you obtain the four empowerments—outer, inner, secret, and thatness—in this very seat. The four empowerments totally pacify adverse conditions, misdeeds, obscurations, and obstacles you have accumulated through separate and joint activities of body, speech, and mind. Trust that for now you are authorized to practice the paths of the four empowerments. Ultimately, you become imbued with the fortune to accomplish the state of the four kayas!

Communicating that, sing the following with a melodious tone of voice in order to invoke the heart-samaya:

HUNG HRIH!
Padmasambhava, the emanation of the victorious ones,
Considering all the people of Tibet with kindness,
Prophesied his concealed treasures, representatives of his body and
    speech,
And entrusted the realization of his mind to the destined disciples.

When conferring the empowerment of the guru to protect against
    suffering,
Bestow your blessings upon all the fortunate ones!
May the kindness of the guru bestow blessings upon you!
May the affection of the guru guide you on the path!
May the realization of the guru grant you the siddhis!
May the powers of the guru dispel your obstacles!
Clear the outer obstacles of the four elements externally!
Clear the inner obstacles of the channels and winds internally!
Clear the secret obstacles of dualistic fixation into dharmadhatu!
Bestow your protection on the fortunate disciples!
Grant your blessings, empowerments, and siddhis right now!

OM AH HUNG BENZA GURU PEMA TOTRENG TSAL BENZA SAMAYA DZAH
SIDDHI PHALA HUNG AH
KAYA VAKA CHITTA SARVA SIDDHI ABHIKHENTSA OM AH HUNG HRIH

Uttering this, place the torma at your three places. Then say:

> In order to recognize the torma as being the accomplishment during the conclusion, trust that by tasting this clear, potent nectar—the torma food into which the torma deities have dissolved—the nature of the accomplishment permeates all your channels and elements, fills your being with unconditioned bliss, and bestows all the supreme and common siddhis, without exception.

Now, in order to receive the consolidating auspicious empowerment of longevity to tame beings, repeat this supplication three times:

> Protector of Beings, Padma Amitayus,
> Buddhas of the Three Times, Lords of Longevity and your
> Consorts,
> I supplicate you; dispel the obstacles for long life!
> Bestow the empowerment of immortal vajra life!

Having made this supplication, summon the vitality and gather back the essences, by imagining that within your heart centers, in the middle of a vajra cross, amidst a sun and moon sphere, is the letter HUNG, the support for longevity. In its nook is the letter NRI marked with the letter A.

Your devotion to the master invokes rays of light that radiate from his heart center, summoning the minds of all the mandala deities. From the heart centers of the five families of Amitayus and their consorts, visualized in their five places, red beams of light stream forth in the form of hooks and *gyokma* goddesses, as many as dust motes in sun light. They gather back all the vitality and life energy you have lost as well as all the essences of longevity, merit, grandeur, affluence, wisdom, and qualities of the worlds and content of samsara and nirvana, without exception. Dissolving completely into you, these light rays confer the accomplishment of immortal life. Dissolving into the articles of longevity in front, they imbue these articles with the extract of the nectar of immortality!

Communicating that, wave the arrow with silken streamers. Then say:

Hung Hrih!⁞

Vairochana and consort, I invoke your heart samaya...⁞

Chant the extensive summoning of longevity, as above; if you are unable to do that, say this invocation:

Hung Hrih!⁞

Five supreme families, I invoke your heart-samaya from the dharmadhatu!⁞

Bring forth the power of the hosts of *gyokma* emissaries!⁞

Collect the vitality, merit, and splendor of the buddhas, bodhisattvas, rishis, and vidyadharas⁞

And of mundane beings endowed with merit!⁞

Collect the vitality plundered by the guardians of the ten directions!⁞

Collect the essence of the five elements and all the supreme vitality of the five families!⁞

Let it flow together into the auspicious vase of longevity!⁞

Perform the activity of stabilizing our vitality and life force!⁞

Bestow the accomplishment of the longevity of indestructible immortality!⁞

Om amarani jivantiye svaha⁞

Om buddha ayur gyana tshe bhrum om⁞

Om padma ayur gyana tshe bhrum hrih⁞

Om vajra ayur gyana tshe bhrum hung⁞

Om ratna ayur gyana tshe bhrum tram⁞

Om karma ayur gyana tshe bhrum ah⁞

After this invocation, say:

Now, for the main empowerment, imagine that this vase of longevity is the host of longevity deities of the Three Roots, seated one above the other in the form of Lord Amitayus.

The rays of light shine forth from their heart centers, gathering back all your life energy and vitality, which have been cut, damaged, or dwindled away, as well as the essences of longevity of samsara and nirvana. It all enters into the vases in their hands, boils, and overflows, so that this radiant nectar of immortal life flows down through the crown of your head and fills your body. Trust that it completely purifies the fear of untimely death along with its tendencies, and that you achieve all the accomplishments of immortal life and wisdom, without exception.

Place the vase of longevity at the crown of your head and say:

Hʀɪʜ Hʀɪʜ Hʀɪʜ!॰

Lord Amitayus, you who have abandoned both birth and death,॰

Fivefold Lords of Longevity and your Consorts,॰

Chandali, goddess of wisdom space,॰

Vidyadhara Padmakara, you who have achieved the body of immortality,॰

Vimalamitra, master of unchanging life,॰

Mandarava, mudra for accomplishing the path of longevity,॰[21]

Tsogyal, consort who obtained the empowerment of the wisdom of great bliss,॰

Lhasey Rölpa Tsal, receiver of the transmission of longevity,॰

Root Guru, embodiment of the entire Triple Refuge,॰

Root and lineage masters of the level of vidyadhara life,॰

Consider this place kindly from your invisible realm॰

And bestow the accomplishments of immortal life and wisdom!॰

Oᴍ ᴀᴍᴀʀᴀɴɪ ᴊɪᴠᴀɴᴛɪʏᴇ sᴠᴀʜᴀ॰

Vᴀᴊʀᴀ ɢʏᴀɴᴀ ᴀʏᴜᴋʜᴇ ʜᴜɴɢ ʙʜʀᴜᴍ ɴʀɪ ᴊᴀʜ sᴀʀᴠᴀ sɪᴅᴅʜɪ ᴘʜᴀʟᴀ ʜᴜɴɢ॰

By taking the pill of longevity, the substance of *means*, in your right hand, trust that you attain the accomplishment of indestructible life, the *means*, which is the most eminently unchanging great bliss.

---

21 The following three lines were composed by the emanated great treasure revealer.

Hrih

By this wisdom enjoyment of immortal life,
The gathered nectar of all unchanging essences,
May unconditioned bliss increase in your minds
And may you forever enjoy the splendor of longevity!
Om vajra gyana ayukhe bhrum nri jah sarva siddhi phala
hung

By taking the nectar of longevity, the substance of *knowledge*, in your left hand, trust that you attain the accomplishment of indestructible life, the *knowledge*, which is the most eminently unchanging emptiness.

Hrih

All the deathless vidyadharas who appeared in the past
Reached accomplishment by means of the nectar-essence of the
    wine of longevity.
By giving it today to you, the fortunate ones,
May you achieve the empowerment of unceasing longevity!
Om vajra gyana ayukhe hung bhrum nri jah sarva siddha
phala hung

By receiving this empowerment, the inside of your entire body is filled with the nectar of immortal life. All of this essence dissolves completely into the syllable nri in your heart center, making it shine with five-colored light. The sun and moon sphere becomes free from cracks. On the outside, the spokes of a vajra cross are fastened together above, while the vajra cross is tied three times with a red dharani cord, securing mastery over vajra life.

At the tip of the vajra spokes, the mighty Hayagriva appears, holding knife and skull cup. Trust that he protects against obstructors and obstacle-makers for your life span. Imagining this, rest evenly in the innate state of dharmata.

Hᴜɴɢ Hʀɪʜ!⸴

All the life force of samsara and nirvana dissolves into the five
    elements,⸴

Increasing the strength of flesh, blood, heat, breath, and mind.⸴

By sealing the unchanging essences with ɴʀɪ,⸴

May you be endowed with the vajra life of immortality.⸴

Oᴍ ʙʜʀᴜᴍ ʜʀɪʜ ʙʜʀᴜᴍ ʜᴜɴɢ ʙʜʀᴜᴍ ᴛʀᴀᴍ ʙʜʀᴜᴍ ᴀʜ ʙʜʀᴜᴍ
ᴠᴀᴊʀᴀ ᴋʀᴏᴅʜᴀ ʜᴀʏᴀ ɢʀɪᴠᴀ ʀᴀᴋsʜᴀ ʀᴀᴋsʜᴀ ʙʜʀᴜᴍ⸴

*Having uttered this, scatter flowers and stabilize, by chanting the Dharani
mantra and the Essence of Causation mantra.*

Now, in order to bring forth auspiciousness, imagine that the
master, the Three Roots, and all the deities of immortal life
sing vajra songs with verses of auspiciousness and shower
down a rain of flowers. Imagine that the light of such virtuous goodness pervades and stabilizes throughout all time and
space.

Oᴍ⸴

May the life of vajra wisdom be accomplished!⸴

Changeless, indestructible, and permeating all of space,⸴

Infinite qualities and activities surpassing the thought,⸴

May Lord Padma Amitayus swiftly be attained!⸴

*Also, chant any other suitable version of lines of auspiciousness from the
extensive or medium length sadhana, and shower down a rain of flowers. Play
melodious music for a long time.*

Thus, by means of these steps, I have now completed the brief
actions for conferring the empowerment of the mandala of
Lamey Tukdrub Barchey Künsel, which is the extract of the
heart of the Glorious Dharma King of Uddiyana and the single unique treasure below the earth in Tibet. Therefore, with
the firm determination to observe the samayas and keep the
precepts, which you have received and pledged, repeat the following three times:

Tso wo jitar ka tsalpa ...

Now present a mandala offering as the gift of thanksgiving for the guru's kindness in letting us fully receive this profound empowerment.

Once again, imagine that your body, wealth, and ocean of virtues multiply into the magnificent abundance of the kingdom of a universal monarch. Repeat the following with the thought, "Please accept all this as your enjoyment, down to the tiniest detail!"

Deng ney tsam teh ...

Now dedicate all together the virtuous roots of having received this empowerment, dedicating it toward the essence of enlightenment:

Sonam diyi ...

Thus seal, by dedicating the virtuous roots toward the essence of enlightenment.

Conclusion

Now perform the concluding steps of the sadhana, from enjoying the feast through the end.

May all who enter with this key for empowerments,
Which opens up the door for the Secret Mantra of great methods,
Have their minds saturated with the ripening empowerment
And be established in the state of the four kayas of liberation!

Having received the command to write this by my older brother, Samten Gyatso, a master with a sublime character, I, Tersey Tulku, noted this by means of embellishing the exact words of the Omniscient Manjuvajra, with some necessary additions. May it bring forth virtuous goodness!

NOTES

1. *Light of Wisdom, Volume II,* translated by Erik Pema Kunsang. Rangjung Yeshe Publications, Hong Kong, 1995, page 39.
2. Ibid., page 106
3. Ibid., page 40.
4. *A Practice of Padmasambhava,* translated by Dharmachakra Translation Committee, Snow Lion Publications, Ithaca, New York, 2011.
5. For the mantras of each, please refer to *The Practice Manual for Approach and Accomplishment, the Dzabkyi Köljang.*
6. *The Six Wondrous Teachings,* by Vidyadhara Padmasambhava, are found in Vol. CHA of the Chokling Tersar, pages 277–361, in various versions of sadhana and applications. *The Reading Method for the Lotus Essence Tantra,* arranged by Jamyang Khyentse Wangpo, is found on pages 183–196 in Vol. GA of the Chokling Tersar. It is also available as a practice booklet from Rangjung Yeshe Publications.